Palgrave Macmillan Studies in Banking and Financial Institutions

Series Editor: **Professor Philip Molyneux**

The Palgrave Macmillan Studies in Banking and Financial Institutions are international in orientation and include studies of banking within particular countries or regions, and studies of particular themes such as Corporate Banking, Risk Management, Mergers and Acquisitions, etc. The books' focus is on research and practice, and they include up-to-date and innovative studies on contemporary topics in banking that will have global impact and influence.

Titles include:

Mario Anolli, Elena Beccalli and Tommaso Giordani (*editors*)
RETAIL CREDIT RISK MANAGEMENT

Rym Ayadi and Emrah Arbak
FINANCIAL CENTRES IN EUROPE
Post-crisis Risks, Challenges and Opportunities

Rym Ayadi and Sami Mouley
MONETARY POLICIES, BANKING SYSTEMS, REGULATORY CONVERGENCE, EFFICIENCY AND GROWTH IN THE MEDITERRANEAN

Caner Bakir
BANK BEHAVIOUR AND RESILIENCE
The Effect of Structures, Institutions and Agents

Alessandro Carretta and Gianluca Mattarocci (*editors*)
ASSET PRICING, REAL ESTATE AND PUBLIC FINANCE OVER THE CRISIS.

Dimitris N. Chorafas
BASEL III, THE DEVIL AND GLOBAL BANKING

Dimitris N. Chorafas
HOUSEHOLD FINANCE
Adrift in a Sea of Red Ink

Dimitris N. Chorafas
SOVEREIGN DEBT CRISIS
The New Normal and the Newly Poor

Stefano Cosma and Elisabetta Gualandri (*editors*)
THE ITALIAN BANKING SYSTEM
Impact of the Crisis and Future Perspectives

Joseph Falzon (*editor*)
BANK PERFORMANCE, RISK AND SECURITISATION

Joseph Falzon (*editor*)
BANK STABILITY, SOVEREIGN DEBT AND DERIVATIVES

Juan Fernández de Guevara Radoselovics and José Pastor Monsálvez (*editors*)
CRISIS, RISK AND STABILITY IN FINANCIAL MARKETS

Juan Fernández de Guevara Radoselovics and José Pastor Monsálvez *(editors)*
MODERN BANK BEHAVIOUR

Franco Fiordelisi and Ornella Ricci *(editors)*
BANCASSURANCE IN EUROPE
Past, Present and Future

Josanco Floreani and Maurizio Polato
THE ECONOMICS OF THE GLOBAL STOCK EXCHANGE INDUSTRY

Jill M. Hendrickson
FINANCIAL CRISIS
The United States in the Early Twenty-First Century

Otto Hieronymi and Constantine Stephanou *(editors)*
INTERNATIONAL DEBT
Economic, Financial, Monetary, Political and Regulatory Aspects

Paola Leone and Gianfranco A. Vento *(editors)*
CREDIT GUARANTEE INSTITUTIONS AND SME FINANCE

Bernardo Nicoletti
CLOUD COMPUTING IN FINANCIAL SERVICES

Özlem Olgu
EUROPEAN BANKING
Enlargement, Structural Changes and Recent Developments

Fotios Pasiouras
GREEK BANKING
From the Pre-Euro Reforms to the Financial Crisis and Beyond

Daniela Pîrvu
CORPORATE INCOME TAX HARMONIZATION IN THE EUROPEAN UNION

Ramkishen S. Rajan
EMERGING ASIA
Essays on Crises, Capital Flows, FDI and Exchange Rate

Gabriel Tortella and José Luis García Ruiz
SPANISH MONEY AND BANKING
A History

The full list of titles available is on the website:
www.palgrave.com/finance/sbfi.asp

Palgrave Macmillan Studies in Banking and Financial Institutions
Series Standing Order ISBN 978–1–403– 94872–4
You can receive future titles in this series as they are published by placing a standing order. Please contact your bookseller or, in case of difficulty, write to us at the address below with your name and address, the title of the series and the ISBN quoted above.

Customer Services Department, Macmillan Distribution Ltd, Houndmills, Basingstoke, Hampshire RG21 6XS, England

Monetary Policies, Banking Systems, Regulatory Convergence, Efficiency and Growth in the Mediterranean

Rym Ayadi
Centre for European Policy Studies, Brussels, Belgium

and

Sami Mouley
University of Tunis, Tunisia

First published 2014 by
PALGRAVE MACMILLAN

Palgrave Macmillan in the UK is an imprint of Macmillan Publishers Limited, registered in England, company number 785998, of Houndmills, Basingstoke, Hampshire RG21 6XS.

Palgrave Macmillan in the US is a division of St Martin's Press LLC, 175 Fifth Avenue, New York, NY 10010.

Palgrave Macmillan is the global academic imprint of the above companies and has companies and representatives throughout the world.

Palgrave® and Macmillan® are registered trademarks in the United States, the United Kingdom, Europe and other countries

ISBN 978-1-349-43424-4   ISBN 978-1-137-00348-5 (eBook)
DOI 10.1057/9781137003485

This book is printed on paper suitable for recycling and made from fully managed and sustained forest sources. Logging, pulping and manufacturing processes are expected to conform to the environmental regulations of the country of origin.

A catalogue record for this book is available from the British Library.

A catalog record for this book is available from the Library of Congress.

Contents

List of Tables

List of Figures

Acknowledgments

This book was directed and edited by Dr Rym Ayadi, Senior Research Fellow, Head of the Financial Institutions and Prudential Policy Research Unit at CEPS and Scientific Director of MEDPRO – Mediterranean Prospects Research Network – in collaboration with Professor Sami Mouley, Professor of International Finance at the University of Tunis and Expert in Banking Strategies and Central Banking.

Other contributors include Emrah Arbak and Willem Pieter De Groen, Researchers in the Financial Institutions and Prudential Policy research unit at CEPS, Barbara Casu Lukac, Reader in Banking at the Cass Business School in London and Sami Ben Naceur, Associate Professor at the University of Tunis.

The book was produced with financial assistance from the European Union within the FEMISE programme 2009–10. Established in June 2005, the Forum Euroméditerranéen des Instituts de Sciences Économiques (FEMISE) is a Euro-Mediterranean network consisting of more than 80 economic research institutes, representing the 37 partners of the Barcelona Process.

Introduction

Monetary policies and international standards and norms on banking regulations have, once again, leaped to the forefront of the policy discussion in developed nations due to the recent crisis in the world's financial markets. This discussion is far from new, nor does it apply exclusively to the world's most advanced economies. A stable monetary policy, and a sound and well-enforced regulatory regime, can help developing nations to channel financial resources more efficiently into investments. For open economies, it can also act as a buffer, an important stability factor in today's shaky market situation.

Against this backdrop, this book assesses the challenges of the conduct of monetary policies and central banks independence, explores banking systems and examines the impact of monetary policy and banking sector regulations on bank efficiency and economic growth in the Southern and Eastern Mediterranean countries (SEMC), while exploring the level of convergence of regulatory practices and efficiency to EU Mediterranean1 standards.

In particular, the book first delves into monetary policy in the region and the evolving role of central banking; it then compares the banking sector and financial and regulatory reforms of the region to international standards, using measures on the adequacy of regulatory and supervisory practices. Second, banking efficiency and the level of convergence to best practices are examined using Data Envelopment Analysis (DEA) and complemented by Meta Frontier Analysis and the β-convergence and σ-convergence methodologies.

1

Third, the impact of the monetary and regulatory environment on the efficiency of banks is investigated using the developed measures of regulatory and supervisory practices. In addition to the regulatory details, the performance analysis also considers the legal and institutional characteristics of the SEMC. Fourth, the book explores how compliance with these standards and norms may influence the growth potential of each country.

Chapter 1 delves into monetary policy and central banking in the SEMC. Chapter 2 provides a descriptive analysis of the banking sectors of the region. Chapter 3 then develops measures of regulatory adequacy in a number of areas and provides comparisons with the EU-MED. Chapter 4 summarises the analysis of efficiency and convergence between the SEMC and EU-MED. Chapter 5analyses empirically the determinants of the efficiency scores, paying special attention to monetary policy and the regulatory adequacy measures developed. Chapter 6 provides a similar analysis for economic growth. The final chapter concludes and puts forth the main policy recommendations.

1
Monetary Policy and Central Banking Independence

The recent global financial crisis coupled with the post Arab spring instability effects have called for a rethinking of monetary policies and the role of central banking in the Mediterranean region. This chapter assesses the challenges of the conduct of monetary policies and central banks' independence. It also explores new elements towards the rethinking of the central banking role and evolving rules in the aftermath of the recent crisis and changing macroeconomic environment in Mediterranean countries. It outlines important lessons for monetary policies and central banking, in particular with respect to inflation targeting. The contribution makes a case in favour of central banks' independence from budgetary authorities and the importance of this independence to achieve inclusive growth.

1.1 Operational frameworks of monetary policies conduct

An analysis of the tools for the implementation of monetary policies by central banks in Mediterranean countries reveals an apparent homogeneity in their operational frameworks, albeit with differences in details and varying degrees of progress. Although price stability remains the announced final objective, weaknesses in terms of regulation and control of interest rates as an operational objective mean that the monetary authorities are required to adopt quantitative approaches based on targeting monetary and credit aggregates as intermediate objectives.

3

Differences are nevertheless discernible in the oil exporting countries (Algeria and Libya in particular) with restrictive monetary policies in place to control the monetary base and absorb the structural liquidity surplus in the banking system. In other countries, restrictive monetary policies are used by raising key interest rates in order to maintain a positive real interest rate in the money market. Generally, we can discern a lower level of interest rate in the dynamics of growth, except in the case of crisis exit strategies (Tunisia, Egypt), and measures for diversification of the instruments of monetary policies, with gradual recourse to underlying and core indicators.

Limited operational independence and slow migration to systems for formal inflation targeting characterise most of the central banks, with the exception of Turkey and Morocco. The excessive use of subsidy and price control mechanisms seems to be the main obstacle to the adoption of explicit inflation targets.

Regarding exchange rate policies, targeting the real effective exchange rate is the operational rule in the case of countries choosing managed floating schemes, while fixed anchoring of the nominal exchange rate is the primary instrument in the pegging regimes to the dollar or to Special Drawing Rights.

In this context, reforms of the monetary and financial systems in these countries have certainly progressed, but are still characterised by latent deficiencies. In particular, although there has been some improvement, the levels of intermediation are relatively low, lying below the average of those in the East Asia and Pacific Region or the levels in the advanced economies of OECD countries. Overall, contributions of capital markets are weak but are progressing in some countries (Turkey, Morocco, Lebanon and Egypt) (see Chapter 2).

Programmes aimed at restructuring of banking systems (supervision, prudential norms and so on) for better resilience have been initiated, but recurring vulnerabilities remain concentrated on the portfolios of nonperforming loans with insufficient provisioning (except in the particular case of Morocco) (see Chapter 3). In addition, the attractiveness of foreign investment in most countries is lessened by several constraints, in particular the slow pace of capital accounts liberalisation and the lack of management structures for systemic liquidity.

Generally, economic and financial governance in these countries is clearly an incomplete process, as evidenced by the widespread deficiencies in business and investment climate and weakness in the quality of institutions.

In Algeria, a cautious monetary policy has been pursued over the last few years, in line with the official objective of controlling

Table 1.1 Operational framework for monetary policy in southern Mediterranean countries

	Final objective	Intermediate objective (target)	Instruments of control	Operational framework
Algeria	Inflation rate	Stability of real exchange rate	Central bank's key interest rate	Liquidity rate control
Egypt	Inflation rate	– Stability of nominal exchange rate – Core inflation index	– Central bank's key interest rate – Rules of broad money control	– Monetary targeting – Implicit mechanism of inflation targeting
Jordan	Inflation rate	Monetary base	Reserve requirement ratios	Nominal exchange rate targeting
Lebanon	Inflation rate	Stability of nominal exchange rate	Liquidity rate	– Sterilisation mechanism – Control of treasury bonds rate
Morocco	Inflation rate	Stability of real exchange rate	Central bank's key interest rate	Formal mechanism of inflation targeting
Tunisia	Inflation rate	– Stability of real exchange rate – Monetary base	– Reserve requirement ratio – Central bank's key interest rate (call for bids rate)	Monetary targeting
Turkey	Inflation rate	Stability of real exchange rate	Central bank's key interest rate	Formal mechanism of inflation targeting

Source: Author's compilations.

inflation. Hence, the Bank of Algeria has continued to absorb the structural liquidity surplus of the banking system through auctions to counterbalance budgetary stimulation and the rapid growth in bank deposits by the national oil company. The expansion of credit in the economy has slowed significantly.

Egypt had an extremely high rate of inflation, reaching 16.2 per cent in 2008–9 before falling to 11.7 per cent in 2009–10. Inflationary pressures appeared in the summer of 2006, accelerating at the end of 2007, and especially in the spring of 2008, because of the rise in the price of wheat, increases in salaries and a partial reduction of subsidies on fuels. At the end of August 2008, the consumer price index (CPI) reached a peak of 23.6 per cent on a year-on-year basis. Monetary policy was thus accommodative and reactive, as it was during the global financial crisis when in 2009 the central bank introduced six increases of the key interest rate to contain inflationary pressures and ensure macroeconomic stability. In fact, since 2003 monetary policy has undergone in-depth restructuring with the enactment of a law modernising the conceptual and operational framework, by steering it towards price stability and by strengthening the autonomy of the central bank. The central bank has also begun a gradual process of migration towards a formal system of inflation targeting by developing new monetary instruments to allow a new target rate to be set. In 2009 the central bank launched a core inflation index based on the unadjusted CPI.

In Jordan the annual average inflation rate, determined by the CPI, stabilised at 4.1 per cent during the last decade (6.3 per cent in 2006 and 13.9 per cent in 2008[1]), and responds mainly to the trend in oil and food prices. Also, the depreciation of the US dollar observed since 2006 partially contributed to the increase of the inflation rate during this period, due to the pegging of the local currency to the dollar. In order to manage inflationary pressures, the Central Bank of Jordan adopted a monetary policy based on price stability.[2] In 2009 it lowered its key interest rate three times (by 0.5 per cent each time), decreased the reserve requirement rate and suspended the depositary certificate's issues to strengthen the liquidity of the country's financial system.

During the first half of the last decade Lebanon had low inflation rates. However, due to the hike in world food and oil prices observed since 2006, inflation rose sharply to reach 10.8 per cent in

2008 before dropping to 4.5 per cent in 2010. The Central Bank of Lebanon is pursuing a monetary policy totally oriented to stabilising the exchange rate of the local currency against the dollar by controlling the volume of liquidity. Against this backdrop a downward trend in the level of interest rates was recorded, combined with measures to combat the inflationary effects of capital inflows. The monetary sector performed well, reflecting the positive trend in the real sphere and recording a massive reconversion of assets into local currency, estimated at more than 10 thousand million dollars in 2009 (against 8 thousand million in 2008), resulting in a *de facto* reduction in the dollarisation rate of deposits at 63.2 per cent in 2010 (the lowest level for 10 years). Moreover, these reconversions considerably strengthened the foreign currency assets of the central bank, which reached an envelope of 29.6 thousand million dollars in 2010 (10.3 months of imports and roughly 80 per cent of GDP) against 28.3 thousand million in 2009 and 19.7 thousand million in 2008. However, this generated an abundance of liquidity in Lebanese pounds, hence lowering the interest rates on local currency deposits. The banking system is structurally supported by the increase in deposits at a steady pace (approximately 11 per cent in 2010) due to the attractiveness of the remuneration rates and the confidence inspired in depositors by tying the Lebanese pound to the dollar. Nevertheless, Lebanese banks prefer to cover the major part of the financing needs of the State rather than grant credits to the private sector. This means they are exposed to sovereign risk and also vulnerable to strong dollarisation of deposits.

In Morocco over the last two years, inflation trends were marked by a significant easing of the pressures inherent in the demand. The inflation rate stabilised in 2009, as well as in 2010, at only 1 per cent, compared to 3.7 per cent in 2008. This moderate trend can mainly be explained by the weak pressure from internal demand and the performance of monetary policy, as well as continuous intervention by the government through social welfare funds. Trends in the monetary sector have been characterised by marked slowing in the money supply and credit. Indeed, the growth of the monetary aggregates (M3) money supply slowed down in 2010 at 4.8 per cent compared to 7 per cent in 2009 and 13.5 per cent in 2008. Bank loans to the economy followed the same trend, increasing by only 10 per cent in 2010, compared to 12 per cent in 2009 and 23.4 per cent in 2008. This downswing shows a return to levels in compliance with the fundamentals of the economy and this took place after the strong growth of these two indicators observed during the period 2005–7. Monetary policy is based on the mechanisms of quantitative regulation. Its main objective is to control inflation in line with economic development. It was a major factor in maintaining the inflation rate at a low level, in conserving foreign balances and strengthening the stability of the real exchange rate of the Dirham. According to the IMF, the Central Moroccan Bank now generally satisfies the prerequisites for inflation targeting: it has operational independence, the expertise and the necessary statistical resources as well as a full range of monetary policy instruments which it continues to improve. Its analytical and operational framework is very close to that of the central banks, which have adopted explicit inflation targets.

In Tunisia, the implementation of monetary policy is characterised by a trend in the interest rate that is dependent on the mechanism of managing banking liquidity. Thus, in spite of the amendment to the statutes of the Central Bank of Tunisia (CBT) in May 2006, which sets price stability as the ultimate objective of monetary policy implementation, the current operational framework is still dominated by a two-fold device. The first is a result of targeting the real effective exchange rate with the objective of achieving a competitive depreciation; therefore the CBT intervenes daily in a discretionary manner, even by way of indication, in order to correct the value of the nominal effective exchange rate in a band of 1 per cent between the bid price and the selling rate of the dinar vis-à-vis the main foreign currencies. The second device focuses on a system of intermediate control of monetary aggregates in the broad sense as a stage to be later transformed into a system that formally targets inflation, but where the factors and prerequisites are far from being verified.[3] In particular, since the key interest rate is not fully under control as an operational objective, the CBT continue to use, as a temporary measure, a quantitative approach which is based on M3 targeting as an intermediate objective, by influencing the monetary base as the operational objective, and essentially by controlling the instruments of the key interest rate (call for bids rate) and the required reserve rate. At the same time, the problems inherent in the mechanism in place of the predictability of banking liquidity do not allow sufficient flexibility in the money market rate because the existing scheme of financial programming used by the CBT is based on monetary targeting for the purpose of projecting an annual, and later a monthly, target for M3 monetary aggregate (intermediate objective).

At the level of the institutional framework for controlling banking liquidity, the choice of monetary policy mechanisms has privileged indirect fine-tuning instruments in the form of call for bids operations. The other instruments are only minimally operational and have limited efficiency.[5] Indeed, and since the genuinely operational instrument which the central bank uses is liquidity volume, the equilibrium in the interbank money market and control of the money supply are ensured by daily injections (or repurchasing) of liquidity. Managing liquidity needs in this way permits adjustment of supply to the demand for central bank money without a significant variation in the interest rate.

The forecast mechanism for banking liquidity is based on monetary targets and is constrained by the inherent difficulties in the current system. In fact, the financial programming plan used as a basis for setting the annual target for M3 monetary aggregate (intermediate objective) and for projecting banking liquidity depends on the estimation of a money demand function which integrates specifically the annual projections for GDP[6] and those of bank credits stemming from macroeconomic development plans and annual budgets.[7] Once the parameters of the money demand function are stable,[8] it is then a question of deriving the profile or the monthly target for M3 aggregate from the estimate of its cyclical trend, its seasonal component and its irregular (residue) component.

For the refinancing needs of the CBT, a target for the monetary base (operational objective since 2004) is deducted at the end of December by applying the monthly multipliers between M3 and the monetary base throughout the current year; this allows a ratio between the estimated monthly target for M3 and the monthly target for the monetary base to be established. This latter estimated variable is used as control variable for fine tuning monetary policy operations. In particular, projection of banking liquidity and consequent refinancing operations are made on the basis of forecasts of autonomous liquidity factors, with maintenance of an average short-term interest rate for the money market band within a band of +/−12 basis points of variability as objective.

Nevertheless the current forecasting mechanism shows some weaknesses. In particular, the multipliers of the monetary base (and of the adjusted monetary base) for M3 aggregates[9] were higher compared with the forecast multipliers,[10] especially in recent years; the accumulated deviations were not subject to any monthly corrections. Therefore the deviations between the monthly target of the monetary base, which is estimated from the M3 monthly growth target and monetary policy interventions, are not eliminated from one month to the next. This results in increasing cumulative differences between M3 and its intermediate target, which were the cause of increasing excess liquidity in the banking system. Furthermore, the cumulative differences between growth rates of the monetary base and the M3 aggregate have led to large deviations since 2004 between forecasted compared with the observed target of monetary aggregates, and have therefore contributed to excess of liquidity.[11]

At the same time, the difficulties inherent in *de facto* monetary targeting ensue, as well the lack of a model in the CBT to make its own macroeconomic projections. Similarly, liquidity management is also dependent on banks' respective demand forecasts for banknotes and coins in circulation, which is wholly disconnected from macroeconomic fine tuning of the monetary base. In practice, and instead of relying on the estimated standards of its operational objective of the monetary base, the CBT plans its refinancing operations on the basis of liquidity requirements of banks which are not set by the departments in charge of monetary policy.

Another recurring problem concerns the forecasts of international reserves, which are not taken into account when calculating external financing and which are nevertheless a decisive variable for projecting operations of monetary policy intervention and liquidity management undertaken by the CBT. All this additional liquidity, which appears to be unconnected with basic economic data, is also the reason for the excess liquidity which was prevalent in the banking system. Ultimately, the variations in the estimated monetary base were no longer suitable for explaining the fluctuations in M3, which hence is not fully controlled in the short term by the CBT. Therefore, various technical assistance reports from the IMF have already rightly concluded total exogeneity of the monetary base in dealing with inflation dynamics in Tunisia.[12]

The interest rate policy is relatively inefficient so that the fall in the key interest rate has no significant effect on growth, which is more influenced by the competitiveness of the export sectors. Furthermore, instead of expecting a positive effect on investments through lower costs of bank loans to businesses, the result was instead an increase in personal loans. Likewise, although all international ratings for the business and investment climate and also for the regulatory frameworks have always mentioned the difficulty of accessing bank loans in Tunisia, a week elasticity or rather total inelasticity of private investment[13] to the interest rate in Tunisia is clearly demonstrated.

Furthermore, the range of monetary policy instruments is of limited efficacy, which would suggest a review of the existing regulation. In particular, the gradual liberalisation of bank conditions[14] ended with banks being free to set the debtor interest rates applied to all forms of credit irrespective of maturity, increased by exchange and guarantee equalisation commissions. On the other hand, the partial liberalisation of credit conditions still limits the rate of return on savings to the average monthly rate of the money market minus two percentage points.

The margins applied to the granting of bank loans to companies and private individuals are indexed to the average monthly rate for the money market published regularly by the CBT. Nevertheless, to protect borrowers, the Ministry of Finance regularly updates its communication by specific orders with a list of excessive interest rates for all types of loans and credit maturities. As it is commonly established that bank margins finance their costs of resources and that commissions cover their operating costs, then the costs of financing provided by banks to Tunisian companies are directly dependent on the money market rate that responds to the management of the banking liquidity by the CBT and in particular to evolution of the call for bids rate (TDAO) which represents the central bank's key interest rate. Nevertheless, in practice, the evolution of the TMM was characterised by three tendencies: (i) initially, full indexation to the TDAO previously fixed at 5 per cent; (ii) then, partial de-indexation of the key interest rate raised to 5.25 per cent; and finally (iii) the beginning of a full de-indexation of the key rate reduced in February 2009 by 75 basis points to settle at 4.50 per cent.

In fact, this de-indexation is not only linked to the drop in the key interest rate but, above all, to the introduction of two new money market instruments during the same period in accordance with the CBT circular to credit institutes N°2009–07 dated 19 February 2009. It concerns credit and deposits standing facilities for 24 hours for banks, allowing them to cover their needs or place temporary liquidity surpluses. The deposit facility is remunerated at a rate equal to the CBT's key rate minus a margin.

A band (corridor) of 100 basis points is set between the interest rate on the deposit facility (TFD 24h), set at 4 per cent, and the interest rate on the credit facility (TFP 24h), set at 5 per cent. Since the CBT turned away from fine tuning in February 2009, convergence between the money market rate and TFD 24h occurred. Therefore, instead of inferring a flexibility to a drop in the money market rate, these new instruments totally de-indexed the money market rate of the CBT's key rate (call for bids rate, TDAO) and led to a *de facto* and gradual convergence of it with the interest rate on deposit facilities, which remains high considering the financing needs of companies by structurally inducing disproportionate loan costs.

Finally, in the 1970s the economy of Turkey was characterised by a chronic inflation level considered as inertial[15] and induced by monetary financing of public sector deficits. It was only from 2004 onwards that Turkey managed to bring its inflation rate under the symbolic bar of 10 per cent. In 2005 the economy was considered stable enough to introduce the new pound (equivalent to a million former pounds). Afterwards inflation stabilised between 8.2 per cent and 9.6 per cent, until 2008 when it accelerated to 10.4 per cent, impacted by the rise in the imported inflation. In 2009, despite a context of strong growth in food and energy prices, Turkey enjoyed its best performance regarding inflation for years. The inflation rate stabilised at 6.3 per cent. In 2010 inflationary pressures were highly exacerbated due the global hike in prices for basic products and also due to the increase in locally managed prices (the price of gas in particular). Consequently inflation reached 8.6 per cent.

The monetary policy implemented by the Central Bank of Turkey has, since the economic and financial crisis of 2001, undergone deep transformations, both regarding its objectives and at the functioning level. In fact, according to its new organic law adopted in

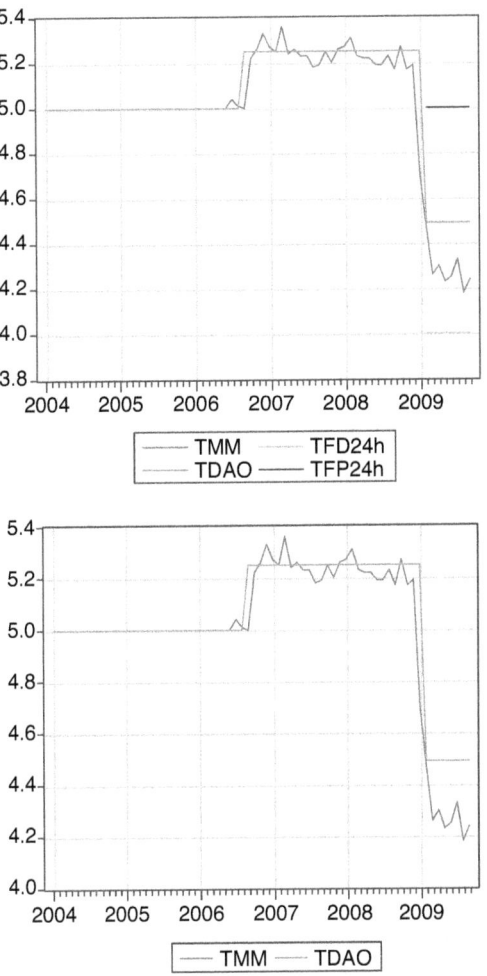

Figure 1.1   Convergence of deposit rates 2006–9 in the case of Tunisia

May 2001, the central bank became an autonomous institution in operational terms, vested with the legal mandate to assure price stability.

At the same time, as part of its efforts to cope with the world crisis and its global repercussions, an unprecedented softening of the monetary policy was noted from November 2008 until December 2009 with a drop in the key rate of 1025 basis points.

1.2 Determinants of inflation and transmission channels of monetary policies

Although inflation in the Mediterranean countries is globally dependent on the international prices for energy and food, as well as pressures inherent in domestic demand, analysis of inflation determinants and especially the transmission channels for monetary policies is based on a combined approach. Hence structural factors induced by inflationary components of monetary origin, cyclical factors (imported inflation, output gap) and external factors (cyclical position) were superposed. A modelling based on Vector Autoregressive Models (VAR) and Vector Error Correction Model (VECM) systems and on simulations of impulse shocks led to the conclusion of the primacy of monetary channels (bank loans and nominal effective exchange rate) in the transmission of monetary policies. Generally it illustrates the difficulty of using the interest rate as an operational objective (except in certain countries).

Analysis of inflation determinants is a major issue when attempting to formulate monetary policy appropriately, as well as for understanding its main mechanisms and transmission channels. Short and long-term inflation determinants are different. Although in the long term it is generally agreed that inflation is a purely monetary phenomenon,[16] in the short term inflation responds to several explanatory factors.[17] Macroeconomic models applied to this issue generally use two complementary approaches:

- estimation of the indirect impact of money supply on the general price level based on the demand for money function, or
- direct estimation of the impact on inflation of the nominal and real shocks which can affect aggregate demand compared with aggregate supply,[18] but also the effect of the price expectation mechanisms which can cause inertia behaviour (or a price – salary spiral).

In the same way, econometric works turn to alternative statistical methods which consist in estimating permanent and transitory components of inflation series by breaking them down into trends (or unobservable components) and cycles.[19] Of these methods, literature generally deals with the following areas.

The non-structural univariate approaches are based on statistical procedures rather than referring to economic theory. Their advantage is that they require less information than methods based on theory. These univariate methods (typically non-parametric) are mainly smoothing or filtering methods which do not use external information.[20] These include the first difference filter, the Henderson filter, the Christiano and Fitzgerald filter (2003), the Hodrick Prescott filter (1997),[21] the Baxter and King filter (1999), the phase-average trend (Bry and Boschan, 1971), the Stock and Watson decomposition (1988), the Harvey decomposition (1985) and the Beveridge and Nelson decomposition (1981).[22] The use of filters means that certain choice frequencies can be eliminated.

Structural and parametric approaches based on time series models which use either VARs (structural VARs) by integrating constraints dictated by economic theory, or (Autoregressive Integrated Moving Average (ARIMA) Seasonal ARIMA Model (SARIMA)) modelling.

Non-structural multivariate approaches, based on multivariate analysis methods for time series which use either the Beveridge and Nelson decomposition or a multivariate version of the Hodrick Prescott filter[23] or Harvey's multivariate method of unobservable components (1985).

Notwithstanding the anticipatory mechanisms, the theoretical determinants of inflation can be divided into three groups:[24]

(1) The first group deals with structural factors induced by inflationary components of monetary origin. According to the monetary approach of the balance of payments, these components mainly concern (i) the expansive effects of monetary counterparts (claims on the economy and net assets abroad), (ii) money gaps (real and autonomous) and (iii) inflationary pass-through effects.

(2) The second group concerns cyclical inflation factors or inflationary components induced by internal demand such as (i) imported inflation (in particular linked with energy, raw products and other imported intermediate inputs)[25] and (ii) the output gap (here understood as a resumption increase recorded

by global GDP compared with its long-term potential level, or a positive output gap, synonymous with an economic upswing, can cause inflationary pressures resulting from demand).[26]

(3) The third group pools external factors (or variables of the external environment) as well as other indicators of inflation, and in particular (i) variations in the cyclical position of the economy (or cyclical concordance indicators) and (ii) specific qualitative indicators of confidence, business climate or of early warning, and so on.

1.2.1 Selection of indicators and econometric methodology

The statements that follow summarise the theoretical and applied arguments developed by Mouley, S. (2011). The determinants of inflation address simultaneously (i) inflationary components of monetary origin; (ii) inflationary components induced by internal demand (or cyclical factors); and (iii) early indicators linked to exogenous factors. In our case practice, the non-availability of all data on a monthly basis (specifically for GDP, import prices index[27] to detect imported inflation and pass-through or other specific qualitative indicators) means that valid proxies must be selected.

1.2.2 Construction of variables and series used

First of all, taking Tunisia as the reference case, an evaluation of the impacts of specific economic determinants on the behaviour of inflation was made on a monthly frequency basis for the period 01:2004 to 12:2009. In particular, the following battery of determinants for inflation in Tunisia was used.[28]

- At the level of structural factors or inflation components of monetary origin, behaviour of loans to the economy (CREDEC) and the trend in the nominal effective exchange rate (TCEN)[29] were selected to determine the mechanism ascribed to the exchange rate pass-through effect.
- At the level of domestic demand components or cyclical inflation factors, initially imported inflation was used. In this context we referred to fluctuations in the international price for energy imports (PENERGI).[30] Generally speaking, variability of international prices of main imported raw materials (energy

and non-energy) is considered as a proxy not only for imported inflation but also of exogenous supply shocks.[31]

- Finally, the cyclical position of the economy is evaluated based on variance in real GDP at constant prices approximated by the industrial production index (IPI)[32] base 100:2000. Because of a high correlation rate between the growth rate of quarterly GDP and the growth rate of the IPI, the latter was in fact used as a direct proxy for monthly GDP.[33] Also, using the IPI means agriculture can be excluded from production since it is a sector which is heavily dependent on the vagaries of the weather and would tend to distort the results of the econometric estimations.[34]

The inflation rate (TINF) is based on monthly inflation with year-on-year rates and is calculated from the monthly consumer price index (IPC).[35] We have added the trend in the monetary market rate (TMM) to these determinants, to allow for monetary policy intervention in the interbank market, as well as the trend in the stock market index (TUNINDEX) base 100:2000. On the other hand, at the level of exogenous variables, besides the price for energy imports (PENERGI), we have added variability of foreign supply, approximated by the fluctuation in the industrial production index of the eurozone (IPIZE). All the data used are expressed as logarithms in terms of levels except for the interest rate.

1.2.2.1 VAR modelling

The procedures of augmented Dickey-Fuller tests (ADF) applied to variables converted into logarithms (except for money market rate) enabled the rejection of the null hypothesis of the unit root for all variables which are therefore non-stationary in level. However, first differences show a stationary behaviour. A non-stationary state of variables in level means making econometric estimates in a multivariate frame. In the absence of cointegration relationships between the variables used, a VAR model in terms of level[36] is estimated without restrictions on the estimated coefficients.[37] Since all variables are I(1) in level and thus I(0) in first difference, the VAR(p) model estimated in level is expressed as

$$Z_t = A(L)Z_{t-1} + B(L)X_t + \mu_t$$

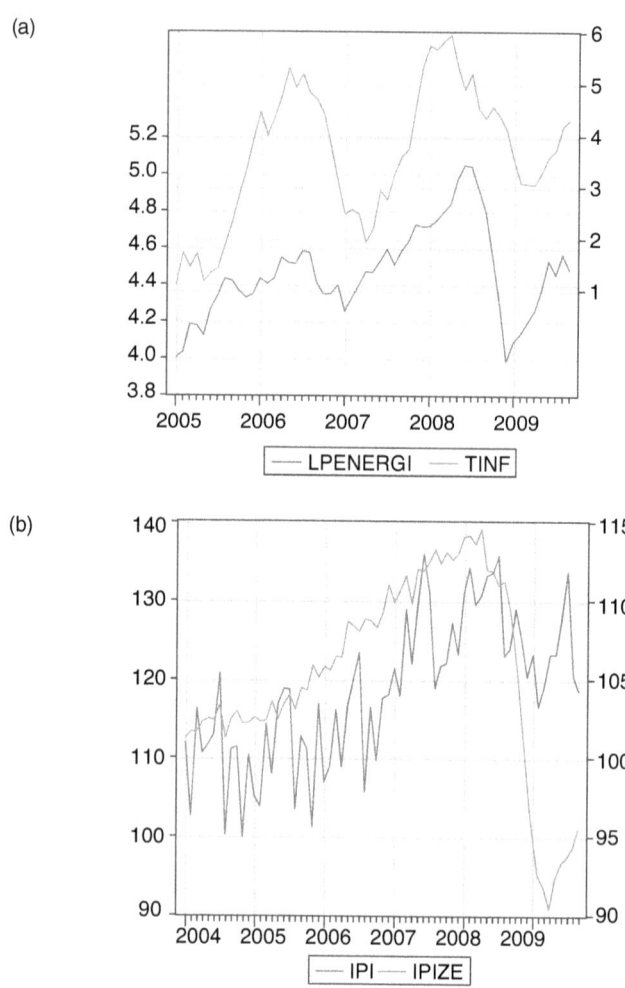

Figure 1.2 Comparison of trends for inflation and industrial production – case of Tunisia. (a) Comparison of trends for inflation and volatility of imported energy prices; (b) Comparison of trends for industrial production indexes, Tunisia – eurozone

Source: Mouley, S. (2011).

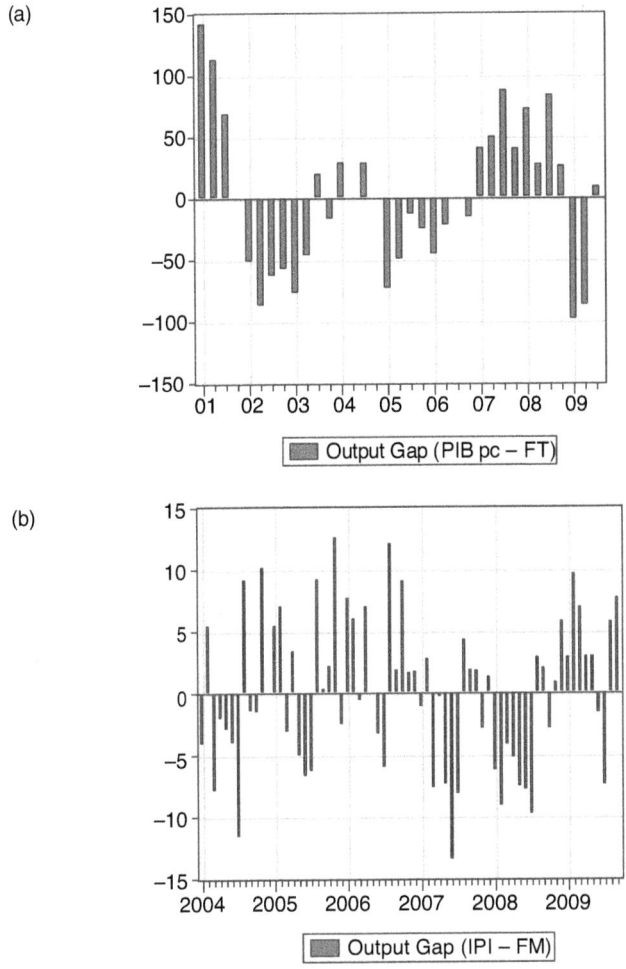

Figure 1.3 Output gaps (real GDP and IPI) – case of Tunisia. (a) Output gap (real GDP with constant prices on quarterly data); (b) Output gap (IPI on monthly data)

Source: Mouley, S. (2011).

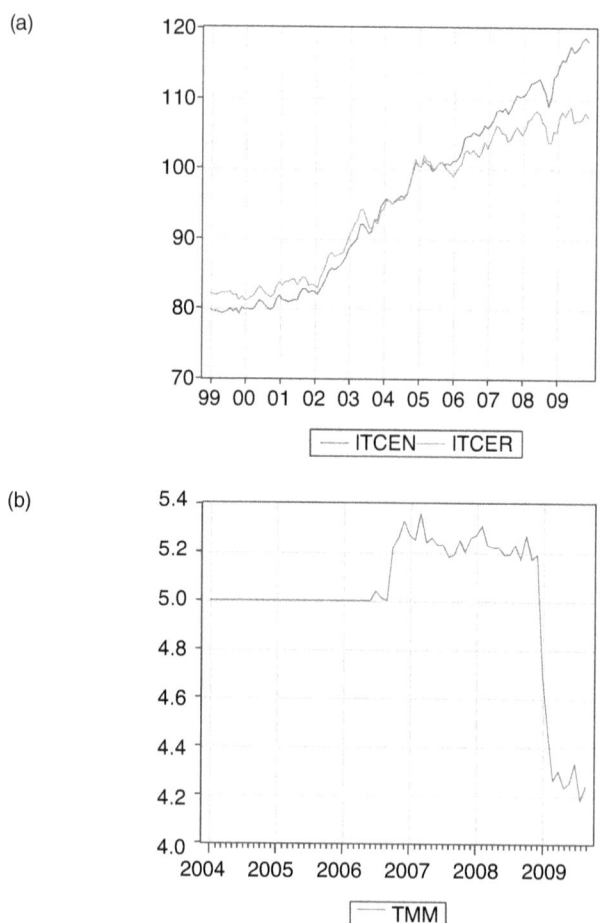

Figure 1.4   Effective exchange rates – case of Tunisia. (a) Evolution of nominal (ITCEN) and real (ITCER) effective exchange rate indexes; (b) Average monetary market rate

Source: Mouley, S. (2011).

where Z_t is the vector of endogenous variables, X_t a vector of exogenous variables and μ_t is a residual vector. The structure of the lags or the number of optimal lags in the VAR model was determined using Akaike's AIC information criterion as well as using the likelihood

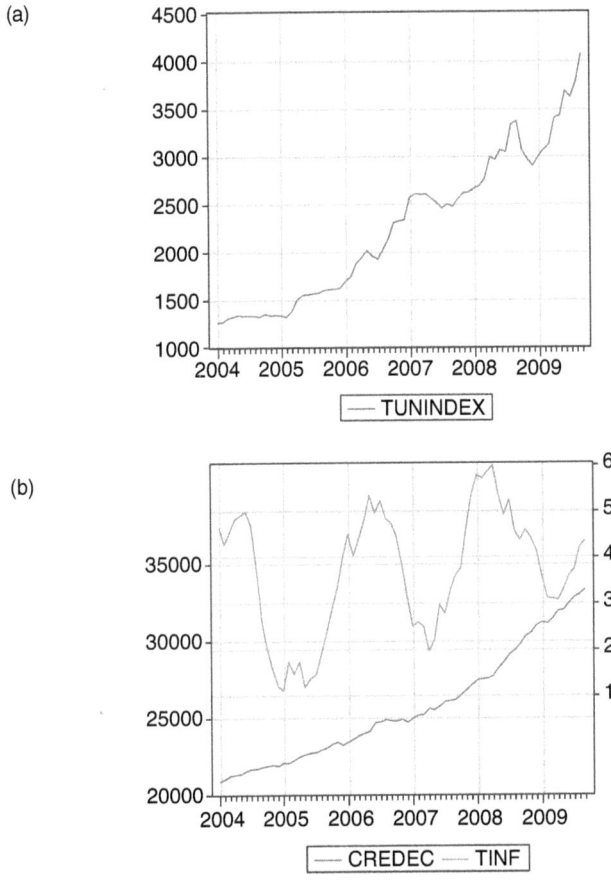

(a)

(b)

Figure 1.5 Stock exchange index, credit to economy and inflation – case of Tunisia. (a) Stock exchange index; (b) Comparison of the trend of inflation and credit to economy

Source: Mouley, S. (2011).

ratio test (LR) which consists in comparing two alternative lags according to the following set of hypotheses:

$$\begin{cases} H_0 : p = p_0 \\ H_1 : p = p_1 \end{cases} p_1 > p_0$$

The test statistics can be expressed as follows:

$$LR = -2\left(\hat{L}_0 - \hat{L}_1\right) \equiv T\left(\log\left|\hat{\Omega}_0\right| - \log\left|\hat{\Omega}_1\right|\right) \to \chi^2_{(q)}$$

where $\hat{L}_0$ and $\hat{L}_0$, respectively are the log likelihoods relating to the estimation of VAR(p_0) and VAR(p_1) models, $\hat{\Omega}_0 \, et \, \hat{\Omega}_1$ are variance-covariance matrices of the residual estimation of the VAR(p_0) and VAR(p_1) models respectively which are expressed as

$$\hat{\Omega}_i = \frac{1}{T}\sum_{t=1}^{T}\hat{\varepsilon}_t\left(p_i\right)\hat{\varepsilon}_t{}'\left(p_i\right) \qquad i = 0,1$$

$|\cdot|$ indicates the determinant of $\hat{\Omega}_i$, $i = 0,1$, $q = n^2\left(p_1 - p_0\right)$ indicates the number of restrictions under a null hypothesis H_0 and (n) is the number of equations or endogenous variables.

By comparing specifications of VAR(1) and VAR(2), the preceding tests enabled us to conclude that dynamics are better expressed by the specification VAR(1).[38]

1.2.3   The transmission channels of monetary policy

The effects of the impulses and the implementation of monetary policy on the level of inflation are generally transmitted through the following channels.[39]

- The interest rate channel: in the sense that a variation in the real interest rate affects the decisions of economic agents through higher costs of financing consumption and investment.
- The exchange rate channel:[40] a modification of the intervention measures of the monetary policy acting on the interest rate results in reallocation of financial portfolios, which impacts on the exchange rate[41] in an open economy with capital mobility. It results price-effects of the exchange rate on foreign trade.
- The bank credit channel: in an economy where financing is dominated by banking intermediation, intervention measures of monetary policy act directly on the potential volume of loans offered by the banking system, and consequently modify the amount of deposits and reserves.

- The price of financial assets channel: modification of the instruments of monetary policy impacts the price of financial assets as a result of portfolio arbitration that companies carry out between prices of equities and bonds[42] or wealth arbitration which the consumer households perform between holding currency and holding securities (liquidity effect).[43]
- The balance sheet channel: by affecting the value of guarantees (or collateral) due on bank loans, the decisions of monetary policy affect the profitability of companies and the solvency of consumers, which leads banks to adjust their volume of loans.[44]

1.2.3.1   Tunisia

With the VAR(1) level model[45] estimated, the impulse response functions or the domestic shock effects[46] of monetary policy equivalent to an innovation of one standard deviation at the level of domestic prices with a confidence interval of 95 per cent are given as follows.

- A monetary shock of a temporary and unexpected increase of credit to the economy will lead to an immediate inflationary impact on the level of prices, which will stabilise and becomes permanent from the fifth month.
- At the level of the pass-through effect, a temporary and unexpected drop in the nominal effective exchange rate will induce a temporary rise in the inflation. This is accompanied by the same effect, but of a more limited extent, of an increase in the price of energy imports.
- A rise in the interest rate (restrictive monetary policy) temporarily reduces inflation but induces a subsequent contraction of short-term activity, which then helps to stabilise the level of medium and long-term prices (sacrifice ratio). Conversely, any real supply shock, and thus an expansion of activity, will lead to inflationary pressures on the general level of prices (augmented Philips curve) which nevertheless tend to become neutral from the 10th month and end with a NAIRU. Although the interest rate channel appears to be verified, the amplitude of the reaction of prices to a temporary and unexpected shock of a rise in the interest rate is low and short term and the restrictive effect tends to become neutral at the end of the fourth month.

- As a consequence, it seems that the standard mechanism of action via the interest rate collides with an inverted phenomenon of Keynesian trap to liquidity, in the sense that implementation of a restrictive monetary policy that involves an increase in the interest rate proves ineffective by generating disinflation only in the very short term. In the medium term, however, the supply of liquidity specifically via bank loans will tend to increase in spite of the adjustment to higher interest rates, which is likely to contribute to a resumption of inflation.[47] Moreover, several academic studies have confirmed the low elasticity or total inelasticity of gross fixed capital formation at the interest rate in Tunisia, irrespective of the specifications adopted by the investment function. The extent of the reaction of prices to a temporary and unexpected shock of the interest rate is lower than that caused by a monetary shock (bank loans or nominal effective exchange rate).[48]
- Finally, the financial assets price channel seems totally inoperative in Tunisia. In theory a modification of the monetary policy instrument (for example a drop in the interest rate) would cause a rise in inflation that would lead to a rise in the price of financial assets as a result of portfolio arbitrage, and specifically the wealth (liquidity) effect which would follow (increasing preference for the holding bonds and debentures against holding currency). In

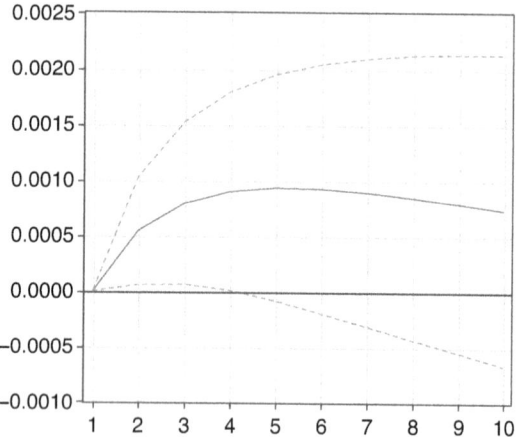

Figure 1.6   Response of LIPC to one SD LCREDEC innovation

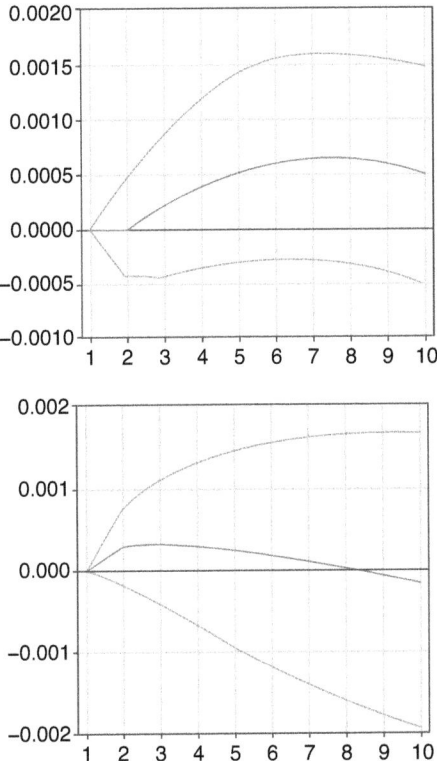

Figure 1.7 Response of LIPC to one SD LTCEN innovation (top) and one SD LENERGI innovation (bottom)

this case, an increase in the TUNINDEX index is associated with a drop in inflation, which makes the impact of this transmission channel contrary to the expected theoretical effect.

We can also analyse the behaviour of variables other than IPC, and in particular the impact of a depreciation of the exchange rate on economic activity. Specifically, an effective depreciation of the nominal exchange rate would induce a temporary increase in inflation and create a short-term expansion of activity; however, the medium-term effect would be gradually contractionist. The same results

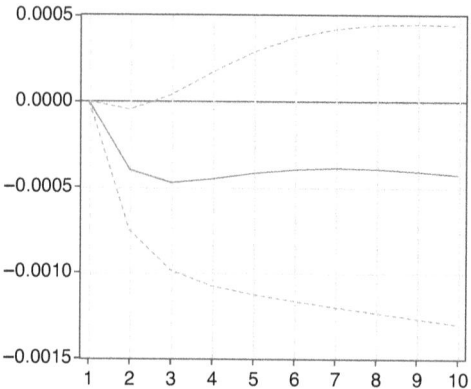

Figure 1.8   Response of LIPC to one SD TMM innovation

were noted as previously mentioned for the augmented Philips curve. In other words, in the logic of the Kaldor-Vernon generalised model (KVGM), a competitive depreciation of the exchange rate produces a positive elasticity-price effect on exports, without these contributing significantly or lastingly to economic growth.[49]

Therefore the monetary channels (bank loans and nominal effective exchange rate) are the main transmission channels of monetary policy in Tunisia. On the other hand, and because of delays in transmission of monetary policy to inflation, the interest rate channel appears to be weak. Consequently, in order to influence banking liquidity, a modulation of the monetary policy would be useful with temporary intervention mechanisms targeting the monetary transmission channels – exchange rate and bank loans. Another striking fact concerns blocking of transmission channels for monetary policy. Monetary policy influences the conditions of financing provided by banks to companies and brings transmission mechanisms into play that interfere with their investment decisions and affect their profitability. In fact, an increase in the interest rate (monetary policy tightening) temporarily reduces inflation. Nevertheless the response range of prices is weak and short term in Tunisia. This basic result reveals the difficulty of using the interest rate as an operational objective. Moreover, the response range of prices to the interest rate is much weaker than that induced by a monetary shock (bank loans or nominal effective exchange rate).

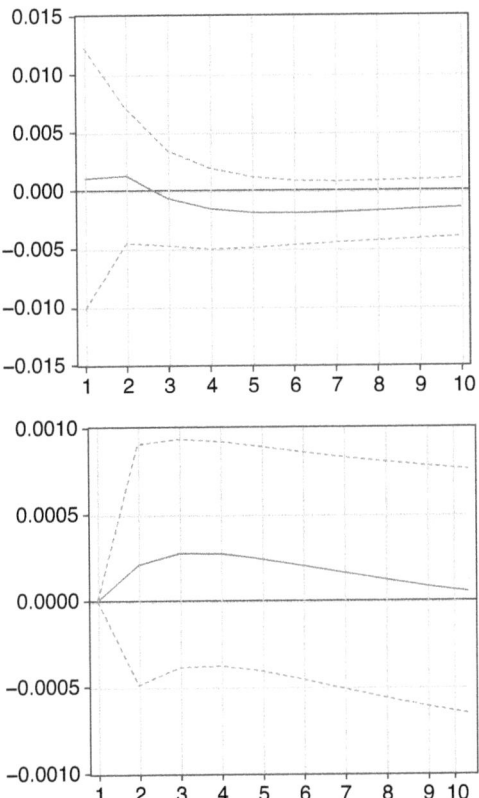

Figure 1.9 Response of LIPI to one SD TMM Innovation (top) and one SD LIPI Innovation (bottom)

Specifically, although the CBT undertakes to influence the short-term nominal interest rate (or money market rate) by fixing its key rate or its call for bids rate (depending on the level of banking liquidity), the relevant interest rate that should be analysed is rather the long-term real interest rate, which represents the real cost of loans in the case of investment financing by banks. However, in this context there is a time inconsistency between current implementation of monetary policy and the expectations of Tunisian companies. Lowering the interest rate puts the economy in a liquidity trap because operators no longer decide between money and securities

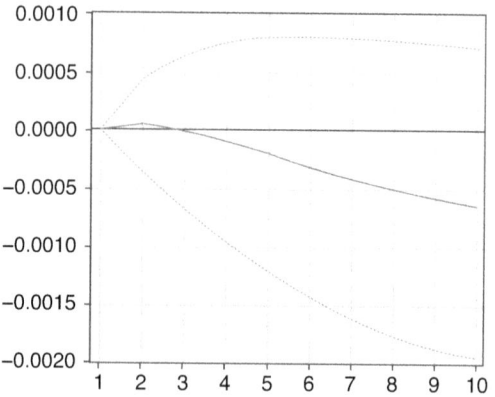

Figure 1.10   Response of LIPC to one SD LTUNINDEX Innovation

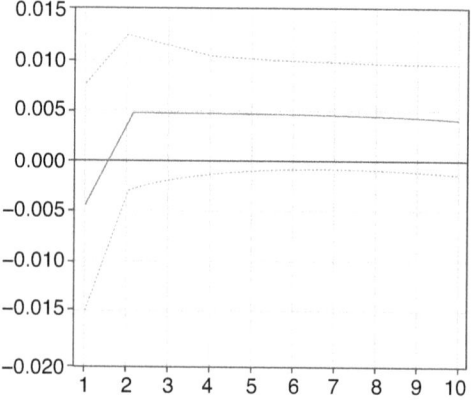

Figure 1.11   Response of LIPI to one SD LTCEN Innovation

so that an increase in the money supply (injection of money) is without effect on real activity. In situations of deflation crises, where a real interest rate close to zero would be useful, this rate cannot be obtained. This suggests having a target of positive inflation.

In reality, there is no single interest rate but an outfit range in which each rate corresponds to a term (maturity) and a category of specific borrowers. The sequence of rates used for various outlooks constitutes the curve of rates, which is still not yet available in the banking system. In such circumstances the intervention of the CBT at the short end of the curve, by fixing the reference rate for operations on a day-to-day basis (key rate) has no effect on debtor rates according to which loans are calculated. Freeing up the interest rate channel requires implementation of unconventional mechanisms and measures.

1.2.3.2 Comparisons with Mediterranean countries

A comparative analysis of the transmission channels of monetary policy impulses concentrates solely on interest rate and exchange rate channels. Estimates are given on a quarterly frequency for a longer period Q1:1990 to Q4:2008, according to the approach developed by Neaime, S. (2008).

The inflation rate which refers to quarterly inflation with year-on-year trends is calculated on the basis of quarterly IPC.[50] All variables are expressed in logarithms except the interest rate.[51] Unit root tests applied to variables converted into logarithms mean that the null hypothesis of a unit root for all variables can be rejected, which are therefore not stationary regarding level. On the other hand, the initial differences display stationary behaviour. The non-stationary nature of the variables in level requires econometric estimates to be studied in a multivariate context. In the absence of cointegration relationships between the retained variables, a VAR(1) level model[52] is estimated without restrictions on the coefficients of each country. The response functions[53] or domestic shock effects of monetary policy equivalent to an innovation of one standard deviation in the level of domestic prices with a confidence interval of 95 per cent yield the following results.

In Egypt, the prices respond quickly to an exchange rate appreciation via their tradable goods prices component. The exchange rate appreciation is inevitably transformed into a lowering of the interest rate to unblock contraction pressures on domestic output. On the other hand, a fall in the interest rate also reduces capital inflows and helps, in the medium term, to lower the exchange rate appreciation which could handicap export competitiveness.

In Jordan, a shock on the exchange rate has a significant effect on output, on prices and on the interest rate. This is mainly attributable to the rigidity of monetary policy, which focuses only on the

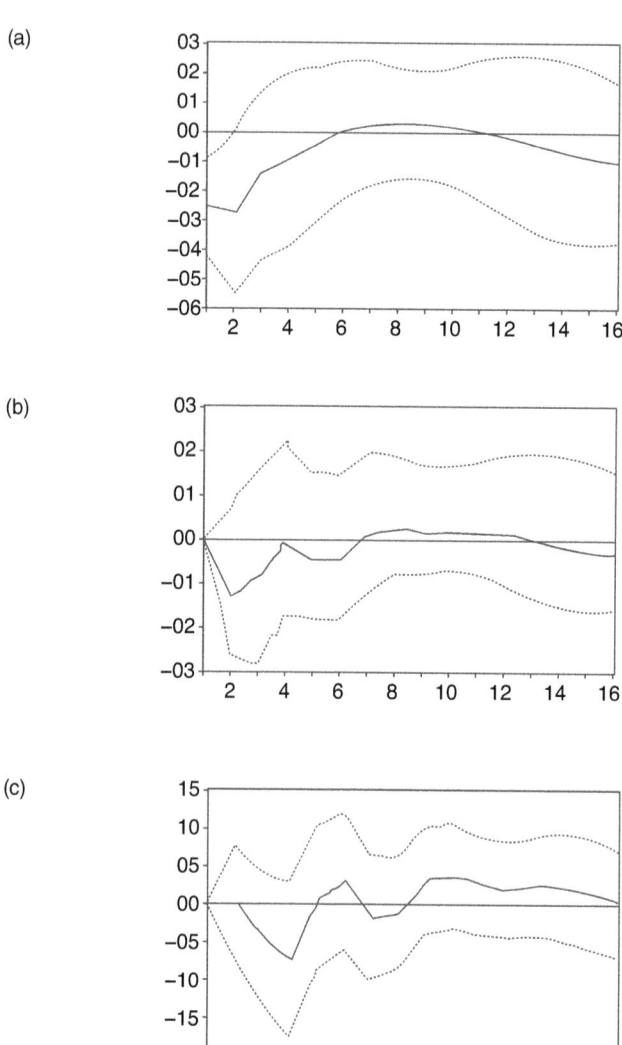

Figure 1.12   Continued

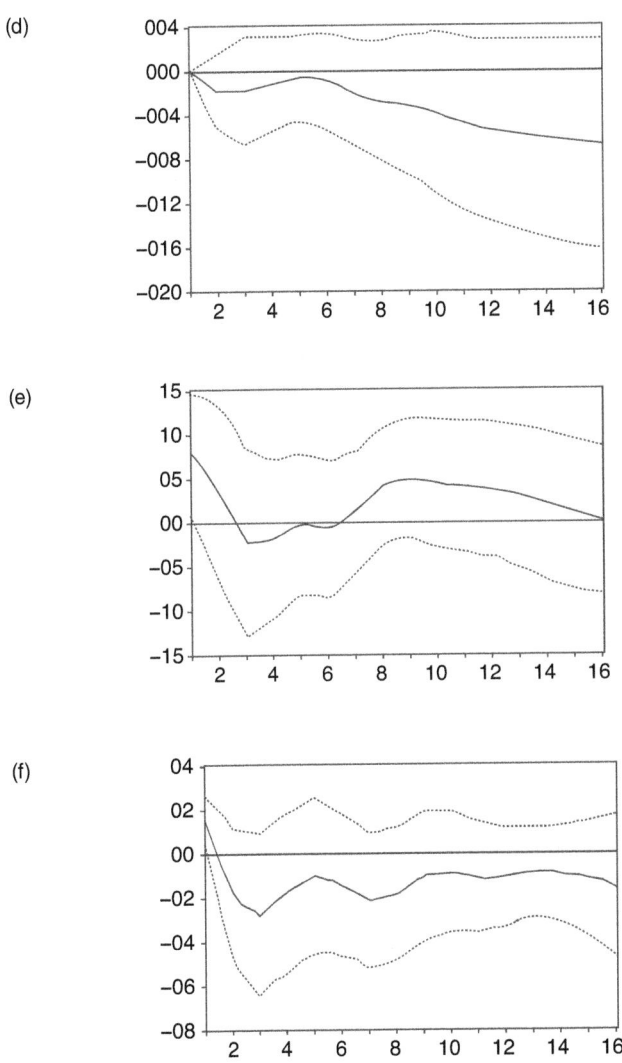

Figure 1.12 Response of CPI, TB and GDP to ER and TB in Egypt. (a) Response of CPI to ER; (b) Response of GDP to ER; (c) Response of TB to ER; (d) Response of CPI to TB; (e) Response of GDP to TB; (f) Response of ER to TB

exchange rate targeting and does not allow fine tuning of the macroeconomic situation by easing monetary conditions. The effect of a shock on the interest rate appears to be the most significant for GDP, where transmission is fast and with no adjustments delays.

In Lebanon, inflation is affected significantly by a shock on the exchange rate, so that a rise in the interest rate inevitably translates into a nominal appreciation. In fact, this adjustment mechanism is due to the control of the treasury bonds rate by the central bank as an operational instrument of monetary policy in order to stabilise the exchange rate of the national currency.

In Morocco, prices respond quickly to any exchange rate appreciation which is followed by a significant and permanent response to a lowering of the interest rate. Besides prices, real domestic output also decreases in the short term as a consequence of the interest rate shock and causes contractionary pressures. Lowering of the interest rate reduces capital inflows and contributes in the medium term to lowering the exchange rate appreciation which could handicap export competitiveness.

Finally, in Turkey the exchange rate trend appears to be disconnected from GDP dynamics, from inflation and from the interest rate as a result of recent currency crises. The interest rate channel has become neutral compared with the exchange rate channel.

1.3 The response functions of central banks

1.3.1 From simple functions to augmented functions

The well know example of simple rules is Taylor's rule (cf. Taylor J. B., 1993),[54] which is used by central banks when evaluating the optimum level of the interest rate instrument for efficient implementation of monetary policy. It formulates an inflation target and a growth target, and can be expressed as follows:[55]

$$i_t = r^* + \pi^* + \alpha \cdot (\pi_t - \pi^*) + \beta \cdot (y_t - y_t^*) \tag{1}$$

where

i_t is the short-term nominal interest rate;

r^* is the real equilibrium (or neutral) interest rate, that is a rate which is compatible with the long term equilibrium growth rate (or potential growth rate);

π_t is the inflation rate;
π^* is the targeted inflation rate;
y_t is the output (GDP) (in log);
y_t^* is the potential output (in log);
$y_t - y_t^*$ is the output gap.

The central bank manipulates the interest rate according essentially to the deviation of inflation from its target or anticipated value. In particular Taylor's equation is used frequently to evaluate the suitability of monetary policy to fundamental economic data. It has therefore necessarily been subject to numerous developments. Taylor's rule has been the subject of numerous studies by several authors. This rule relies in fact on a purely monetary conception in the sense that the real interest rate must equal, in equilibrium level, the real growth rate of the economy. Nevertheless, the prospective and operational impact of this rule relies on the selection of variables and on their scheduling (Jaillet, 1998), and seems therefore debatable. Taylor's previous simple rule does not specify any adjustment mechanisms. In practice central banks adjust their key rates gradually. The interest rate is not only dependent on a notional or desired rate (derived from Taylor's rule) but on the rate prevalent in the previous period:

$$i_t = \varphi \cdot i_{t-1} + r^* + \pi^* + \alpha \cdot (\pi_t - \pi^*) + \beta \cdot (y_t - y_t^*) \qquad (2)$$

where φ is the smoothing coefficient.

Alternative rules exclude production gaps because of inaccuracies of measurements and take into consideration only the inflation rule (Orphanides, 1998; Orphanides et al., 2000):

$$i_t = r^* + \pi^* + \alpha \cdot (\pi_t - \pi^*) \qquad (3)$$

In order to best represent the behaviour of central banks, other approaches also take into account the specifications of the framework for implementation of monetary policy. Besides the ultimate goal of price stability, the authorities can adopt a strategy of monitoring a monetary aggregate at a transitional stage. The response functions of an augmented Taylor type take then the following forms.

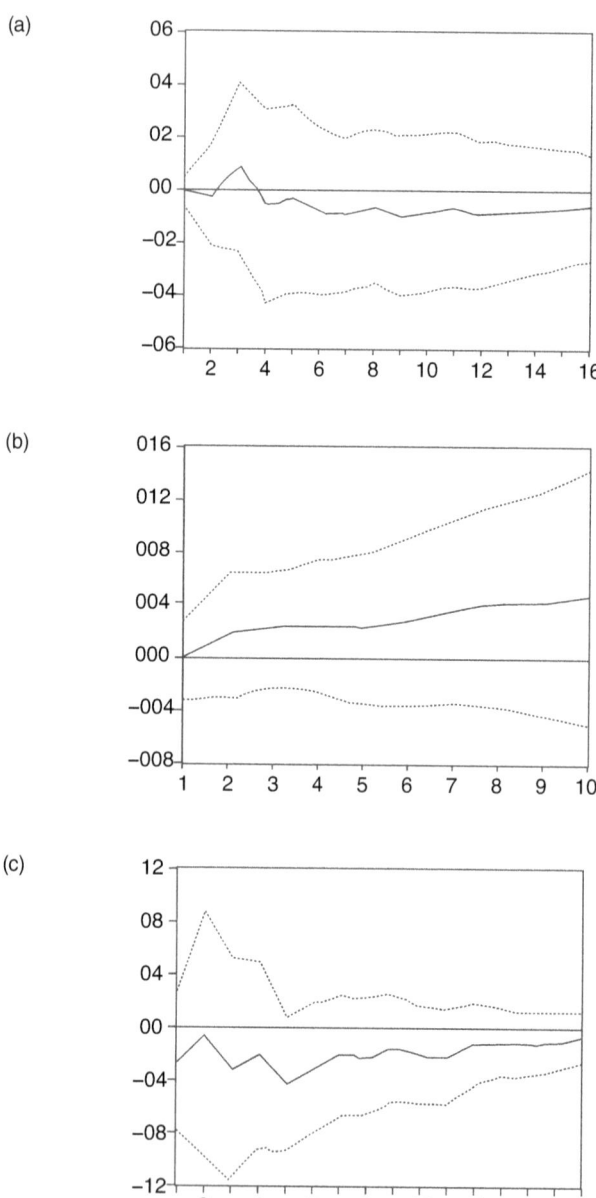

Figure 1.13   Continued

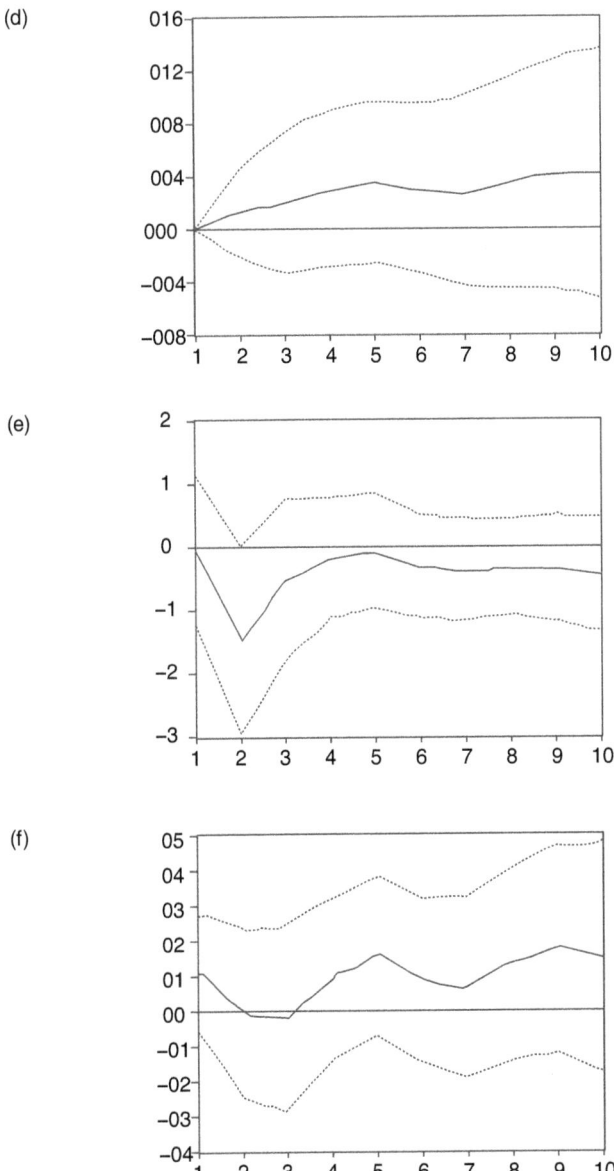

Figure 1.13 Response of CPI, TB and GDP to ER and TB in Jordan. (a) Response of CPI to ER; (b) Response of GDP to ER; (c) Response of TB to ER; (d) Response of CPI to TB; (e) Response of GDP to TB; (f) Response of ER to TB

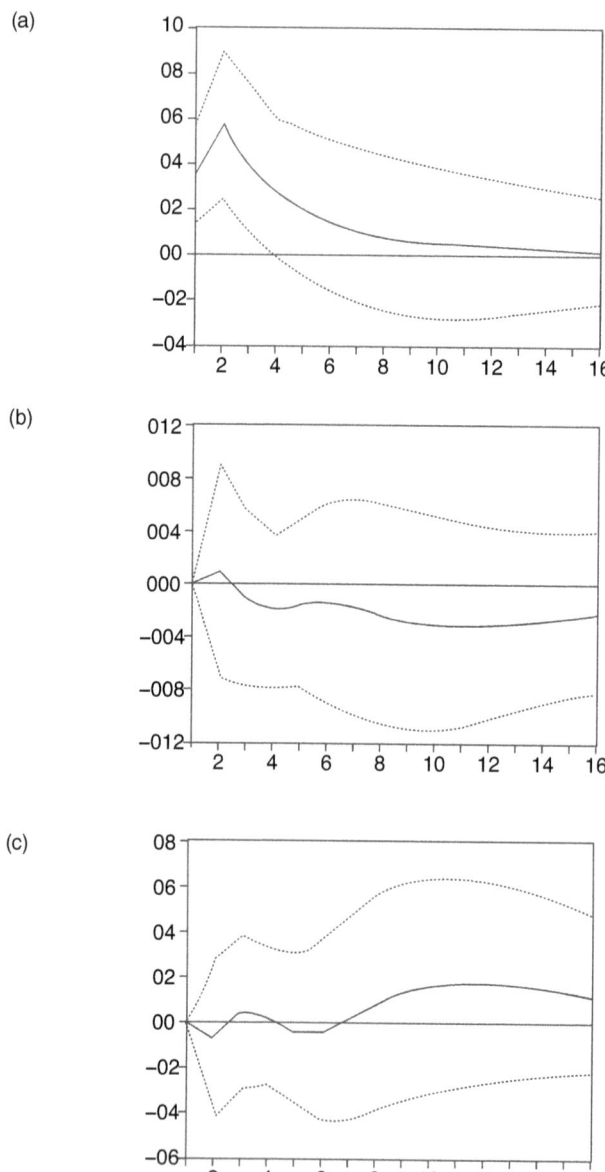

Figure 1.14   Continued

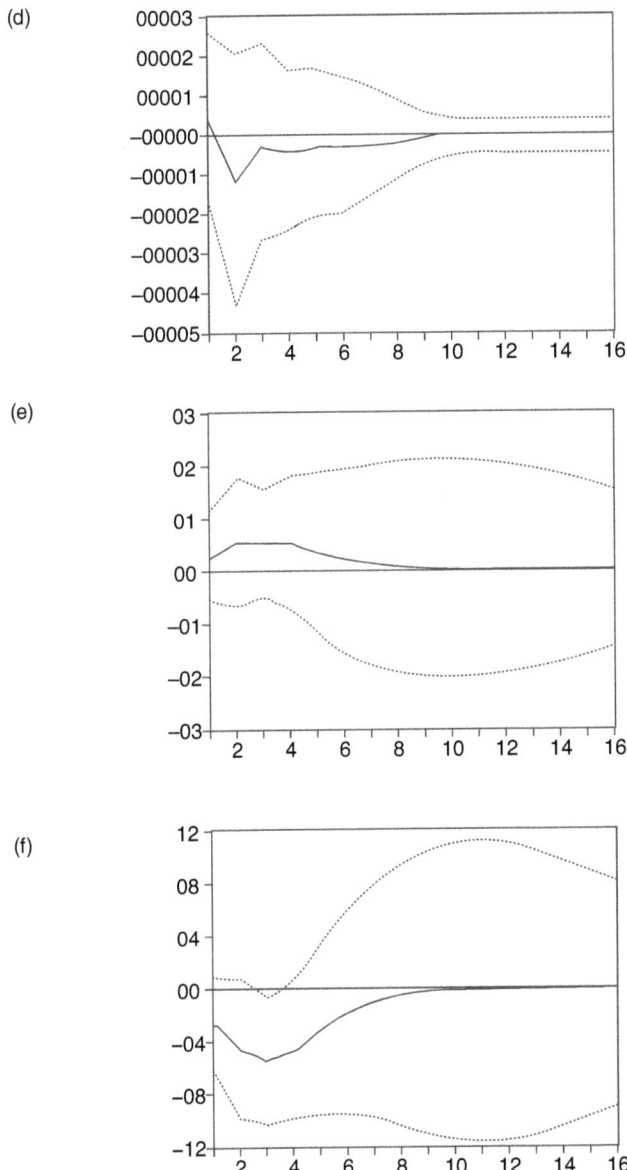

Figure 1.14 Response of CPI, TB and GDP to ER and TB in Lebanon. (a) Response of CPI to ER; (b) Response of GDP to ER; (c) Response of TB to ER; (d) Response of CPI to TB; (e) Response of GDP to TB; (f) Response of ER to TB

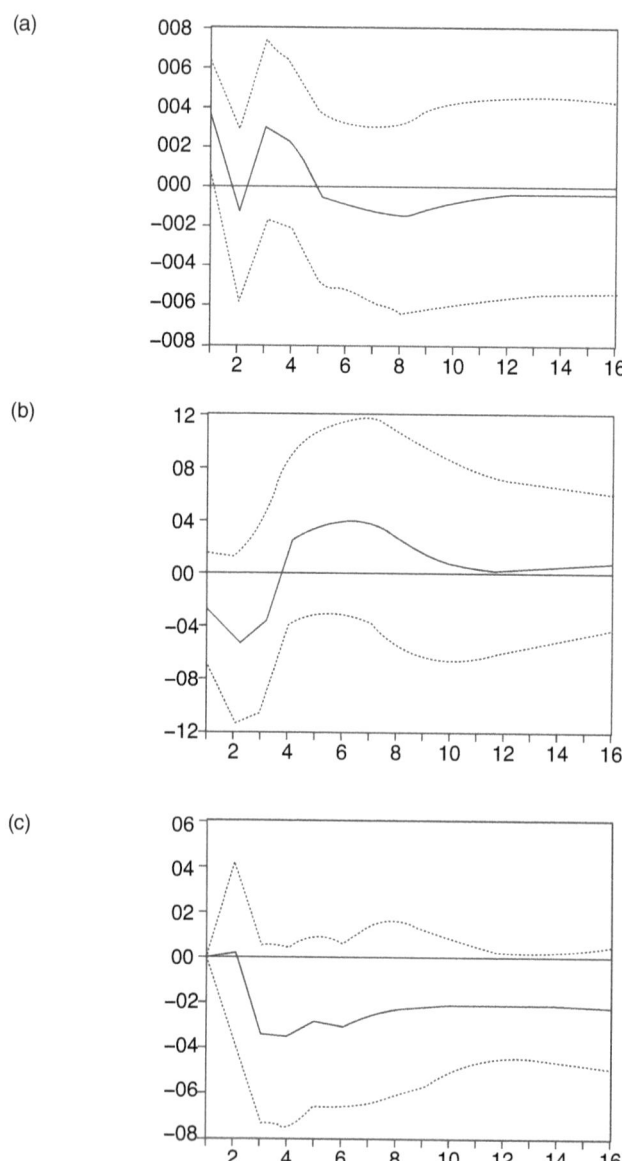

Figure 1.15   Continued

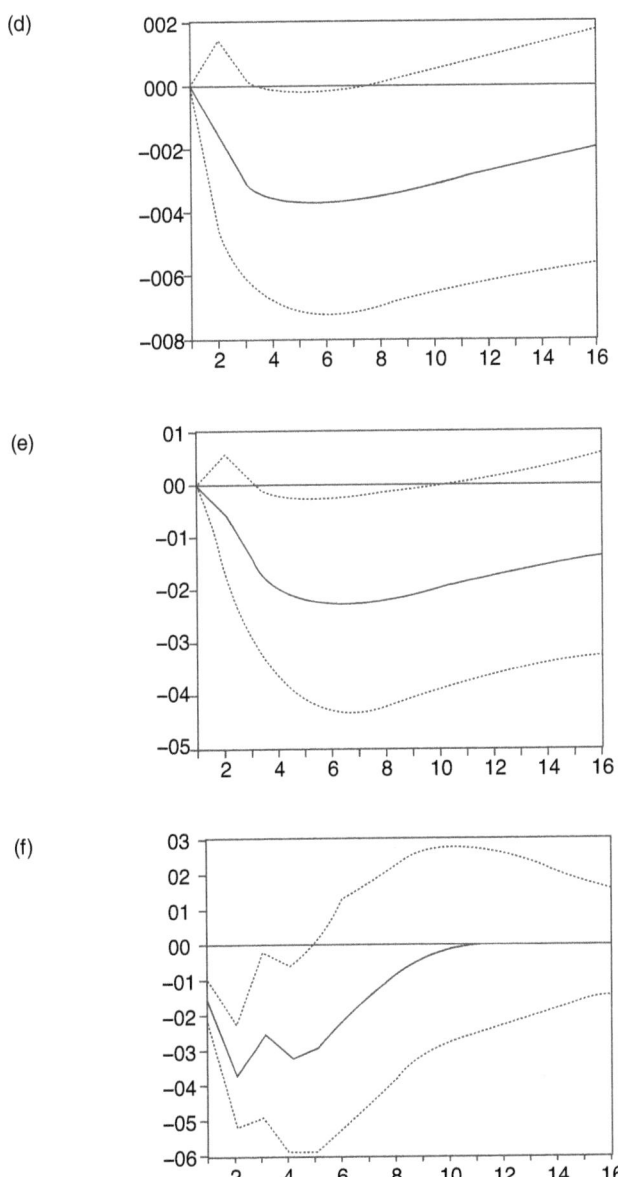

Figure 1.15 Response of CPI, TB and GDP to ER and TB in Morocco. (a)
Response of CPI to ER; (b) Response of GDP to ER; (c) Response of TB to ER; (d)
Response of CPI to TB; (e) Response of GDP to TB; (f) Response of ER to TB

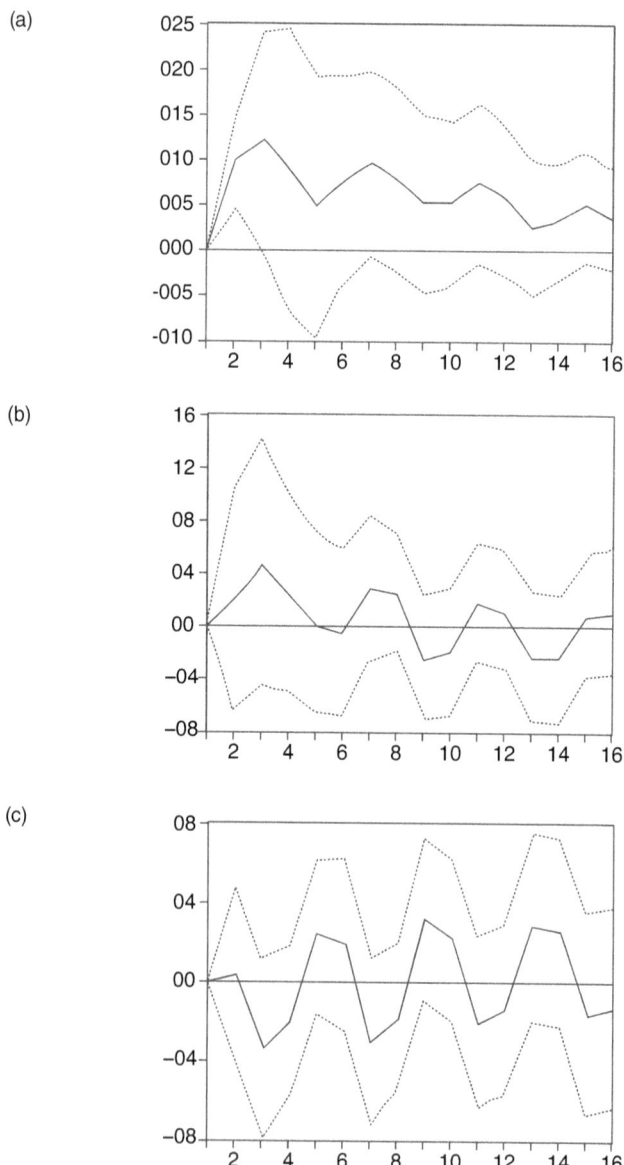

Figure 1.16   Continued

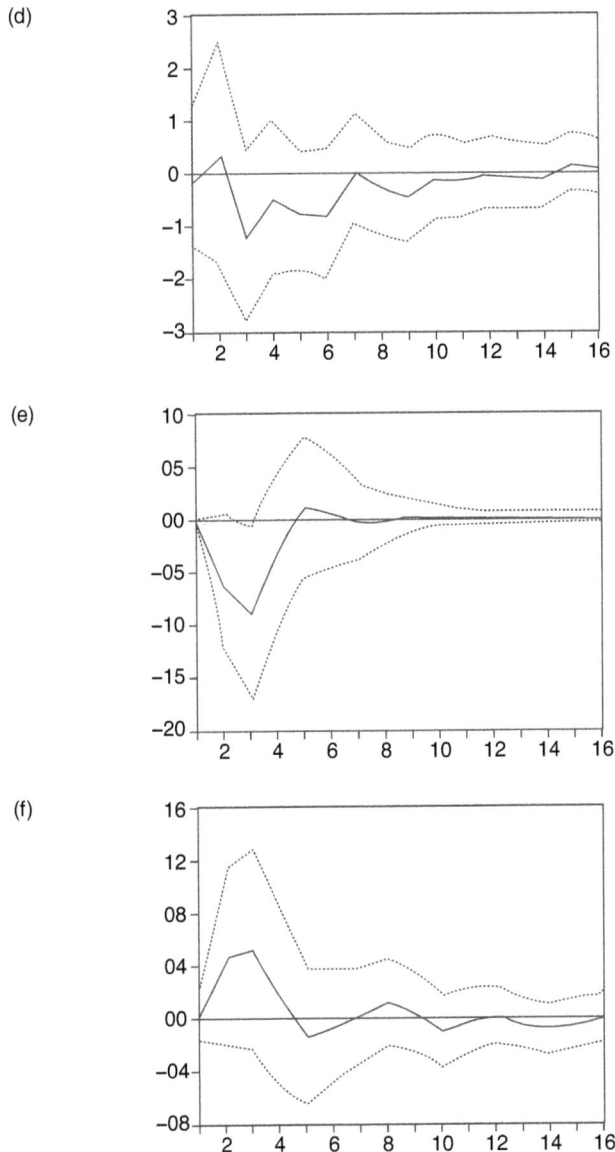

Figure 1.16 Response of CPI, TB and GDP to ER and TB in Turkey. (a) Response of CPI to ER; (b) Response of GDP to ER; (c) Response of TB to ER; (d) Response of CPI to TB; (e) Response of GDP to TB; (f) Response of ER to TB

Monetary targeting:

$$i_t = \alpha + \varphi \cdot i_{t-1} + \beta \cdot (\Delta m_t - \Delta m_t^*) + \gamma \cdot (y_t - y_t^*) + \xi_t \tag{4}$$

Implicit inflation targeting:

$$i_t = \alpha + \varphi \cdot i_{t-1} + \beta \cdot (\pi - \pi_t^*) + \gamma \cdot (y_t - y_t^*) + \xi_t \tag{5}$$

where ξ_t is a term of error which is by definition orthogonal to all available information and follows a normal law.

Similarly, according to the NAIRU process,[56] other authors have suggested improving Taylor's rule by including not only the inflation level but also its variation (as proxy for the output gap). Leitemo and Lønning (2001) advocate the following formula for that purpose:

$$i_t = r^* + \pi^* + \alpha \cdot (\pi_t - \pi^*) + \gamma \cdot (\pi_t - \pi_{t-1}) \tag{6}$$

In particular, the McCallum rule (1987, 1993) is an alternative monetarist rule in terms of nominal GDP for evaluating NAIRU (corresponding to the long-term real growth rate).[57] The central bank acts on the level of the monetary base depending on the gap between nominal GDP and its potential level. Nominal GDP is the target variable while the monetary base represents the instrument. The growth rates of the monetary base are fixed every quarter in order to keep the growth of nominal GDP close to a NAIRU corresponding to the long-term real growth rate. The response function specifies the adjustment that the central bank has to make with respect to the deviation of effective GDP compared with target GDP. In other words, the central bank manipulates the interest rate according to the inflation gap but also the output gap:

$$i_t = r^* + \pi^* + \alpha \cdot (\pi_t - \pi^*) + \gamma \cdot (u_t - u_t^*) \tag{7}$$

where u_t and u_t^* respectively represent the current and the natural unemployment rates in the sense of the augmented expectations Phillips' curve.

This relation between production and unemployment is known as Okun's law and allows the output gap to be substituted by the unemployment gap. However, this rule has some limits, as pointed out by several authors. First of all, in order to make this rule operational, it is necessary to estimate the natural unemployment rate with very different and complex concepts (structural, equilibrium, NAIRU (Non-accelerating inflation rate of unemployment), NAWRU (Non-accelerating wage rate of unemployment), and so on). Then, as rightly demonstrated by Kahn, G. A. (1988), the response of the authorities to short-term shocks with a nominal GDP objective depends on the nature of the shock. If a nominal GDP objective can mitigate the effects of short-term demand shocks, it is not necessarily the same for supply shocks.

A positive demand shock (lowering of tax rates or improvement of confidence) entails a rise in prices together with short-term quantities, while a positive supply shock (lowering of inflation forecasts or a drop in the price of raw materials) entails a drop in prices and an increase in short-term quantities. However, McCallum (1995a) states that these shocks exist irrespective of the objective and that a nominal GDP rule is the most efficient to mitigate the effects. Furthermore, GDP statistics are not available quickly and are often revised. Moreover, this rule refers to a very particular institutional context where the authorities have perfect control over the monetary base (Woodford, 1994). Should the opposite occur, certain authors suggest taking into account concepts of financial stability by substituting the output gap by the credit flows, formalising the gaps between the growth rate in credits to the economy and its potential growth rate (Bårdsen et al., 1999):

$$i_t = r^* + \pi^* + \alpha \cdot (\pi_t - \pi^*) + \Psi \cdot (\Delta c_t - \Delta c^*) \tag{8}$$

where Δc represents the growth in domestic credit and Δc^* its trend.

1.3.2 Empirical applications

The empirical study which follows illustrates the response functions of the CBT in two referential scenarios. Firstly, in the current framework for implementing of monetary policy in a managed floating system, thus authorising competitive depreciation of the nominal exchange rate and hence misalignments to its fundamental equilibrium norm. Subsequently, in a more advanced framework of capital account liberalisation.

1.3.3   Monetary policy in an exchange control scenario

We adopted an alternative or augmented form of Taylor's rule, following methodologies regularly used by central banks, in particular Board of Governors of the Federal Reserve System (FED) and European Central Bank (ECB).[58] To do so, besides smoothing the key rate (TD) and the inflation gap, we introduce the production gaps (GAPPIB) and exchange gaps (discrepancy between the nominal effective exchange rate and its fundamental equilibrium norm: GAPTCEN). At the expected inflation level in particular, we use the estimated forecast inflation in a model where residues follow an ARMA process.[59] In a second phase, an implicit inflation targeting at 3 per cent is introduced as follows.

Inflation targeting (ARMA forecast):

$$i_t = \alpha + \varphi \cdot i_{t-1} + \beta \cdot (\pi - \pi_t^*) + \gamma \cdot (y_t - y_t^*) + \lambda \cdot (s_t - s_t^*) + \xi_t \tag{9}$$

Implicit inflation targeting:

$$i_t = \alpha + \varphi \cdot i_{t-1} + \beta \cdot (\pi - 3\%) + \gamma \cdot (y_t - y_t^*) + \lambda \cdot (s_t - s_t^*) + \xi_t \tag{10}$$

where

$(y - y^*)$ is the output gap, where y designates the logarithm of real GDP and y^* the potential GDP subject to Hodrick and Prescott's filter,

$(s - s^*)$ is a misalignment of the exchange rate, where s is the nominal exchange rate and s^* is the equilibrium exchange rate estimated using the Fundamental Equilibrium Exchange Rate (FEER) method.[60]

The results are shown in following tables.

These two iterations lead to almost the same results. The estimated coefficient of the smoothing parameter, which expresses the adjustment mechanism of the interest rate, is statistically significant but relatively low compared with those from international comparisons, especially in the practices of central banks such as ECB and FED,[61] which means low volatility of the interest rate in response to fluctuations in prices. The estimated parameter of inflation gaps

Table 1.2 Augmented Taylor's rule (with inflation forecast ARMA)

Dependent variable: key interest rate

Method: least squares
Sample(adjusted): 2004:02, 2009:09
Included observations: 68 after adjusting endpoints

Variable	Coefficient	*t*-Statistic
C	0.398088	1.442492
TID(-1): Smoothing	0.091048	2.139474
TINF-TINFFARMA	0.686670	2.438096
GAPPIB	0.122597	1.368413
GAPTCEN	0.386312	2.392599
R-squared	0.843703	
Adjusted R-squared	0.833779	
LM(1):0.34 LM(2):0.41		

Table 1.3 Augmented Taylor's rule (with implicit inflation targeting)

Dependent variable: key interest rate

Method: least squares
Sample(adjusted): 2004:02, 2009:09
Included observations: 68 after adjusting endpoints

Variable	Coefficient	*t*-Statistic
C	0.828564	1.812489
TD(-1): Smoothing	0.128301	2.725142
TINF – 3 per cent	0.632910	2.377566
GAPPIB	0.060030	1.628018
GAPTCEN	0.381739	2.062192
R-squared	0.843293	
Adjusted R-squared	0.833343	
LM(1):0.31 LM(2):0.43		

is significant and higher than 0.5 (rise in interest for the objective of price stability). Finally, the GDP gap is weak and not significant, while the exchange rate gap (GAPTCEN) is higher and significant which means that exchange rate stability is more important for the CBT than real stability. The reliability of these forecasts is measured using the root-mean-square error (RMSE), with a low value in

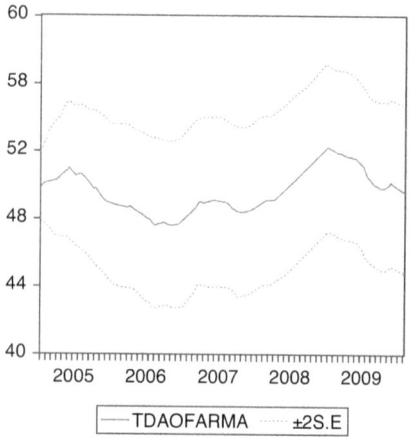

Forecast: TDAOFARMA	
Actual: TDAO	
Sample: 2004:022008.08	
Include observations: 68	
Root Mean Squared Error	0.270551
Mean Absolute Error	0.217508
Mean Abs. Percent Error	4.391372
Trail Inequality Coefficient	0.027010
Bias Proportion	0.095344
Variance Proportion	0.165412
Covariance Proportion	0.739244

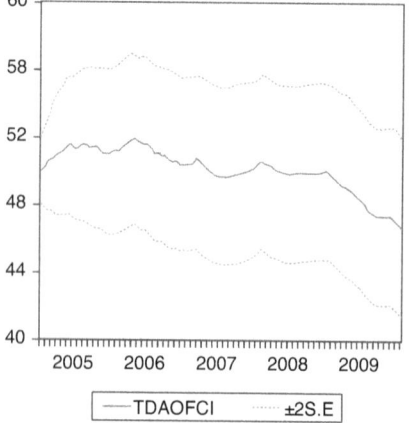

Forecast: TDAOFCP	
Actual: TDAO	
Sample: 2004:022008.09	
Include observations: 68	
Root Mean Squared Error	0.212550
Mean Absolute Error	0.192187
Mean Abs. Percent Error	3.802843
Trail Inequality Coefficient	0.021118
Bias Proportion	0.027945
Variance Proportion	0.277888
Covariance Proportion	0.894367

Figure 1.17   Root-mean-square error

both cases (0.27 and 0.21) that confirms the good quality of the forecasts.

The comparisons between the observed trend of the key rate and the two response functions of the central bank are shown in the graphs and table below.

The results show a gap between the effective key rate and its estimated value of 25 basis points (with regard to the response function

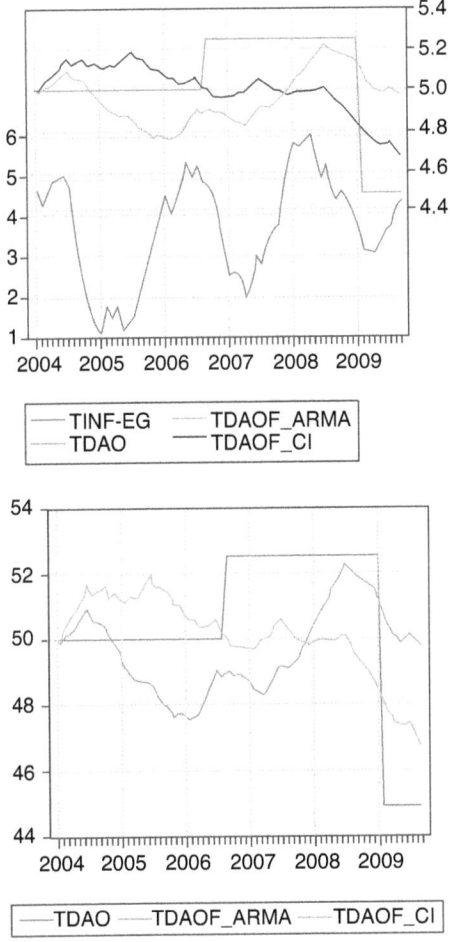

Figure 1.18 Key rates, central bank rates and response functions

according to implicit targeting) and of 50 basis points (in relation to the one from the ARMA model). At the same time, it would be convenient to implement implicit targeting of inflation by keeping the underlying inflation rate at 3 per cent. Other measures can be useful, especially concerning the implementation at a transitory stage of an Index of Monetary Conditions (IMC) as an operational objective.[62] In this

Table 1.4   Analysis of gaps in basis points

		TD – ARMA		TD – implicit targeting	
	TD	Value	Spread	Value	Spread
2009:02	4.50	5.08	+0.58	4.81	+0.31
2009:03	4.50	5.03	+0.53	4.78	+0.28
2009:04	4.50	5.01	+0.51	4.76	+0.26
2009:05	4.50	4.98	+0.48	4.74	+0.24
2009:06	4.50	4.99	+0.49	4.73	+0.23
2009:07	4.50	5.02	+0.52	4.75	+0.25
2009:08	4.50	4.99	+0.49	4.71	+0.21
2009:09	4.50	4.97	+0.47	4.68	+0.18
Average			+0.50	Average	+0.25

way monetary authorities can influence IMC in the short term while ensuring that monetary aggregates evolve in a coherent path with the long-term objective of price stability and of full employment.

1.3.4   Monetary policy in a capital account liberalisation scenario

We use an augmented Taylor's rule, incorporating a qualitative indicator of capital account liberalization,[63] of the type

$$i_t = cte + \rho i_{t-1} + \mu(\pi - \pi^*)_t + \gamma(y - y^*)_t + \delta(e - \bar{e})_t + \lambda lib_t + u_t \quad (11)$$

where:

i_t is the key interest rate on date t, taken at a level;
i_{t-1} is the key interest rate delayed by one period
π is the inflation rate on the date t;
π^* is an implicit inflation rate target fixed at 3 per cent per year;
$(y - y^*)$ is the production gap;
$(e - \bar{e})$ is the misalignment of the exchange rate;
Lib is a capital account liberalisation index.

Finally, u_t is a term of error reflecting an imperfect adjustment of the interest rate.

This equation shows how the central bank adjusts the interest rate according to the state of the economy described by the inflation gap, the output gap, the exchange rate misalignment and the index of capital account liberalisation. The introduction of i_{t-1} aims at smoothing the interest rate to reduce the risks of financial instability linked with strong variations (Mishkin, 2008).

The first question concerns the method of estimation to be used. Should we use the Ordinary least squares (OLS) or instrumental variables? The last line of the following table supplies a set of test statistics which enables us to determine the relevance of our estimations. The first test, which here acquires crucial importance, is the LM test of Breusch-Godfrey on the absence of a serial correlation of residues. P-values relative to this test reveal unambiguously the absence of self-correlation, as White's test concludes the absence of heteroscedasticity. Besides, Ramsay's RESET test reveals the absence of specification errors which can be attributed to an omission of pertinent variables, bad specification of the model or a non-exogeneity of certain explanatory variables. According to the p-value associated with this latter test, our model appears to have been specified correctly. The evaluation method using OLS is thus justified compared with the method of instrumental variables.

We also reported the p-value associated with the statistics of the ADF test applied to the residue series for this model. This test, which was carried out only as a rough guide, allows us to conclude the stationary nature of these residues. In fact, our concern results from the presence in this regression of variables I(0), such as the output gap and the exchange rate gap, and variables I(1) as the inflation rate and the liberalisation index. The fact that residues are stationary eliminates the risk of fallacious regression. We multiplied stability tests of parameters (CUSUM, CUSUM2, recursive residues, recursive coefficients) but we were not able to reject this hypothesis.

We can see at a glance that all signs of the estimated coefficients concur with the theory. The smoothing parameter, which represents the adjustment mechanism of the interest rate, is statistically significant but relatively low compared with other countries, which means a slow variance in the interest rate in response to fluctuations in prices. On the other hand, a capital account liberalisation scenario would result in a monetary policy tightening, which would require us (i) to favour the interest rate as an operational instrument and (ii) to implement sterilisation mechanisms by opting for gradualism when relaxing exchange controls.

Table 1.5   Evaluation results of the augmented Taylor rule

Variables	Coefficients	p-value
C	0.017	0.019
i_{t-1}	0.489	0.001
$(\pi-\pi^*)$	0.126	0.401
$(y-y^*)$	0.128	0.222
$(e-e^*)$	0.059	0.099
Lib	0.035	0.002

$R^2 = 0.94$; LM (1): (0.3); LM(2): (0.46); RESET(1): (0.15);
White: (0.53); ADF: (0.0001)

1.4   Inflation targeting in Mediterranean countries

1.4.1   Theoretical reference

At the beginning of the 1990s, some developed countries (in particular Canada, the United Kingdom and New Zealand) gave up all policies with intermediate objectives and chose to target inflation directly. Previously, the traditional method consisted of targeting an intermediate objective of a monetary aggregate (more or less broad). But given the instability of the demand for money function, partly due to financial innovations, the links between currency and prices, and even between currency and aggregated income, became less close. In this context it became harder to implement a money aggregate policy to reach a sustainable low inflation situation.

Generally speaking, the implementation of a monetary policy based on a direct inflation target has three particularly important characteristics.[64] First, monetary authorities clearly announce a quantitative inflation objective, generally as a range of price variations.[65] Secondly, no explicit intermediate objective is set. This characteristic is a consequence of the instability of demand for money function, which indicates that a direct relation between inflation and the instruments of monetary policy has greater stability than that of the relation between money aggregates and instruments.

In a direct inflation target scenario, the delays which affect the transmission of monetary policy mean that inflation does not react immediately to the application of monetary policy instruments. From this we can infer the third characteristic of this monetary strategy, which is essential from the perspective of information variables: a forward-looking approach prevails. The implementation of monetary policy is based on inflation forecasts. There is a consensus to consider that a minimum horizon of two years is appropriate. When identifying relevant information variables, such a variable must precede inflation by a sufficient period (between four and eight quarters) to be usable by monetary authorities. If the forecast is too short (a quarter or less) or too long, it cannot be considered as an information variable.

Applied in developing countries and especially in emerging economies, direct targeting of inflation is based on a number of prerequisites which can make this strategy difficult to implement (Eichengreen B., 1999). A direct inflation target is based on the capacity of a central bank to implement monetary policy independently. In fact, it's the functional independence (or independence of instruments), rather than organic (or institutional) independence that is essential.

Yet monetary authorities can manage monetary instruments with full independence only if the policy mix is appropriate. This implies (i) a financial policy which ensures sustainability of the budgetary position of the state; (ii) a sufficiently developed fiscal system to diversify public revenue; (iii) a sufficiently deep financial system to allow the state to finance budget deficits through debenture loans; (iv) no commitment to any other nominal anchor, that is the central bank has to renounce to exchange rate targeting; and (v) respect of the conditions for implementation of a direct inflation target.

When the first two conditions are met, the direct inflation target must be implemented by complying with the following four core elements: (i) definition of an explicit inflation objective for the future; (ii) clear and unambiguous indication that inflation is the only objective of the authorities; (iii) elaboration of a model to forecast inflation based on information variables; (iv) a strategy of a forward-looking monetary policy identification of instruments which depends on the estimation of future inflationary pressures.

In other words, a direct inflation target presupposes that the central bank has the expertise and the technical means necessary for its implementation. This technical question, which is very important to ensure that target is credible, is made more complicated by the fact that the economic environment central banks are faced with in developing countries is more complex than that of developed countries. They generally have to cope with a deficient fiscal system. Besides, financial repression conditions can make lending of resources by the state in the domestic market very difficult. The banking systems are often in a precarious situation, with a very significant budgetary cost, when monetary authorities have to intervene to contain banking crises. Nevertheless, and although it seems difficult to implement a monetary policy based on a direct inflation target, important progress has been recorded for the adoption of such a strategy, in particular in emerging countries (Chile, Brazil, Mexico and Turkey) or countries in transition (Czech Republic, Poland and Hungary).

1.4.1.1 A new paradigm: strategic monetary policy and central banking theory

In an environment characterised by the risks of a rise in inflation and signs of fragility in financial systems, the preoccupation with price stability led to a rethink of inflation targeting plans with a view to guarantee the credibility of monetary policies and the reputation of the monetary authorities that implement them. As such, the study of the transmission channels of monetary impulses focused on a review of the determining factors of the behaviour of central banks and private agents in a strategic context, thus bringing interaction and interdependence among these players to bear in the form of game where every player considers the current and expected behaviour of the others.

The attitudes of private agents, thus their expectations and, ultimately, the impact of monetary policy are all conditioned by the degree of credibility of a disinflation objective. In fact, central banks can orient private expectations by announcing a rule of future behaviour and then implement a discretionary policy, that is, the one that optimises their behaviour *ex post*, once the announced rule is integrated into private expectations. Hence the efficiency of monetary policy is linked to the fact that agents "believe" in it, and thus in the credibility of the announced rule of monetary regulation (cf. McCallum B. T., 1984). Artus, P. (1987) gives a double definition of credibility: an announcement of future choice (of monetary policy) is credible if private agents believe that central bank will not renege on the announced choices. In other words, the credibility of the announced policy depends on the expectation of rational agents that the authorities have a possible incentive to "cheat" them.

In particular, a negative connection between inflation and unemployment means that a disinflationary monetary policy entails economic costs (effects of redistribution, job and production losses) which are, however, lower when policy implementation is credible. For Blackburn and Christensen (1989), the credibility of monetary policies can be distorted by three constraints: (i) a technological constraint due to the fact that monetary control can be weakened by incomplete data, imperfect control of instruments or unpredictability of their effects on the monetary objectives; (ii) an institutional constraint where an inadequate regulatory framework can limit the manoeuvre of monetary authorities; and finally (iii) a strategic constraint ensuing from the interdependence between private behaviour and public decisions via the expectations of private agents regarding future monetary policies.

In particular, in a situation with asymmetry of information, the most frequent case where central bankers have an information advantage, monetary authorities possess privileged information about shocks affecting the economy. In such conditions, the deviation of an effective monetary policy from the announced strategy will ensue from two alternatives: either (i) the decision-makers have adopted deviating behaviour which they attribute to exogenous disturbances; or (ii) the observed gap is effectively the likely consequence of such exogenous disturbances. Private agents must be capable of discriminating between these two alternatives before formulating their expectations regarding inflation. In this sense, private agents ignore the real preferences of central banks, and "lax" monetary authorities can mask their bad choices to acquire a fallacious reputation of "restrictive (or conservative)" authorities. Alternately "restrictive" authorities can adopt more rigorous strategies than their preferences would suggest in order to distance themselves from "lax" authorities.

1.4.1.2 Information asymmetry on the random preferences of central banks

In the research carried out by Cukierman (1986, 1992) as well as Cukierman and Meltzer (1986a), asymmetric information concerns the random preferences of central banks which display by hypothesis discretionary behaviour. This temporarily coherent behaviour is not enough to ensure their credibility, since their preferences change over time. The respective weightings of effective monetary growth and predicted monetary growth are random variables. This random modification of monetary preferences is coupled with an exogenous stochastic shock on the money supply, and the authorities partly lose control over the money aggregates.

Private agents will ignore the authorities' current preferences, and therefore are unable to detect immediately the origin of excessive monetary creation. Monetary slippage results sometimes from an imperfect control over the money supply, and sometimes from a change in preferences. The objective function of a central bank (or monetary authorities) is deduced from the maximisation of the expected value of the following equation:

$$MaxJ = MaxE\left[\sum_{i=0}^{\alpha} \beta^i \left[x_i \cdot \phi \cdot (N * - N_i) - \frac{\pi_i^2}{2} \right]\right] \tag{1}$$

$$\begin{cases} 0 \le \beta \le 1 \\ \phi(N * - N_i) = \begin{cases} N * - N_i & \text{for } N * - N_i \ge 0 \\ 0 & \text{or else} \end{cases} \end{cases}$$

Under the constraint of the following short-term Phillips relationship:

$$N - N_n = \alpha(\pi - \pi^e) \quad \alpha > 0 \tag{2}$$

where:
N is the current unemployment rate;
$N*$ is the desired or notional unemployment rate;
N_n is the natural unemployment rate;
π^e is the forecast inflation rate;
π is the current inflation rate;
β is the discount factor;
x_i is the measure of the aversion of monetary authorities to deviate from the desired unemployment level $N*$ compared with their aversion to deviate from price stability.

The hypothesis of the information asymmetry is analysed basically from an employment perspective. The equilibrium equation (2) means that in the absence of inflationary surprises, $(N^* - N)$ will be equal to $(N^* - N_n)$. When the desired level of employment rises above its natural level, the monetary authorities will stabilise in a spread where $N^* - N > 0$.

The possibilities of deviating from preferences of an employment objective to a price stability objective, or one contrary to the continuity of these preferences, are formalised by the stochastic variable x_i which is expressed as:

$$x_i = A + p_i \quad A > 0 \tag{3}$$

where:

$$
\begin{cases}
p_i = \rho.p_{i-1} + v_i, \\
v_i \to N(0;\sigma_v^2),
\end{cases}
\tag{4}
\tag{5}
$$

$0 < \rho < 1$ (positive auto-regression coefficient), v_i is white noise that measures the degree of instability of central bank objectives and ρ measures the degree of continuity of the objectives, A is the average value $\bar{x}_i$ of x_i, and p_i is the stochastic component of x_i. In a period i, implementation of A is only known by the monetary authorities. Like private agents, they do not know future modifications of preferences v. The future forecasts of x by monetary authorities are, however, more precise because they know the current value of x and p.

Equation (3) defines the mechanism of continuity of preferences. The specification of v_i implies a high probability that the objectives of the central bank will vary by a small amount and there is little probability that they will vary significantly. In strategic games models for monetary policy, these comments are illustrated by a range of relative weightings assigned to employment and inflation objectives by various types of decision makers. In the approach of Cukierman, A. (1986, 1992) the nature of the central banker (strict or concerned only with price stability, or else lax) is revealed by the implementation of x_i which depends on deviations and on changes in the preferences of the monetary authorities.

Private agents manage asymmetry of information (private information that monetary authorities have about their changes in preferences) through a learning mechanism. They do not know about implementation of A but know the stochastic structure of the process which has led to variations in x_i. In other words, they know about σ_v^2 and the auto-regression coefficient ρ. By linking this knowledge with past observations of monetary growth rates, they then formulate their expectations of the future inflation rate. Their past observations are short term because private agents are supposed to have a precise observation over the two previous periods of p, that is p_{i-2} at the beginning of period i before concluding wage agreements for the same period.

However, private agents have no information on p_{i-1}, which observation is estimated by the monetary growth rate in the same period ($i-1$), which allows them to estimate the inflation rate in period i. This learning process is fundamental because if the authorities increase the current monetary expansion rate, inflationary expectations for the later period will increase accordingly.

The central bank then has to take into account the adverse effect of its current decisions on the objectives for future periods. However, this approach is valid only for a restrictive hypothesis of an immediate and symmetric effect of an increase in the money supply on the inflation rate. This raises a more sensitive problem which relates to the nature of the control applied by the central bank to monetary growth.

1.4.1.3 Imperfection of information and monetary control

Central banks in particular do not have perfect control over monetary aggregates and hence over the inflation rate. This imperfection of monetary control is illustrated in the following stochastic equation:

$$m_i = m_i^P + \Psi_i \qquad (6)$$

where:

m_i^P designates projected or planned monetary growth rate for period i;

m_i is the current monetary growth rate for the period i, or the monetary inflation rate for the same period;

Ψ_i is the random error of monetary control, known only by the central bank.

The game of monetary policy illustrated by this imperfect control over the money supply aggregates is a non-cooperative game according to Nash: at the beginning of period i, the contracts for nominal wages are concluded on the basis of the expected inflation rate for the duration of the contract. Then the central bank chooses m_i^p, supposing that the wage contract and expectations are given. When implementing monetary policy, authorities make an error in control and the monetary inflation rate m_i is determined by equation (6).

Because private agents detect the variations in objectives by their learning process based on current inflation, they take into consideration the effect of their current choice on future expectations. This method of private expectations forming is supposedly given for the monetary authorities that choose the value of monetary growth, which they control in order to maximise the expected value of the objective function of the equation (1).

This provides a discretionary decision rule which implies that the current inflation rate π depends on the current state variables of the central bank and on the current implementation of the error of control ψ. Private agents know the structure of this decision rule but ignore the current state p of the objectives of monetary authorities. They then use this information in an optimal way to estimate the minimal variance of the inflation rate. The decision rule for monetary authorities depends on this private process for elaborating expectations and which depends on the decision rule. The decision-making process is thus symmetric, and this circularity defines a simultaneous Nash equilibrium, as shown by the following system:

$m_i = m_i^p + \Psi_i$ (central bank)

$m_i^p = B_0 \cdot A + B \cdot P_i$ (private agents)

B_0 and B (constant)

$$\Rightarrow m_i^p = B_0 \cdot A + BP_i + \Psi_i \tag{7}$$

In other words, private agents do not directly observe m_i^p but only the current rate of monetary inflation m_i. The expectation of m_i, in view of the state of information I_i, is given by:

$$E(m_i | I_i) = B_0 \cdot A + B \cdot E\left[p_i | I_i \right] \tag{8}$$

since $\begin{cases} E(B_0 \cdot A) = B_0 \cdot A \\ E(\psi_i) = 0. \end{cases}$

Information I_i contains previous monetary growth rates until m_{i-1} and the value of p_{i-2}.

However,

$p_i = \rho \cdot p_{i-1} + v_i$ $0 < \rho < 1$

$\Rightarrow p_{i-1} = \rho \, p_{i-2} + v_{i-1}$

$\Rightarrow p_i = \rho [\rho \, p_{i-2} + v_{i-1}] + v_i$

$$\Rightarrow p_i = \rho^2 p_{i-2} + \rho v_{i-1} + v_i \tag{9}$$

$$\Rightarrow E(p_i | I_i) = \rho^2 p_{i-2} + \rho E[v_{i-1} | I_i] \, E[v_i | I_i] \tag{10}$$

(Here, p_{i-2} is already included in the state of information I_i.) Then, as no information on v_i is included in I_i, this gives:

$E[v_i | I_i] = 0$

$$\Rightarrow E(p_i | I_i) = \rho^2 p_{i-2} + \rho \cdot E[v_{i-1} | I_i] \tag{11}$$

We know that

$\begin{cases} p_i = \rho \cdot p_{i-1} + v_i \\ m_i = B_0 \cdot A + B \cdot p_i + \psi_i \end{cases}$

$\Rightarrow m_{i-1} = B_0 \cdot A + B [\rho \cdot p_{i-2} + v_{i-1}] + \psi_{i-1}$

$\Rightarrow m_{i-1} = B_0 \cdot A + [B \cdot v_{i-1} + \psi_{i-1}] + B \rho \, p_{i-2}$

$$\Rightarrow m_{i-1} = B_0 \cdot A + y_{i-1} + B \rho \, p_{i-2} \tag{12}$$

where $y_{i-1} = B \cdot v_{i-1} + \psi_{i-1}$, and since (p_{i-2}) is included in the state of information I_i, observation of m_{i-1} is equivalent to observation of the linear combination y_{i-1},

$$B \cdot v_{i-1} = y_{i-1} - \psi_{i-1}$$
$$\Rightarrow v_{i-1} = \frac{1}{B} \cdot y_{i-1} - \frac{1}{B} \cdot \psi_{i-1}$$

Therefore,

$$\rho \cdot E\left[v_{i-1} \middle| I_i\right] = \rho E\left[v_{i-1} \middle| y_{i-1}\right]$$
$$= \rho \cdot E\left[\left(\frac{1}{B} \cdot y_{i-1} - \frac{1}{B}\psi_{i-1}\right) \middle| y_{i-1}\right] \tag{13}$$
$$= \rho \frac{\theta}{B} \cdot y_{i-1}$$

where $\theta = \dfrac{B^2 \cdot \sigma_v^2}{B^2 \cdot \sigma_v^2 + \sigma_\psi^2}$

Equation (13) is the regression equation of v_{i-1} over y_{i-1}, and (θ/B) is the regression coefficient

$$E(p_i | I_i) = \rho^2 \cdot p_{i-2} + \rho \cdot \frac{\theta}{B} \cdot y_{i-1}$$

Since

$$E(m_i | I_i) = B_0 \cdot A + B \cdot E\left[p_i | I_i\right]$$

$$\Rightarrow E(m_i | I_i) = B_0 \cdot A + B \cdot \rho^2 \cdot p_{i-2} + \rho \cdot \theta \cdot y_{i-1} \tag{14}$$

equation (14) then defines the optimal estimator of m_i by private agents: private agents anticipate m_i because current inflation is determined by monetary inflation m_i. Therefore, and considering the minimum state of information they have access to I_i (hypothesis of asymmetric information), private agents have to anticipate all the components of equation (2), which leads to equation (15) in which y_{i-1} is used as an indicator of v_{i-1} or the proxy variable. Finally,

$$\begin{cases} E\left(m_i | I_i\right) = \pi_i^e = m_i^e \\ m_i = \pi_i. \end{cases}$$

The Phillips short-term relationship then becomes

$$N - N_n = \alpha \left(m_i - m_i^e \right)$$

and the objective function of the central bank is expressed as

$$J = E \left[\sum_{i=0}^{\alpha} \cdot \beta^i \cdot \left[x_i \cdot \left(N^* - N_i \right) - \frac{\pi_i^2}{2} \right] \right]$$

Since $N^* - N_i \geq 0 \Rightarrow \phi \left(N^* - N_i \right) = N^* - N_i$

$$\Rightarrow J = E \left[\sum_{i=0}^{\alpha} \cdot \beta^i \left[x_i \cdot \alpha \cdot \left(m_i - m_i^e \right) - \frac{m_i^2}{2} \right] \right]$$

because $N - N_n = N^* - N_i$ (in the absence of any inflation surprise).

The maximisation of this objective function ensues from a problem of optimisation without constraint because the Phillips equation is already incorporated in the modified objective function, and knowing that:

$$m_i^e = E(m_i | I_i) = B_0 \cdot A + B \cdot \rho^2 \cdot p_{i-2} + \rho \cdot \theta \cdot y_{i-1} \tag{15}$$

In this optimisation, the state variable J and control variable (m_i^e) depend on various parameters $(\alpha, \rho, \beta, \theta)$ and the first-order conditions are deducted from Euler equations.

Condition of transversality:

$$\lim_{i \to \infty} \beta^i . E \left[\alpha . x_i - \alpha . \beta . \rho . \theta . E(x_{i+1}) - m_i \right] = 0$$

Euler equation:

$$\alpha \cdot \left[x_i - \beta \cdot \rho \cdot \theta \cdot E(x_{i+1}) \right] - m_i = \alpha \cdot \left[x_i - \beta \cdot \rho \cdot \theta (A + \rho \cdot p_i) \right] - m_i = 0 \quad i > 0$$
$$\Rightarrow m_i = \alpha \cdot \left[(1 - \rho \cdot \beta \cdot \theta) \cdot A + (1 - \rho^2 \cdot \beta \cdot \theta) \cdot p_i \right]$$
$$\Rightarrow m_i = \alpha \cdot (1 - \rho \cdot \beta \cdot \theta) \cdot A + a \cdot (1 - \rho^2 \cdot \beta \cdot \theta) \cdot p_i$$
$$\Rightarrow m_i^* = B_0 \cdot A + B \cdot p_i$$

with $B_0 = \alpha \cdot (1 - \rho \cdot \beta \cdot \theta)$

$\quad B = \alpha \cdot (1 - \rho^2 \cdot \beta \cdot \theta)$

The optimal solution for the central bank depends on the model parameters:

$B_0 = f(\alpha, \rho, \beta, \theta)$

$B = g(\alpha, \rho, \beta, \theta, \sigma_v^2, \sigma_\psi^2)$

Finally, formalisation according to Cukierman, A. (1986, 1992) is a representation of a strategic game of monetary policy in a situation of asymmetric information. In this context, the credibility of a disinflation monetary policy is not conversely symmetric to its risk of temporary incoherence as in the game models with perfect information. On the contrary, it is conditioned by a continuous process which ensues from the private learning mechanism. The credibility of a disinflation monetary policy or the reputation of a conservative central banker is measured according to the gap (with a minus sign) as an absolute value between the projected monetary growth rate announced by the monetary authorities and the pertinent expectations of private agents. In period i credibility C_i is measured by

$$C_i = -\left| m_i^p - E\left(m_i^p \,\middle|\, I_i\right)\right| \tag{16}$$

If $C_i = 0$, credibility is perfect. The more the absolute value of the gap increases, the more credibility decreases. When monetary authorities have a greater preference for an inflation objective relative to an unemployment objective, they must invest in their reputation; the credibility of their monetary policy must be high. In other words, the absolute value of the gap between (m_i^p) and $(E(m_i^p \,|\, I_i))$ must be low. The public has to believe that the employment level is lower than the natural rate N_n.

At the beginning of the 1980s, the policy of disinflation implemented by Paul Volcker, then governor of the Federal Reserve (FED) was greatly facilitated by a period of high credibility due to the low relative gap (as an absolute value) between the announced monetary expansion rates and the rates expected by private agents. However, besides the restrictive hypothesis of symmetry between the monetary growth rate and the current inflation rate, Cukierman's model supposes that private agents can accurately perceive the changes in preferences of monetary authorities after two game periods.

However, in practice a degree of uncertainty can continue over several periods. Credibility will depend then on the learning speed of private agents, which depends on changes in the preferences of authorities.[66] In fact the scenario in terms of a Nash non-cooperative strategic game between a central bank and private operators does not reflect reality. On the contrary, because of its higher analytical and technical capability and its privileged access to monetary and financial information relating to the functioning of the economy, the central bank acts as a "dominant" player or "leader" by knowing in advance the best reply function of private agents to its choice of monetary policy. The central bank thus incorporates this knowledge in its decision making. Private agents are "followers" and ignore the influence of their strategy on that of monetary authorities. This non-cooperative game as developed by Stackelberg seems more appropriate for illustrating the inherent difficulties when implementing a disinflation policy.

In the same way, previous approaches describe "central banks" (or monetary authorities) and "governments" in a non-differentiated manner in order to designate the only decision maker of monetary policy when faced with strategic behaviours of private agents. More recently, theories abandoned this fiction of the only public decision maker and extended the analysis to a "temporarily coherent coordination" of monetary and budgetary policies, and introduced an additional conflict of objectives between two different decision makers determining and implementing budgetary policy and monetary policy, namely the budgetary authorities (treasury, government or central government)[67] and the monetary authorities (central bank). Every decision maker possesses, in principle, their own field of intervention, their own objectives and their own representation of the economy, as well as their own time frame. This means that the time consistency of optimal monetary and budgetary policies is less a problem of coordinating objectives and alternative instruments by a single decision maker and more a problem of cooperation between monetary and budgetary authorities.

1.4.2 Prerequisites for inflation targeting: compared scenarios and progress in Mediterranean countries

We previously demonstrated that only Turkey and Morocco have adopted operational frameworks for monetary policy which favour formal inflation targeting, while Egypt has implemented a gradual scheme of implicit targeting. The other economies are some way behind because of non-compliance with several technical and institutional prerequisites. The evaluation of compliance with the constituent elements of formal inflation targeting in Mediterranean countries is analysed in the table of comparison, which breaks them down into four blocks: (i) institutional elements, (ii) operational elements, (iii) technical elements and (iv) organisational elements.[68]

1.4.3 What perspectives in the aftermath of the international economic and financial crisis?

The field for implementation of economic policies at an international scale was a major factor in demonstrating the break in the decoupling inflation and monetary policy both in advanced economies and in developing economies.

It is therefore advisable to contemplate, using the terminology of Blanchard,[69] rethinking and redefining all macroeconomic policies in the aftermath of the financial crisis. Several leading ideas on this question were swept away by the crisis. Such is the case of the hypothesis according to which monetary policy should only address the volatility and level of inflation. New approaches suggest that central banks should accept and even target inflation rates beyond the objectives of 2 per cent, and combine monetary policy and macroprudential policy more closely in a more countercyclical manner than before. Monetary policy would then focus more on financing growth for lack of prudential instruments, allowing the credit spillovers towards assets markets to be controlled. More particularly, as economies with formal targeting mechanisms have defined them according to inflation rates, the question is whether it would be better to target the level of prices. A target focusing on the level of prices offers several advantages, including (i) reduction of uncertainty regarding the level at which prices will stabilise for long-term forecasts and (ii) less variability in production.

Table 1.6 Compliance with constituent elements of inflation targeting

		Levels of compliance					
	Algeria	Egypt	Jordan	Lebanon	Morocco	Tunisia	Turkey
1. Institutional components							
1.1. Mandate focusing on price stability as the priority objective of the central bank	High	High	High	High	High	High	High
1.2. De facto autonomy versus de jure autonomy of central bank	Low	Intermediate	Low	Intermediate	High	Low	High
1.3. Accountability of central bank and transparency of monetary policy	Low	Intermediate	Low	Intermediate	High	Intermediate	High
2. Operational components							
2.1. Stability of the macroeconomic framework							
2.1.1. No budget (fiscal) dominance	Low	Intermediate	Low	Low	High	Intermediate	High
2.1.2. Strength of external position	High	Low	Low	Intermediate	High	Low	High
2.2. Stability and efficiency of the financial system							
2.2.1. Efficiency of financial market	Low	Intermediate	Low	High	High	Low	High
2.2.2. Efficiency of monetary market	Intermediate	Intermediate	Low	Intermediate	High	Low	High
2.2.3. Efficiency of foreign exchange market	Intermediate	High	Low	Intermediate	High	Intermediate	High

2.2.4. *Stability and efficiency of banking system*	Low	Intermediate	Low	Intermediate	Low	High
2.3. Efficiency of monetary and exchange operations of central bank	Intermediate	High	Intermediate	Intermediate	Intermediate	High
2.4. Efficiency of the interest rate transmission channel	Low	High	Low	Inter-mediate	Low	High
3. Technical components						
3.1. Infrastructures needed for inflation targeting						
3.1.1. *Availability of a measure of inflation targeting*	Low	Intermediate	Low	Low	Low	High
3.1.2. *Definition of the inflation target and its duration*	Low	Intermediate	Low	Low	Low	High
3.1.3. *Early indicators of inflation*	Low	High	Low	Intermediate	Low	High
3.1.4. *Technical tools of inflation predictions*	Low	High	Low	Intermediate	Intermediate	High
3.2. Publishing of regular reports on inflation	Low	High	Low	Low	Low	High
3.3. Publishing of regular reports on monetary policy	Low	High	Low	Low	Low	High
4. Organisational components						
4.1. Well-established analytical capacities	Low	High	Intermediate	High	Intermediate	High
4.2. Transparency of the decision-making process	Low	Intermediate	Low	Intermediate	Low	High

Source: Author's compilations.

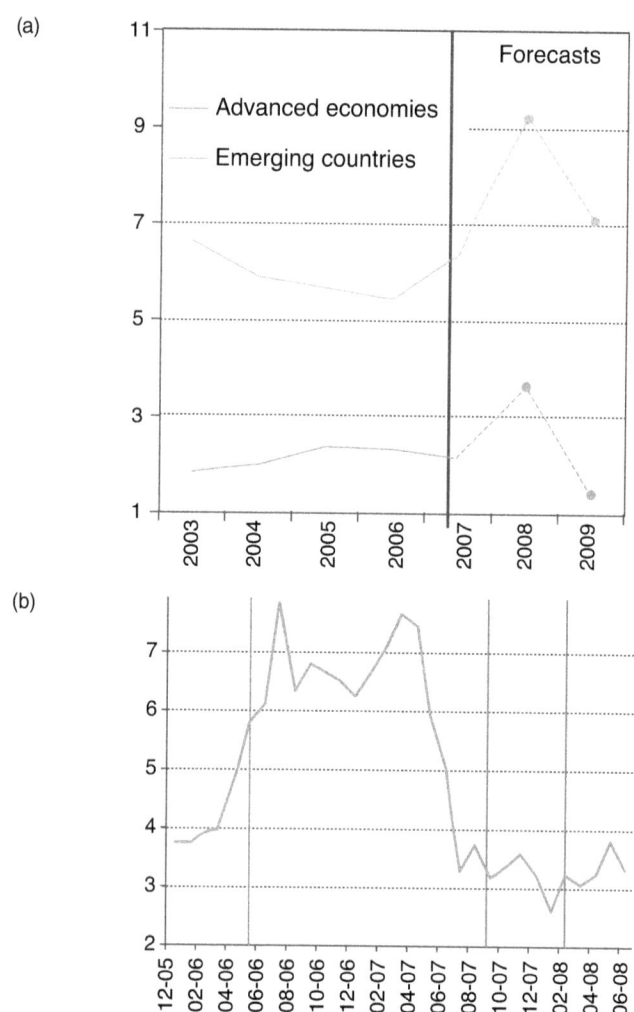

Figure 1.19 Comparative inflation rates. (a) Comparative inflation rates (Average annual variations in % of GDP); (b) Annual variation in % (*)

Note: (*) A significant drop in the inflation gap between economies with targeting and the others.

1.5 Institutional constraints and independence of central banks

The independence of central banks or the choice of a central banker reputed to be "conservative" is a solution to the credibility problem of disinflation strategies. According to Cukierman, A. (2008), commenting in theory on the conduct of central bankers and defining their monetary policies are in fact part of an analysis of the strategic choice between a rule, or commitment towards a disinflation rule, and discretionary conduct (cf. Kydland and Prescott, 1982). The independence of central banks is in fact the result of a set of statutory provisions or customs in which the (central) bank is clearly recognised as being in charge of monetary and price stability and, within the scope of this mission, it should not receive any directives from public authorities. In these terms a measure of independence is calculated by weighting various ranking scales according to both organic and functional criteria. Organic independence includes the conditions of managers' appointments and those relating to the exercise of their functions. Functional independence is measured by the missions and statutory goals assigned to the central bank, its responsibility regarding monetary policy framework and its own financial autonomy or budgetary independence.

1.5.1 Determinist framework

The economic theory of credibility appears to be the foundation for central banks' independence. Commenting in theory on the conduct of central bankers and defining their monetary policies does not avoid the arguments analysed regarding the strategic choice between a rule, or the commitment towards a rule of disinflation, and discretionary conduct. As underlined by Rogoff, A. (1985), the theories on the dynamic temporal inconsistency of inflation develop the possibility that an independent central bank can grow in credibility and reputation without being subject to private trigger strategies.

Reputation is based on the selection of a conservative central banker according to Rogoff (1985); this preference is less inflationary than the "median reference" of the population, as expressed by Aglietta (1992) , or the "median voter" as demonstrated by Alesina and Grilli (1991, 1992) who tried to formalise the effects of independence of the European Central Bank and, before, on the enlarged system of central banks, within the framework of political and economic integration in Europe. Other authors such as Alesina and Summers (1993) likewise try to demonstrate that the independence of central banks also has a positive effect on real variables such as the unemployment or real interest rate, where the objective is to reduce the risk premium which is high in the absence of independence.

However, the core difficulty of all these analyses is firstly to determine a criterion for measuring the degree of independence, which Grilli, Masciandaro and Tabellini (1991) try to develop based on the distinction made between "political independence" (or "institutional independence" according to Cukierman, Webb and Neyapti, 1992) and "economic independence". The first criterion ensues from the ability of the central bank to select its objectives without any governmental influence (or a once-and-for-all determination of objectives), while the second criterion ensues from the use without constraints (free choice) of monetary policy instruments. The conflict around financing the fiscal deficit is essentially influenced by these constraints. In these conditions the measure of independence of a central bank is a weighted average of these two criteria according to the characteristics of each economy. There is a ranking scale of 16 economies made by Alesina (1988) varying from 1 to 4, an updated scale varying from 3 in 13 in Grilli, Masciandaro and Tabellini and an average of these two scales of independence in Alesina and Summers.

The independence of central banks or the selection of a central banker considered "conservative" is a solution to the credibility problem of disinflation's strategies to such an extent, as noted by Dornbusch and Fisher (1993), that a reduction of the inflation rate in New Zealand is linked to an institutional arrangement by which the governor's salary depends on his ability to control and stop inflation. In developing economies the important studies carried out by Cukierman, Webb and Neyapti have strengthened, in many respects, the relation between institutional independence (political or legal) and efficiency of deflation therapies.

In particular, the concept of the independence of central banks finds its theoretical justification in new classic macroeconomics: the currency is neutral in the long term, or even the neutrality of a policy of monetary easing to reach cyclical objectives, while the adjustment of expectations regarding inflation ensures that unemployment reaches a position of equilibrium in the long term (natural unemployment). However, this standard approach of expectation's augmented Phillips curve reveals the cyclical efficiency of monetary policy in the short term since different reasons for adjustment due to inflation surprises are attributed to monetary expansion. These reasons are generally real objectives such as low interest rates, a high level of business activity or employment, financing by seigniorage of the fiscal deficit and prevention of financial crises. In an open economy a depreciation of the nominal exchange rate can be used temporarily to improve the current balance.

These reasons for monetary expansion reveal discretionary implementation of monetary policy. The public anticipates the inflation rate rationally and adopts "preventative measures" in terms of nominal wage contracts. The zero-inflation objective then translates into a situation of dynamic incoherence, which means that a situation of discretion in monetary policy leads to a sub-optimal inflationist bias when one of the above-mentioned reasons for monetary expansion is operative.

The inflationary bias can be mitigated by delegating monetary policy to an independent central bank or a conservative central banker in the sense of Rogoff (1985). There are several selective analyses such as Epstein and Schor (1986) on the relationship between the Bank of Italy and the Treasury, Lined and Strauss-Khan (1987) on the French economy, the comparative analysis between FED and Bank of Japan by Cargill and Hutchison (1990) and finally other non-selective analyses of the concept of the independence of central banks (cf. Goodhart, 1988; or Fazio, 1991). In this way, hypotheses on the theoretical determinants of independence generally ensue from strategic models of monetary policy in which the dynamic incoherence of an optimum policy is corrected by an institutional rule (of independence) versus the discretion of central bankers. The credibility of monetary actions implemented by an independent central bank is then synonymous with an "... unfailing commitment to the search for and the maintenance of price stability ... (in order) ... to isolating the implementation (of monetary policy) from (cyclical) risks, or electoral schedules ... ". (cf. Cartapanis and Bassoni, 1994).[70]

1.5.2 The indices of independence of central banks

If independence of central bankers is generally gauged in industrialised economies through legal independence criteria, this is less the case in emerging and developing economies which tend to favour behaviour criteria such as the revocation or turnover rate of governors. A negative correlation is generally observed between independence and inflation rate in both groups of economies, contrary to the relationship between legal independence and growth, which is low in the first group, while the relationship between behaviour indices and growth is positive in the second. Determination of these indexes is therefore necessary to evaluate the effects of independence on macroeconomic performance.

1.5.2.1 Legal independence

The attempts to codify legal (formal or statutory) independence of central banks in industrialised economies started with Bade and Parkin[71] and were developed by Alesina, A. (1988, 1989). Weightings are attributed according to various criteria of organic autonomy and are relative to: (1) conditions of appointment, composition and duration of the mandate of the directory instances; (2) the gap between the mandate of the governor of the central bank and the average length of an electoral cycle; and (3) the non-synchrony of the governor's mandate with that of the executive power, which ensures the stability of monetary choices and neutralises alternations due to partisan choices (cf. Waller, 1992). Grilli, Masciandaro and Tabellini (1991) propose an index of legal independence and distinguish "political independence" from "economic independence". They focus more on the criteria of relative functional autonomy, first regarding the definition of objectives and implementation of monetary policy and secondly regarding the free choice of the use of instruments.

Based on these two contrasting studies, the first generation of works on the independence of central banks points out multiple possibilities of alternative ranking and arbitrary weightings (Alesina and Summers, 1993). This basic difficulty is largely dependent on the choice of formal criteria of autonomy. According to Cukierman, Webb and Neyapti (1992), the legal or statutory regulations of a central bank are never evidence in themselves of the independence of a central bank. Some practices reveal themselves to be contrary to organic texts; for example, although the mandate of the governor of the central bank of Argentina is supposed to be four years, traditionally the governor resigns if the Minister of Finance changes.

These criticisms were part of the attempts to re-examine empirical evaluation methods of the real degree of autonomy of central banks. In this respect the works of Cukierman, Webb and Neyapti appear to be precursors of the second generation of analyses. In a homogeneous framework for developing economies but also for industrialised countries, classifications by Cukierman (1992, chap. 19) and by Cukierman, Webb and Neyapti provide an aggregated index of legal independence based on 16 legal characteristics organised in four groups of variables (cf. Table 1.7).

Table 1.7 Legal independence of central banks

Groupe de variable	Spécification statutaire des variables	Pondération	Codification Numérique
A-	**Organes directeurs**	0.65	
	1-Durée du mandat	0.2	
	Supérieur à 8 années renouvelables		1
	Entre 6 et 8 années renouvelables		0.75
	5 années renouvelables		0.5
	4 années renouvelables		0.25
	inférieur à 4 années renouvelables		0
	A la discrétion des autorités publiques		0
	2-Nomination	0.15	
	Par un conseil d'administration		1
	Par la législation		0.5
	Par l'éxécutif (e.g. le conseil des Ministres)		0.25
	Par un membre de l'exécutif (e.g. le ministre des finances)		0
	3-Révocation (Turn-over)	0.15	
	Abscence de clauses statutaires		1
	Objet sans rapports à la conduite de la politique économique		0.83
	A la discrétion du conseil d'administration		0.67
	A la discrétion de la législation		0.5
	Inconditionnalité légiférée par la loi		0.33
	A la discrétion de l'exécutif (e.g. conseil des ministres)		0.17

Continued

Table 1.7   Continued

Groupe de variable	Spécification statutaire des variables	Pondération	Codification Numérique
	A la discrétion d'un membre de l'éxécutif (e.g. le Ministre des Finances)		0
	4-Cumul de portefeuilles ministériels ou d'autres fonctions au sein du gouvernement	0.15	
	Aucun cumul possible		1
	Dérogation de cumul		0.5
	Aucune régle d'interdiction		0
B-	**Formulation et conduite de la politique monétaire**	0.25	
	5-Mise en oeuvre et formulation	0.1	
	Délégation exclusive à la Banque Centrale		1
	Participation active		0.67
	Participation consultative		0.33
	Aucune forme de participation		0
	6-Arbitrage des conflits d'objectifs entre Banque Centrale et Autorités budgétaires	0.1	
	Dispositions réglementaires		1
	Sur commission paritaire hétérogéne ou un conseil de membres de la Banque Centrale, de l'exécutif et du législatif		0.8
	Par le conseil d'administration		0.6
	Par le législatif		0.4
	Par l'executif		0.2
	Priorité inconditionnelle à l'éxécutif légiférée par la loi		0
	7-Droit de regard sur l'évolution budgétaire de l'Etat	0.05	
	Dispositions actives de la banque centrale		1
	Absence d'influence		0
C-	**Objectifs de politique monétaire et choix d'instruments**	0.025	
	8-Objectifs et instruments	0.025	
	Objectif statutaire de stabilité des prix		1

Continued

Table 1.7 Continued

Groupe de variable	Spécification statutaire des variables	Pondération	Codification Numérique
	Objectifs compatibles (e.g. stabilité de la valeur de la monnaie Nationale ou stabilité du systéme bancaire)		0.8
	Objectifs incompatibles (e.g. stabilisation conjoncturelle ou plein emploi)		0.4
	Aucun objectif statutaire n'est mentionné		0.2
	Absence, parmi les objectifs statutaires, de celui de stabilité des prix		0
D-	**Restrictions statutaires sur les financements publics**	0.075	
	9-Avances directes et indirectes	0.025	
	Aucune avance n'est permise		1
	Concours au trésor restreints à des taux faibles (e.g. £ à15% du revenu gouvernemental)		0.67
	Taux d'avance élevés (e.g. > 15%)		0.33
	Aucune limite légale aux concours des banques centrales		0
	10-Sécurisation des concours	0.025	
	Absence d'aléa de moralité		1
	Hasard moral (e.g. £ à15%)		0.67
	Hasard moral (e.g. > 15%)		0.33
	Aléa de moralité illimité		0
	11-Structure par termes (maturité, taux d'intérêt et volume)	0.025	
	Contrôle de la banque Centrale		1
	Fixation statutaire des conditions et régimes d'obtention		0.67
	Agrément entre la Banque Centrale et l'exécutif.		0.33
	Décision de l'exécutif		
	12-Spécification des emprunteurs Institutionnels		
	Uniquement le trésor public		0
	Autres institutions gouvernementales		1
	Entreprises publiques		0.67
	Secteur privé		0.33

Continued

Table 1.7   Continued

Groupe de variable	Spécification statutaire des variables	Pondération	Codification Numérique
	13-Type de restrictions		
	Volumes monétaires		0
	Taux sur le capital		1
	Taux sur le revenu gouvernemental (e.g. les recettes fiscales)		0.67
	Taux sur les dépenses publiques		0.33
	14-Maturité		
	A 6 mois		0
	A une année		1
	Supérieure à une année		0.67
	Non spécification statutaire de la maturité des concours		0.33
	15-Taux d'intérêt sur concours des		0.67
	Banques Centrales		
	Supérieurs aux taux minimals		0
	Au taux du marché monétaire		1
	Inférieurs aux taux maximals		0.75
	Aucune indication statutaire		0.5
	Concours sans intérêts		0.25
	16-Rachat de titres publics ou		
	financement type « open-market »		
	Oui		1
	Non		0
TOTAL		1	

Source: Cukierman, Webb and Neyapti (1992).

This is the measure of the degree of institutional independence conferred by statutory legislation on central banks (cf. Parkin, 1986; Alesina, 1988; Grilli et al., 1991). An index of legal independence is then established for 72 economies of the sample used through codification of certain statutory characteristics, for a classification of central banks according to their degree of independence in divergent institutional contexts. A scale of 16 legal (or formal) indices codified from 0 (minimum degree of independence) to 1 (maximum degree of independence) is established from weightings for the four groups of statutory clauses mentioned above. The higher the weighting, the more the statutory frame confers legal independence on the central bank.

Statutory conditions relating to governing bodies confer a higher level of autonomy. Maximum autonomy is given on the scale of indices when the length of mandate is greater than eight years, which can be renewed, appointments are the prerogative of the board of directors, there are no statutory clauses of revocation (of the governor, of deputy governor or of one of the members of council) or there is no accumulation of incompatible functions exercised by the central banker. In the same manner, and in view of the variable "formulation and implementation of monetary policy", central banks which have had sole responsibility for handling of monetary policy delegated to them exclusively (from a statutory point of view), arbitration of conflicts and the right to inspect budgetary balances, are classified as being more independent. In view of the third group of variables "objectives and choice of instruments", maximum independence is linked to the predominance of the statutory objective of price stability in relation to the other statutory objective of the stability of the banking system and, to a lesser degree, of economic policy. We find the concept of "bias of conservatism" in statutes of central banks, to use the terminology of Rogoff (1985). Finally, the fourth group of variables embodies the idea that statutory limitations on public financing constitute an "intermediate objective" in the pursuit of price stability.

1.5.2.2 Turnover and political vulnerability of governors

Next to the index of formal "autonomy" (legal index), Cukierman, Webb and Neyapti apply an index of "real autonomy" (practical index) approximated by the rate of turnover of governors deduced from a questionnaire sent to recognised experts on central banks and concerning their respective practices. The rotation rate of governors can be taken as a proxy variable of the current independence of central banks. However, this rate does not inevitably imply a high level of independence. In particular, a length of mandate of three years, for example, (rate of turnover to the order of 0.33) is not sufficient to reach price stability, which responds with long and variable delays in relation to money. To this end, other subjective or informal factors such as the political vulnerability of governors were used to measure the independence of central banks. With a sample of 67 economies (20 industrialised and 47 developing countries) over the period 1950–89, Cukierman and Webb (1995) demonstrate that the average tendency to replace the governor is higher during political transition. Statistical tests reveal that the appropriate "cut-off" between "political" periods (where the change in governor is due to the last political transition) and "non-political" periods is six months, and that the turnover rate is twice as high in the former type of period as in the latter.

1.5.2.3   Independence of central banks and macroeconomic performance

Alesina and Summers (1993) demonstrated using numerical simulations on the double relation "autonomy/inflation" and "autonomy/ variability of inflation" that legal independence helps to stop inflation. The study by Grilli et al. (1991) of 18 OECD economies over the period 1950–89 distinguishes a "partial index of organic autonomy" and a "partial index of functional autonomy".

By dividing the period of observation into four decades, these authors show the existence of divergent effects: (1) both partial indices have no effect on inflation rates during the 50s and 60s because of the fixed exchange rates; (2) during the 70s, the effect of both indicators is highly significant; and (3) during the 80s, only the "partial index of functional autonomy" has an effect. Statutory provisions, and thus the organic component, seem weak in the face of implementation of monetary policies and the modalities of the choice of instruments.

However, there is no significant relation between distribution of inflation and the indices of legal independence in developing countries (cf. Cukierman (1992, chap. 20) and Cukierman, Edwards and Tabellini (1992). This weakness can be explained by the predominance of current or practical independence, which is not linked to inflation. Based on these findings, it appears that the relation between the inflation and turnover rate is strong and positive, which confirms that the relation between inflation and current independence is negative in developing economies.

Besides, it seems that the relation between inflation and political instability is positive, as demonstrated by Cukierman, Edwards and Tabellini (1992). This relation is either direct or indirect, that is, due to the political influence on the central banker. To answer this question, Cukierman and Webb (1995) regressed inflation and the standard deviation of inflation in relation to: (1) variable of vulnerability of the central bank; (2) non-political "turnover"; and (3) some measures of political instability. The variables of political instability are not significant, in spite of the positive coefficients which characterise them. However, vulnerability coefficients and non-political turnover are always positive and significant, which means that a high proportion of inflation and its variability are rather due to political influence on the central bank (indirect effect) than to the direct effect of political instability on the distribution of inflation.

Finally, the independence of central banks is conversely proportional to the distribution of inflation (that is, to its level and to its variability) both in industrialised economies and in developing countries. However, the measures of independence differ between these two groups of economies: in developed countries, legal independence is used as a proxy variable of autonomy contrary to turnover rate or its two components – vulnerability and non-political turnover – in developing countries. This distinction in the choice of indices ensues from the fact that legal independence is a particularly weak proxy for current independence in the second group because of the substantial deviations between the practice of central banks and the laws which govern them.

It is also advisable to remember the contingent effects of the level of inflation on the management of public finances. Demopoulos, Katsimbris and Miller (1987) in particular noted a negative relation between fiscal deficits (expressed in percentage of GDP and GNP) and degrees of autonomy of central banks. On the other hand, we generally note a low correlation between degrees of autonomy of central banks and public debt (expressed in percentage of GDP or GNP). The Bank of Spain and the Bundesbank, for example, show comparable performances but their degree of autonomy differs considerably.

In fact, (cf. Grilli et al., 1991), the dynamics of public debt depend more on political and electoral domestic structures than on the organic and functional autonomy of monetary authorities. A study focusing on the economies of the European community also confirms this (cf. Daniel, Gubian and Harasty, 1993). On the other hand, with respect to economic growth, several studies underline the absence of a significant relationship between the output growth rate (and variability) and legal independence of central banks (cf. Grilli et al., 1991; Alesina and Summers, 1993).[72] However, other analyses, in particular that of Pollard (1993) but especially the founding article by

Cukierman, Webb and Neyapti (1992), highlight the positive effect exercised by the degree of autonomy to boost economic activity. From the index of real autonomy (practical index) measuring the turnover rate of governors as a "proxy" variable, Cukierman et al. demonstrate a positive correlation between independence and growth in some developing economies, although the variable "political vulnerability of governors" does not show a significant relation with productivity growth (cf. Cukierman and Webb, 1995; Cukierman, Kalaitzidakis, Summers and Webb, 1993).

In addition, Debelle and Fisher (1994) demonstrate that the sacrifice ratio (loss of output per disinflation unit) is positively linked to independence, by showing that it is higher in Germany than in the USA to the benefit of the credibility of the Bundesbank *vis-à-vis* the FED, also during recessionary periods since the first oil crisis. Generally, the absence of an empirical relationship between independence and fluctuations in output is due, according to Alesina and Gatti (1995), to the fact that independent central banks reduce fluctuations in output only, which are linked with the politico-economic cycle. This difficulty is heightened by the uncertainty in transmission channels from independence to growth. Weak independence can reduce investments or be associated with low productivity growth rates. Cukierman et al. (1993) find that private investment in proportion to GDP is even lower when the turnover and political vulnerability of governors is high.

Because of the negative relation between inflation variability and independence of central banks, a negative relationship ensues between legal autonomy and variance of the real interest rates (cf. Alesina and Summers, 1993; Cukierman et al., 1993). However, in developing economies Cukierman et al. (1993) and Cukierman and Webb (1995) identified a positive effect of turnover and vulnerability on the variability of real interest rates.

The various controversies surrounding the expected effects of the independence of central banks on macroeconomic performance raise questions about the theoretical foundations for the approach that independence is the solution recommended in the conventional argument of credibility theory; this being a commitment to an institutional "rule" to be adopted to protect the implementation of monetary policy from the risks of temporary incoherence. A lack of independence leads to "discretion" and, from the perspective of macroeconomic performance, to an inflationary attitude, making any disinflation strategy ineffective. Monetary stability depends primarily on the strategy of money supply, which should not react either to cyclical risks or to the discretionary choices of governments facing electoral schedules (cf. Alesina, 1989). In this sense, the credibility granted by the public to monetary policy depends on the degree of central bankers' autonomy, which is negatively correlated to the inflation level (and variability). Monetary stability, and hence stable management of the money supply, do not constitute the only basic arguments in support of this theory. Added to this is a lack of monetary financing (or monetisation) of public deficits as an institutional solution linked to the independence policy of a central bank, which helps to combat any strategy aimed at cheating and thus of incoherence.

1.5.2.4   Application to Mediterranean economies

By using the classification of Cukierman, Webb and Neyapti (CWN) relating to the aggregated index of the legal independence of central banks, Arnone, Laurens and Segalotto (2006) classified emerging economies and in particular the Mediterranean economies following the aggregation of legal characteristics in four groups of variables (governing bodies, formulation and implementation of monetary policy, objectives of monetary policy and choice of instruments, statutory limitations to public financing) so as to distinguish two sub-indices of legal independence and economic independence as follows.

1.5.3   Stochastic context: flexibility versus credibility

All the conventional theoretical foundations confronted with the controversial empirical reports seen above should, according to Cartapanis and Bassoni (1995), give rise to critical reflections.

Table 1.8   Classification of Mediterranean economies

Partial index of legal independence				Partial index of economic independence			
Tunisia	Morocco	Egypt	Israel	Tunisia	Morocco	Egypt	Israel
0.63	0.5	0.17	0.33	0.75	0.8	0.8	0.8

According to these authors, some questions arise about the foundations of the conventional credibility theory; first is the argument relating to the fragility of the quantitative monetary norms in the face of financial innovations.

Moreover, since the relations between monetary aggregates and macroeconomic performance are not clearly established, monetary authorities prefer nominal anchoring to a set of indices (interest rate, exchange rate, level of debt, and so on). Some authors even suggested monitoring an index of the prices of financial assets (cf. Goodhart, 1992, 1993; Icard, 1992; Aglietta, 1993). This questioning puts in perspective the strategic foundation required to strengthen the credibility of monetary policy by an institutional rule of the independence of central bankers who are excessively focused on price stability. Monetary policy flexibility is necessary to stabilise an economy facing negative productivity shocks. In a stochastic context, arbitration between credibility and flexibility reconsiders and partially rejects the conservatism argument of Rogoff (1985).

In this context, the question of delegation of monetary policy to independent central bankers should be treated with caution when the economy is hit by productivity shocks. Under such conditions, the dilemma of "rules versus discretion" is transposed into terms of "credibility versus flexibility" because it has been demonstrated that flexibility of monetary policy is more beneficial than its delegation to an independent central bank that would make it counterproductive in the case of supply shocks. Monetary policy loses its credibility when it remains overly rigid, that is, its objectives prove to be inconsistent with the long-term equilibria. This point of view was firstly established by Sargent and Wallace (1981). Then, in a stochastic context, the central banks have to define contingent rules for risks (cf. Aubin, 1995).

In the light of these observations, central banks are confronted with the problem of arbitration between the credibility necessary to stabilise inflation and the flexibility required in the managing random exogenous shocks.[73] In this compromise – simplified as a "triangle of indecision" – and since the optimum choice of degree of conservatism depends on the variance of a supply shock, a central banker must not be too conservative. A minimum degree of flexibility is necessary to stabilise the economy in case of shocks, but what should then be the optimum degree of a central banker's conservatism according to variance in supply shocks? To this question, left unanswered by Rogoff, Nowaihi and Levine (1996), these authors add two alternative criticisms to the game of delegation.

It can prove counterproductive in an open economy as a result of external factors putting pressure on the exchange rate (cf. Currie, Levine and Pearlman, 1995, 1996).

It can be disrupted when budgetary (or fiscal) authorities enter the game as a third player and make a commitment to the stabilisation of supply shocks in strategic interaction with an independent or "conservative" central bank (cf. Aubin, 1995).

To this end, the argument for the conservatism of central bankers was extended and reconsidered by Lohmann (1992) who, on the other hand, proposes an "escape rule clause" specifying a rule of zero inflation for weak supply shocks, and a totally discretionary (flexible) conduct when stabilising strong shocks. Lohmann describes the potential costs of the independence of central banks in terms of the arbitration "credibility versus flexibility" of monetary policy. Therefore, the optimal commitment includes the appointment of a central banker of the Rogoff type but who can be objected to by the government if supply shocks are not stabilised adequately. The optimum behaviour of a central bank, which at the same time gives a high weighting to the degree of credibility of a disinflation policy (elimination of dynamic incoherence bias) and also allows some flexibility (stabilisation of real productivity shocks), is a question that Lohmann answers in terms of "partial independence" of a conservative central banker. This alternative is deduced from strategic arbitration among four institutional systems of implementation:

– A discretionary system.
– A system of full and binding commitment to a simple zero inflation rule, or credibility system.
– A system of partial commitment or flexibility, where central bankers accommodate the stabilisation rule for supply shocks.
– A system of pure conservatism as previously demonstrated by Rogoff.

In these conditions, the behaviour of the inflation rate is a stochastic process of a change in system (Flood and Garber, 1983). In other words, this stochastic process allows for arbitration between credibility (disinflation in "normal" or "sustainable" conditions of transmission of a random shock ξ within boundaries $[\underline{\xi}; \overline{\xi}]$) and flexibility (inflationary bias of a partially discretionary strategy or an accommodation of inflation expectation, in the case of unsustainable shocks $\xi \notin [\underline{\xi}; \overline{\xi}]$).

From the report of Lohmann (1992), experts propose a double optimum contract of the central bank, with linear reward of central bankers on their performance regarding disinflation[74] and, with a trigger option of punitive threat in case of non-stabilisation of supply shocks (Walsh, 1995b), where the flexibility of monetary policy is, however, contractually limited by a maximal threshold of inflation or "inflationary bias" which may not be exceeded.[75] This second optimum contract of the central bank thus allows the "credibility versus flexibility" of monetary policy to be associated. In both cases, the optimum contract stipulates that the central bank should maximise a utility function which results in the implementation of a socially optimum monetary rule.

In this base, some experts develop the concept of supporting legal independence of central banks through a commitment of responsibility of central bankers towards the electorate or towards a government agency, for example the Treasury. The independent central bank chooses specific objectives of monetary policy such as numerical inflation targets and fulfils its responsibility in the case of deviation. The central bank thus has "instrumental independence" and not "independence of objectives", such as the model of independence for the reserve bank in New Zealand, copied in projects to reform the statues of central banks in Canada and the United Kingdom (cf. Roll report[76]).

2
Overview of the National Banking Systems and Reforms

A well-functioning financial system is instrumental in attaining balanced and sustainable development. Such a system increases the availability of funding by mobilising idle savings, facilitating transactions and attracting foreign investments. It can also improve the allocation of financial resources by enhancing risk management, transparency and corporate governance practices and reinforcing property and creditor rights. Developed financial systems are crucial in providing funding to more opaque borrowers, such as the first-time and low-income borrowers or small and medium-sized enterprises (SMEs), which represent a significant proportion of economic activity but often lack the internal resources to grow. In short, financial development can serve to ameliorate the distribution of opportunities and improve income equality.

The emerging consensus in the academic literature is that financial development is possible as long as certain conditions are present to ensure that financial intermediaries serve the financial needs of the citizens and the private sector. These conditions include an adequate and operational regulatory structure, a well-defined supervisory authority, legal systems that reinforce property and creditor rights, restrained control of government over the financial system and macroeconomic stability.

Although the majority of the countries in the Mediterranean have embarked upon wide-ranging financial reforms, financial development has remained relatively limited. With mainly bank-driven financial systems, the surveyed countries are "under-banked", that

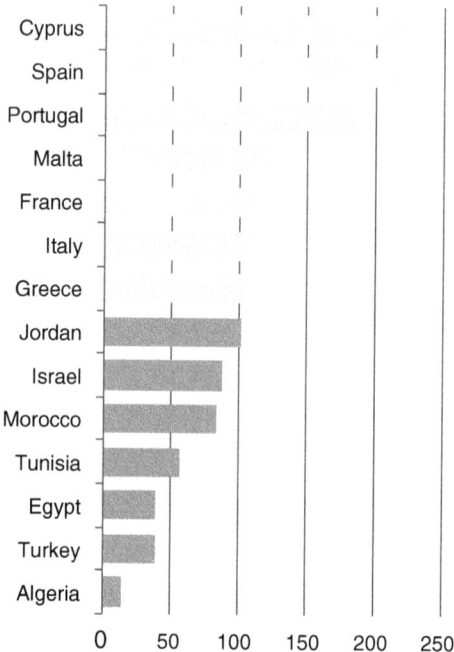

Figure 2.1   Private credit in the Mediterranean and Middle East (per cent of GDP, 2009)

is, the availability of credit to households and businesses is limited. In Algeria and Egypt, these shortcomings are quite severe, with bank loans to private enterprises representing less than half of the country's GDP (see Figure 2.1).

This section provides a descriptive analysis of the financial systems and reforms in the South and East Mediterranean and emphasises key development in four countries in the region, namely Algeria, Egypt, Morocco and Tunisia.

2.1   Banking and capital market development

To a large extent, the Mediterranean region has made substantial progress in financial development over the past few decades. Figure 2.2 confirms that credit to the private sector has grown substantially

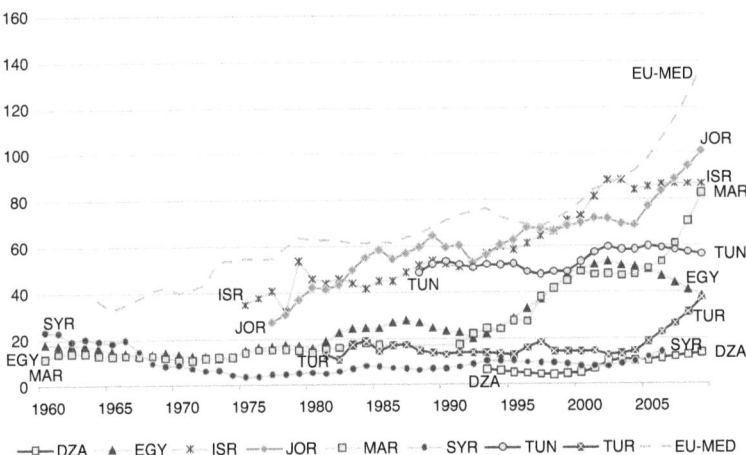

Figure 2.2 Bank credit to private sector, 1960–2009 (per cent of GDP)

Note: The pre-1993 data on Algeria (DZA) has been omitted due to the inclusion of loans to public enterprises.

Source: Beck and Demirgüç-Kunt (2009).

in most of the southern Mediterranean countries. Nevertheless, the share of credit in national income has remained consistently lower than the aggregate EU-MED figures in many South and East Mediterranean Countries (SEMCs). The relative unavailability of credit is particularly noteworthy in Egypt, Turkey, Syria and Algeria.

While credit may not always be available at the aggregate level in some SEMCs, banks appear to have no trouble in getting deposit funding in some of these countries. As depicted in Figure 2.3, in some of the SEMCs, including Egypt, Israel, Jordan and Morocco, the ratio of deposits to GDP is greater than or comparable to the EU-MED countries.

Historically, many reasons may explain these discrepancies. In Israel, the inflation rates remained exceptionally high in the late 1970s and early 1980s, with annual change in the consumer price index (CPI) climbing persistently from an already high 34 per cent in 1977 to nearly 400 per cent in the mid-1980s and finally settling down to about 20 per cent in the late 1980s and early 1990s. The early inflationary period in Israel also overlaps with the introduction

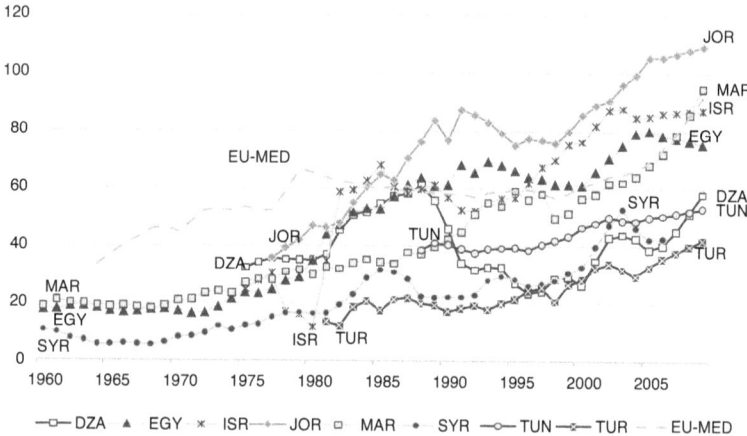

Figure 2.3 Bank deposits, 1960–2009 (per cent of GDP)
Source: Beck and Demirgüç-Kunt (2009).

of dollar-linked deposit accounts (that is, the so-called 'PATAM' accounts), seen as one of the main factors contributing to high inflationary expectations in the following years (Fischer, 1987; Yashiv, 1994). Over the years, as demand for domestic currency was replaced with demand for currency-indexed assets, inflation actually helped total bank deposits to pick up. Meanwhile, credit to private enterprises remained relatively dormant and even decreased slightly as a share of GDP during the same period.

Similarly, Turkey's persistent record with inflation throughout the 1980s and 1990s seems to have had a limited impact on bank deposits. When compared with Israel, Turkey's inflationary period lasted longer, with annual growth in CPI remaining above 50 per cent between 1979 and 2001. As in Israel, however, the period overlapped with a gradual opening of the capital account and an increasing demand for (and availability of) currency-linked assets. The foreign currency deposits accounted for approximately half of the total deposits in Turkey during the 1990s, reaching a staggering 60 per cent in the aftermath of the 2001 crisis (Bahmani-Oskooee and Domac, 2003). As the depositors shifted their money from the Lira-denominated accounts to currency-linked accounts to protect themselves, the total amount of bank liabilities changed little over this period.

In Algeria, the share of deposits was quite high prior to the 1990s and fell substantially afterwards. This could be largely attributable to monetary overhang, which is a characteristic of centrally-planned economies. The liberalisation that took place in the late1980s and 1990s was possibly the main factor that put an end to the excess liquidity in Algeria. Yet, the rise of inflation in the early 1990s could be an added reason for the decline in deposits. Unlike Israel or Turkey, currency convertibility was by and large prohibited until the late 1990s in Algeria, which prevented banks from offering currency-indexed deposit accounts during the inflationary period.

Much like the banking sector, the SEMCs have made substantial improvements in developing their capital markets over the past decades. Figure 2.4 shows that by the late 2000s, Egypt, Israel, Jordan and Morocco achieved larger stock exchanges than the EU-MED countries as a whole, measured in terms of stock market capitalisations as a share of GDP. The next figure (Figure 2.5), however, shows that the activity in the SEMC stock markets was relatively limited. Only Israel, Jordan and Turkey's stock markets showed a level of activity comparable with the EU-MED countries.

Several reasons can be put forward to explain these observations. In most of the region's stock markets, the trading activity takes

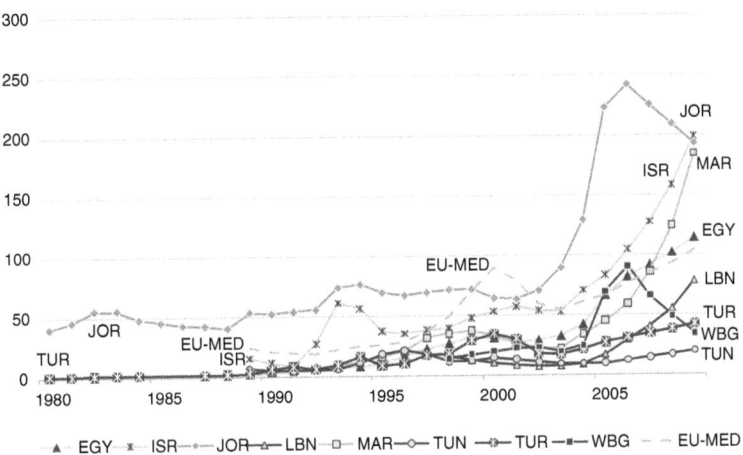

Figure 2.4 Stock market capitalisation, 1980–2009 (per cent of GDP)
Source: Beck and Demirgüç-Kunt (2009).

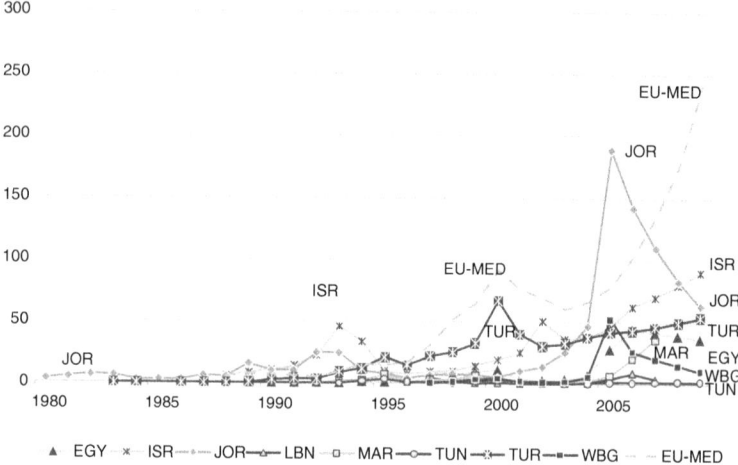

Figure 2.5   Stock market value traded, 1980–2009 (per cent of GDP)
Source: Beck and Demirgüç-Kunt (2009).

place in a few shares. Development of the stock markets has been severely hindered by poverty and inadequate market infrastructure, in particular the absence of credible and strong legal institutions. Some countries have only recently implemented laws to introduce stock markets. For example, Algeria only introduced the legal framework for share trading in 1999 and has not developed much equity trading. In other countries, only a few companies are listed on the market. Public ownership of utility companies and other enterprises has deprived the market of an important source of new issues (Creane et al., 2004). In other cases, the capital markets are used only as the basis for public funding.

2.2   Financial reforms and evolution of institutions

Although other factors may be at play, the persistent growth of private credit in some of these countries overlaps with substantial policy changes in recent decades. Indeed, the Mediterranean region is one of the leading areas of the world where extensive financial reforms have taken place. This is clearly shown in an overview of the financial reform index, constructed by Abiad et al. (2008) for a large number of countries around the globe, which provides evidence that the Mediterranean region, especially the EU-MED countries, has recorded the largest gains in financial reforms over the past three decades (Table 2.1). For most of the countries in the region, the reform momentum was the strongest between the mid-1980s and the mid-1990s (Figure 2.6).

Table 2.1 Evolution of financial reforms index, 1973–2005 (normalised scores)

	1973	2005	Difference (1973–2005)
MED	0.18	0.82	0.64
EU-MED	*0.22*	*0.93*	*0.71*
SEMC	*0.15*	*0.74*	*0.59*
LAC	0.11	0.75	0.64
ADV	0.36	0.94	0.58
EMA	0.17	0.69	0.52
SSA	0.17	0.68	0.52

Note: MED refers to the Mediterranean countries covered in the study, that is, the SEMCs and EU-MED; LAM refers to Latin America; ADV refers to Advanced countries; EMA refers to Emerging Asia; SSA refers to Sub-Saharan Africa.

Source: Abiad et al. (2008).

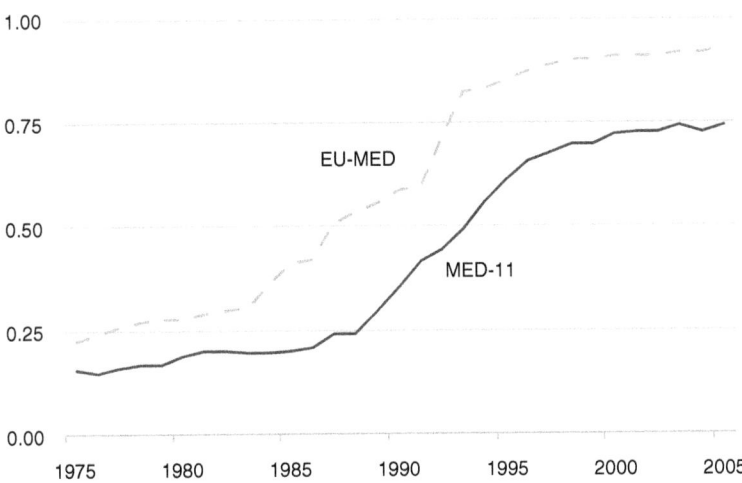

Figure 2.6 Evolution of financial reforms index in the Mediterranean, normalised scores

Note: MED 11 refers to SEMCs.

Source: Abiad et al. (2008).

The reforms appear to have had a positive impact on financial development in the region. For example, private credit and bank deposits are substantially higher in more regulated markets, especially among the SEMCs (Figure 2.7). The same also appears to be the case for stock markets. Although the variation in data is limited, both stock market capitalisation and stock market total value traded seems to be greater in more liberalised markets (Figure 2.**8**).

It is important to highlight, however, that financial reforms are not the only factors that could have had led to financial development in the region. In particular, most of the 11 SEMCs have made some improvement in putting in place strong legal institutions over the past years. However, as the events leading to the Arab Spring have clearly shown, such developments mean little unless complementary progress is also achieved in democratic governance, limiting the power of the executive branch and leading to an even distribution of power. Indeed, none of the financial development indicators seem to respond to the extent to which law and order is enforced in the 11 SEMCs or EU-MED countries (Figure 2.9).

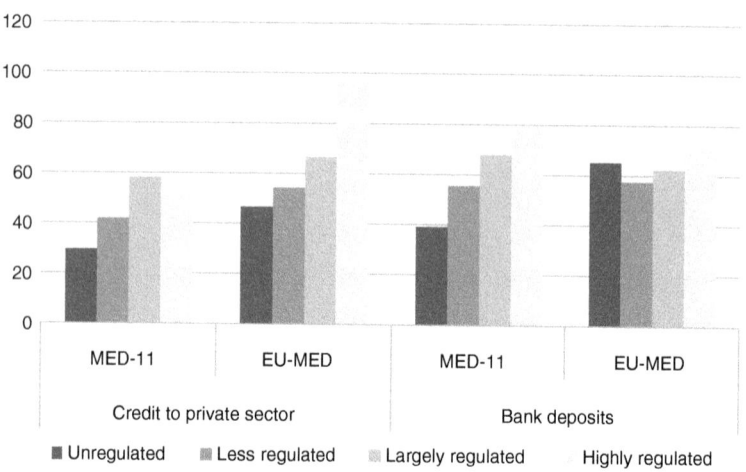

Figure 2.7 Banking sector development and banking reforms (per cent of GDP)

Note: MED 11 refers to SEMCs.

Sources: Abiad et al. (2008); Beck et al. (2009).

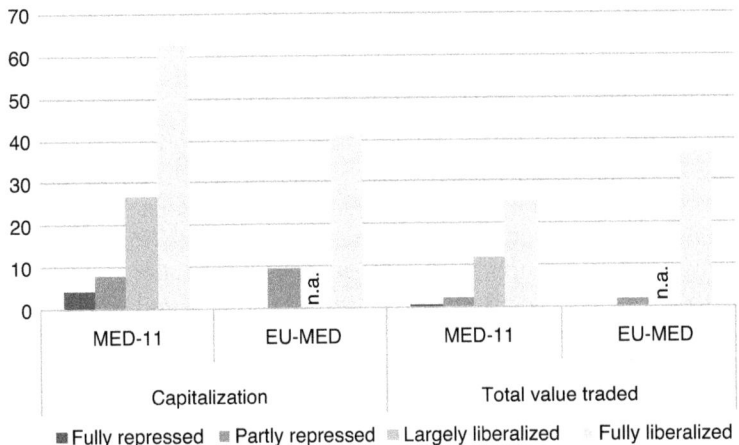

Figure 2.8 Stock market development and capital market reforms (per cent of GDP)

Note: MED 11 refers to SEMCs.

Sources: Abiad et al. (2008); Beck et al. (2009).

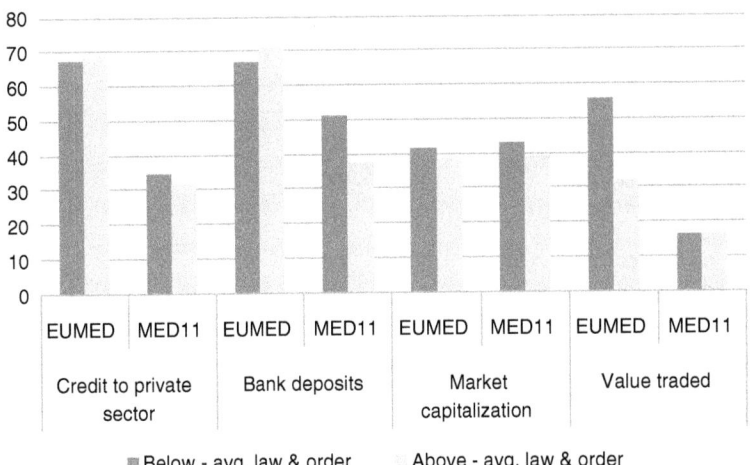

Figure 2.9 Financial development and law and order (per cent of GDP)

Note: MED 11 refers to SEMCs.

Source: PRS Group; Beck et al. (2009).

2.3   Investigation into financial systems of Algeria, Egypt, Morocco and Tunisia

2.3.1   Algeria

Algeria's banking system is characterised by an exceptionally strong and persistent presence of the public sector. The public banks direct the country's vast domestic savings to the state-owned enterprises operating in the country's hydrocarbon sector, which produces the country's chief exports. The Algerian government has expressed interest in liberalising the sector, although these promises are not backed by realistic policies to attract foreign investment. Moreover, although the banks appear to be well capitalised, the loan quality is very low, especially in the portfolios of public banks, requiring constant restructuring. Access to banking services is limited, with over 25,000 inhabitants per branch, or more than twice the regional average (Table 2.2).

Prior to the 1990s, as in most centrally planned countries, Algeria had a financial system that could only be described as "financially repressed". A set of regulations, laws and other non-market restrictions prevented the intermediaries from functioning at their full capacities. The government had full administrative control over the

Table 2.2   Structure of the Algerian economy and banking system

	2005	2006	2007	2008	2009
GDP per capita ($)	3,137	3,470	3,904	4,940	4,027
GDP per capita growth (per cent)	3.37	−0.70	1.20	2.22	0.52
Inflation (per cent)	1.64	2.33	3.56	4.86	5.74
Deposit rate	1.94	1.75	1.75	1.75	1.75
Lending rate	8.00	8.00	8.00	8.00	8.00
Commercial bank assets (per cent of GDP)	56	61	69	66	72
Top-3 banks (per cent share)	48	54	56	57	57
Number of commercial banks	19	18	19	21	21
... of which: public	6	6	6	6	6
Number of branches	1,183	1,227	1,278	1,287	1,301
... of which: public	1,063	1,097	1,126	1,093	1,057
Inhabitants per branch	27,772	27,181	26,489	26,699	26,772

Sources: IMF and Bank of Algeria.

banking sector as a whole, setting credit and deposit interest rates, directing the allocation of credit and having ownership stakes in practically all credit institutions. The banking system had the single aim of providing liquidity for the execution of the objectives of the plan. The directed allocation of credit and high liquidity levels led to an unrestrained monetary expansion.

The sector was partially liberalised in 1990 with the entry into force of the Monetary and Credit Law (Law No. 90–10). The law was designed as a first step to replace the state's direct control over the banking sector, facilitating entry and liberalising interest rates, first the deposit rate and then the credit rate in 1994. Between the years 1995 and 2007, several private banks were formed, almost all foreign-owned subsidiaries of prominent international banks. Although the government has repeatedly renewed its commitment to liberalising the sector, the private banks' role remains limited in terms of the mobilisation and allocation of resources, except for loans to the private sector, where public banks' predominance is lower (Table 2.3).

Several reasons may explain the deficient growth of the privately owned banks in Algeria. First and foremost, the public authorities have been historically hesitant to open the banking sector to competition, since this may divert financing from public entities. As an example, Algeria's ability to attract foreign direct investment (FDI) flows has been severely hampered by the recent Supplementary Budget Law of 2009 (Ordinance No. 09–01, Art. 58). This law requires, among other things, that the majority stake must belong to a domestic partner for all new incoming FDI flows. This new requirement will continue to hamper the privatisation of public banks, which puts in question the government's willingness to liberalise the market.

Table 2.3 Market shares of Algerian public banks

	2005	2006	2007	2008	2009
Total assets	91.4%	91.7%	92.2%	90.8%	–
Private sector loans	85.4%	83.3%	79.4%	77.0%	76.7%
Public sector loans	99.9%	99.9%	99.8%	99.8%	99.9%
Total deposits	93.3%	92.9%	93.1%	92.2%	–
Branches	89.4%	88.1%	84.9%	81.2%	–

Source: Bank of Algeria.

Second, Algeria has traditionally been seen as a risky country, mainly due to political risks. The recent financial crisis appears to have reduced investors' risk appetite, which is often cited as the main reason behind the cancellation of privatisation of Crédit Populaire d'Algérie (CPA), one of the largest public banks in Algeria.

The predominance of state-owned banks leads to a number of problems. First, by providing funding primarily to the public sector, the present structure severely restricts the diversification opportunities for the Algerian economy. According to recent figures, the share of loans to the private sector represents only one-fifth of total banking assets (Table 2.4). A large proportion of the total assets is held in loans to public enterprises, mostly in the hydrocarbons sector, and balances with the state. Although a more effective financial intermediation and diversification of the economy are the key aims of the authorities, progress has been limited in channelling the domestic savings into the real economy, especially to non-hydrocarbon businesses and private enterprises (IMF, 2010a).

A second problem arises from the allocation of credit to inefficiently run public undertakings; in particular, the state-dominated banking sector has been characterised by exorbitant levels of non-performing loans (NPLs), especially for loans to public enterprises (Table 2.5). Owing to their limited role, the public banks lack the institutional framework and experience to promote efficient intermediation. Over the past years, this fundamental weakness has repeatedly threatened the viability of the quality of public banks' portfolios, calling for a frequent clean-up of the balance sheets via government loan purchases. The government implemented such a buy-back program in 2008, when the NPL rate in public banks had dropped from 24 per cent of total loans in 2007 to 20 per cent. Despite these policies, the NPL rates continue to remain high for the publicly-owned banks, not only for their loans to state-owned enterprises but also for the credit they extended to private-sector businesses. In turn, foreign-owned private banks, which have almost no exposures to the public sector businesses, have relatively low NPL rates, except in recent years due to the financial crisis.

In recent years, Algerian authorities have launched a number of additional initiatives aimed at increasing the banking system's lending capacity, increasing the minimum capital requirements for banks, and reducing the level of NPLs through financial restructuring

Table 2.4 Assets and liabilities of Algerian banks (billions of Algerian Dinars)

	2004	2005	2006	2007	2008	2009	2010*
Assets	3,893	4,210	5,229	6,511	7,287	7,327	7,510
Reserves	281	198	274	445	370	340	617
Balances with foreign institutions	77	91	84	108	142	58	55
Balances with state	803	876	1,015	941	678	810	805
...of which: Treasury deposits	15	14	84	46	52	83	64
...of which: Deposits at CCP	11	4	12	7	5	15	10
...of which: Treasury bills	669	644	818	793	491	541	552
of which: Other	109	215	102	95	130	171	180
Loans	1,534	1,779	1,904	2,204	2,614	3,085	3,185
...of which: Public enterprises	858	882	847	989	1,202	1,485	1,570
...of which: Public authorities	0	0	1	0	0	1	1
...of which: Private enterprises	675	896	1,056	1,213	1,411	1,598	1,613
...of which: Private banks	2	1	0	2	1	1	1
Other assets	1,198	1,265	1,953	2,813	3,482	3,034	2,891
Liabilities	3,893	4,210	5,229	6,511	7,287	7,327	7,510
Capital	142	152	161	171	184	302	300
Reserves	25	20	24	28	169	170	173
Liabilities to non-residents	116	84	115	90	134	46	54
Deposits	2,705	2,961	3,517	4,322	4,938	4,732	4,880
...of which: Sight: Public enterprises	697	774	1,164	1,832	2,056	1,427	1,511
...of which: Sight: Private enterprises	274	321	442	563	721	904	910
...of which: Sight: Other banks	157	129	144	166	170	173	165
...of which: Term: Public enterprises	254	366	365	351	394	499	509
...of which: Term: Private enterprises	1,189	1,233	1,271	1,396	1,573	1,723	1,779
...of which: Term: Other banks	134	138	130	14	24	7	8
...of which: Central government	67	99	144	218	400	445	444
Funds by state	49	55	34	29	16	15	14
Other liabilities	790	840	1,236	1,654	1,446	1,618	1,645

Note: *March 2010 figures.

Source: Bank of Algeria.

Table 2.5   The Algerian banking system: key financial soundness indicators

	2005	2006	2007	2008
Regulatory capital (as per cent of RWA)	12%	15%	13%	17%
... of which: public banks	12%	14%	12%	16%
... of which: private banks	19%	22%	18%	20%
NPLs* (as per cent of total loans)	19%	18%	22%	18%
... of which: public banks; all loans	20%	19%	24%	20%
... of which: public banks; private loans	10%	12%	19%	16%
... of which: private banks; all loans	3%	3%	9%	7%
Return on equity	8%	19%	25%	25%
... of which: public banks	6%	17%	24%	25%
... of which: private banks	5%	23%	28%	26%

Note: *Non-performing loans (NPLs) include loans in arrears with 100 per cent provisioning requirement. The figures include all public and private banks, including the branches of foreign institutions.

Source: IMF (2010a).

of public enterprises. The 1990 Monetary and Credit Law foresaw the gradual implementation of the capital requirements set by the 1988 Basel Capital Accord. After several revisions, the minimum capital adequacy ratio of 8 per cent was established in 1999 and has been maintained ever since. Reserve requirements were first implemented in 1994 (Instruction No. 73–94), gradually raised from a minimum of 2.5 per cent of deposits to 8 per cent by 2008.

A deposit insurance scheme was introduced in 1997 (Law no. 97–04), providing a guarantee of up to 600,000 Algerian dinars (approximately €6,200 at end-2010 conversion rates) per depositor with no co-insurance or legally set delays for making payments. The scheme became operational with the creation of Société de Garantie des Dépôts Bancaires (SGDB) in 2003. Under the current regulations, the scheme is funded by an annual premium charged on each bank, which is set at 1 per cent of deposits. The scheme was put to use for the first time in 2004, to reimburse depositors of the now-defunct El-Khalifa Bank, which was a private bank that was founded in 1998. As noted in the World Bank (2004) assessment, there has been some concern that the scheme lacked functional and financial independence, which could result in discretionary decisions on its use.

Turning to legal and informational infrastructure for getting credit, the World Bank's Doing Business (2010) ranking clearly shows that Algeria lags behind others, putting it in 135th position out of a total of 183 countries. The finding is not surprising. Algeria is behind many countries in terms of creditors' rights and information-sharing capacity. In particular, there are no private credit bureaus and the public credit registry's coverage is largely insufficient. Secured creditors' ability to make claims on collateral is ill-defined, severely undermining their rights and more generally the legal framework for credit.

To conclude, Algeria's banking system is dominated by six public banks, which continue to collect over 90 per cent of the domestic deposits and divert a significant proportion to the mostly inefficient public enterprises concentrated in the hydrocarbon sector. Under current conditions, the Algerian financial sector is not providing the necessary funding for its private sector to successfully diversify its economy in the near- to mid-term, in line with the aims set in its 2009 Action Plan and the EU-Algeria National Indicative Plan (NIP) for 2011–13. In addition to hampering growth opportunities, directed credit undermines credit quality and real intermediation. Algeria has ample fiscal space due to its immense hydrocarbon receipts and can continue to engage in risky loans and their restructuration at regular intervals. However, these strategies should be used to resuscitate private sector growth and not to support the ailing public enterprises. In conjunction with steps to liberalise the economy, the government should improve the pre-conditions for easing the flow of credit information and improve creditors' rights. Doing otherwise may hamper credit growth for the traditionally opaque firms, such as SMEs, and may prolong the realisation of the benefits from a well-developed financial sector. The use of an explicit deposit insurance scheme when a substantial proportion of the banking sector is publicly owned should also be assessed.

2.3.2 Egypt

Egypt's banking regulations have undergone significant reforms in recent years. A new banking law (Law no. 88) enacted in 2003 unified all Egyptian banking regulations, reinforcing the independence and regulatory role of the Central Bank of Egypt (CBE), aligning the prudential standards with the Basel II Accord as well as strengthening loan classification rules, remedial powers of regulator, risk-based focus on supervision and capital requirements. More recent reforms have sought to reduce the state-owned stakes in joint-venture and public banks, enhancing credit conditions and increasing access to banking. The pervasiveness of state ownership is one of the key challenges of the Egyptian banking system. The government-controlled banks account for nearly two-thirds of the banking activity. This has undermined competition by obstructing entry, and contributes to inefficiencies, as is evident from the country's high non-performing-loans. By 2006, the reported stock of NPLs amounted to nearly a quarter of gross loans, mainly held in public banks' portfolios. This has resulted in a set of programmes initiated by the CBE to settle these loans by cash injections (funded by privatisation receipts), settlements and investment sales. Although the private banks have been increasing their network in recent years, most of the branches remain in urban areas. Access to banking remains low, as in Algeria, with over 24,000 habitants per branch (see Table 2.6).

Table 2.6   Structure of Egyptian economy and banking system

	2004–5	2005–6	2006–7	2007–8	2008–9	2009–10
GDP per capita ($)	1,283	1,506	1,771	2,160	2,450	1,283
GDP per capita growth (per cent)	2.38	4.90	3.74	4.89	2.62	2.38
Inflation (per cent)	8.80	4.20	10.95	11.70	16.24	8.80
Deposit rate (per cent)	7.23	6.02	6.10	6.58	6.49	7.23
Lending rate (per cent)	13.14	12.60	12.51	12.33	11.98	13.14
Bank assets (per cent of GDP)	131	123	126	121	105	101
Top-3 banks (per cent share)	58	59	57	55	–	–
Public banks (per cent of total assets)	–	–	–	67	–	–
Number of commercial banks	52	43	41	40	39	39
... of which: public	7	7	6	6	5	5
Number of branches	2,841	2,944	3,056	3,297	3,443	3,490
... of which: public	2,185	2,222	2,074	2,089	2,088	2,080
Inhabitants per branch	25,308	25,000	25,360	23,992	24,252	24,212

Note: Deposit rates correspond to interest rates for three-month time deposits.

Sources: IMF, Central Bank of Egypt and Beck and Demirgüç-Kunt (2009).

Under the reform programme initiated in 2004, a number of public-ly-owned banks with high non-performing loans have been elimi-nated by sales, purchases and mergers. In 2006, the country's fifth largest bank, Bank of Alexandria, was successfully privatised with its acquisition by the Italian Sanpaolo IMI group. These measures have reduced the share of the publicly-owned banks. Nevertheless, the state continues to maintain a significant proportion of the banking system, either directly, as in the case of the top-two banks, which are public, representing over one-quarter of total assets, or indirectly via partial stakes, as is the case in a number of specialised banks and joint-ven-ture stakes held by public banks. There are concerns over the future roles of the remaining state banks, as the private banks continue their growth and expansion into underserved sectors (World Bank, 2008).

The state's influence in banking is not limited to its direct or indirect ownership. More broadly, the level of government debt held by banks has been very high in Egypt, accounting for an increasingly greater share in the banks' balance sheets. As of October 2010, the share of public debt and loans represents around 40 per cent of the total assets of Egyptian banks, up from less than a quarter in 2001 (Figure 2.10).

One chief underlying reason for banks' increasing willingness to hold more public debt than private credit is the attractive yields

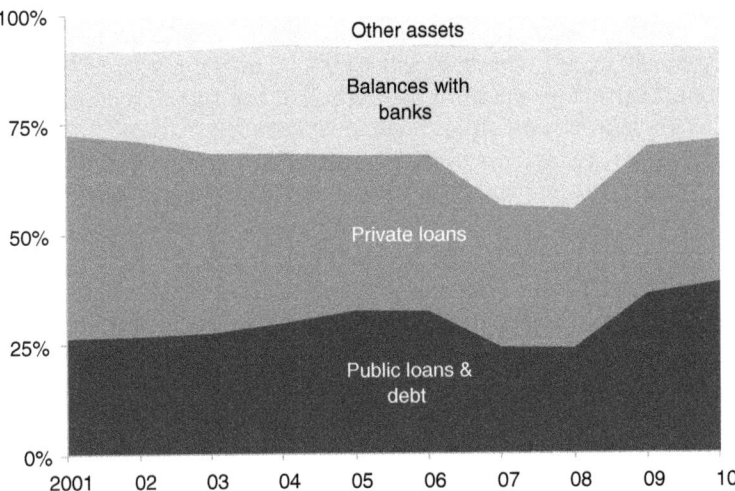

Figure 2.10 Assets of Egyptian banks
Source: Central Bank of Egypt.

offered by the treasury bonds, crowding out credit to other segments. The aggregate information on the banks' balance sheets gives details on the activities of Egyptian banks (Table 2.7). More specifically, public debt held by the banks has increased substantially in recent years and has surpassed the total outstanding private loans as of October 2010. Meanwhile, customer deposits represent nearly two-thirds of the total balance sheet.

There is some evidence that the policies implemented since the early 2000s to diminish NPLs have also made banks more reluctant to lend to the private sector, especially to more risky lines of business. Deficiencies in the availability of credit-worthiness information and managerial skills of most SMEs have also contributed to greater-than-normal risks in the real sector. Outstanding bank credits are by-and-large concentrated in the blue-chip corporations, with retail and SME sectors remaining relatively underserved due to inherent risks. Facilitating bank intermediation remains one of the key challenges in Egypt and has been the main aim of the recent reform initiatives (IMF, 2010b).

In recent years, Egypt has made significant strides in the field of credit information-sharing. The CBE, which supervises the Egyptian banking system, has operated a public credit registry (PCR) since 1957. In 2002, an online system was adopted, permitting banks to extract and transmit information electronically. In 2004, the coverage of the registry was improved by lowering the threshold for reporting credit to E£30,000 (approximately €4,000) (Emerging Markets Group, 2006). In the same year, the CBE required the larger credit institutions to report any credit card delinquencies (defined as 90 days past due and/or with legal proceedings) in an effort to compile a "Negative List Database"; however, the database is not distributed directly by the public registry. Legal amendments introduced in 2006 allowed the public registry to share information with the country's first private credit bureau, I-score, founded by a consortium of the country's main banks in 2005. Other banks, non-bank financial institutions and utility companies have also been invited to join the private credit bureau in 2008. With these changes, the private database is expected to cover a large majority of the lending portfolio of all banks.

Despite significant improvements in credit information sharing, barely any progress has been noted in improving the legal and institutional framework for credit. A number of notable weaknesses exist

Table 2.7 Assets and liabilities of Egyptian banks (billions of Egyptian pounds)

	2001	2002	2003	2004	2005	2006	2007	2008	2009	2010*
Assets	428.4	495.5	577.9	633.4	703.6	761.6	937.9	1,083.3	1,092.0	1,220.7
Cash	3.5	4.5	5.6	5.4	6.6	6.8	7.7	10.3	11.1	12.4
Public debt	71.1	87.7	111.3	137.4	170.7	194.0	176.1	201.9	332.6	405.9
Balances with domestic banks	67.0	83.2	110.9	116.3	125.0	121.7	217.4	278.2	173.5	200.7
Balances with foreign banks	16.3	20.0	29.8	43.3	51.2	72.6	124.4	122.8	77.1	57.4
Loans	241.5	266.1	284.7	296.2	308.2	324.0	353.7	401.4	430.0	466.0
...of which: Public	42.3	45.5	48.2	51.6	59.3	53.6	50.9	57.8	63.6	69.2
...of which: Private	199.2	220.6	236.5	244.6	248.9	270.4	302.9	343.6	366.3	396.8
Other assets	29.0	33.9	35.7	34.8	42.0	42.5	58.6	68.8	67.7	78.2
Liabilities	428.4	495.5	577.9	633.4	703.6	761.6	937.9	1,083.3	1,092.0	1,220.7
Capital	12.0	12.5	18.2	20.3	22.9	27.1	33.0	37.6	41.6	46.6
Reserves	10.2	11.2	11.8	11.5	12.4	13.4	12.6	19.8	21.4	28.5
Provisions	31.2	35.9	40.1	44.6	49.5	55.0	53.5	62.3	69.7	70.4
Long-term loans & bonds	11.9	14.1	14.9	15.0	14.3	17.5	26.4	22.3	22.0	21.7
Liabilities to domestic banks	28.2	35.1	35.6	29.9	22.7	21.5	82.6	98.7	31.0	53.9
Obligations to foreign banks	11.5	11.8	16.2	10.3	12.3	8.8	10.0	13.3	18.2	20.3
Deposits	291.2	340.9	403.1	461.7	519.6	568.8	650.0	747.2	809.7	892.5
...of which: Public	–	–	–	–	108.7	108.2	107.1	126.3	139.9	151.9
...of which: Private	–	–	–	–	410.7	460.9	546.7	624.7	676.4	744.1
Other liabilities	32.2	34.0	38.0	40.1	49.9	49.5	69.9	82.1	78.4	86.8

Note: *October 2010 figures.

Source: Central Bank of Egypt.

in loan enforcement and collateral foreclosure practices, including an incomplete definition of secured transactions that are allowable as collateral. Administrative costs for registering land titles and mortgages remain high, which makes collateralisation difficult. Out-of-court enforcement remains largely unavailable, except for secured claims over securities. In particular, collection of unsecured debt or secured real estate transactions is only possible through complex and lengthy court proceedings. The CBE has sought to address these challenges through the creation of an NPL Management Unit, the launch of a conciliation and arbitration mechanism, and regulatory changes in the real estate finance law. However, these moves are unlikely to be as efficient as a full-scale revision of the legal and institutional framework for credit.

The introduction of an explicit deposit insurance scheme was foreseen under the second phase of the banking sector regulation reform initiated in 2008. Information obtained from the authorities and the CBE's website shows that the scheme aims to protect small depositors. Other details on the scheme, such as the type of funding, risk-responsiveness of premiums and potential government backing are not available. At this moment, no timeline has been provided on when the scheme will become operational.

Other reforms on the agenda that are currently at play include the comprehensive implementation of the Basel II standards along with supplementary prudential measures to limit excessive risk in the financial sector. To that extent, there is some scope for cooperation with the EU for capacity-building purposes. The authorities have also expressed an interest in encouraging banks to publish more detailed information, where cooperation opportunities also exist.

Although the Egyptian government has been actively engaged in a variety of regulatory reforms in recent years, some of the endemic problems in the banking sector continue to exist and may well remain unaddressed in the upcoming years. Indeed, despite the privatisation move, by the end of 2008, the market share of institutions that were wholly- or majority-owned by the state remained over half of the total banking assets (Table 2.6). Although the NPL rates have dropped considerably, they still represent 13.4 per cent of gross loans by the end of 2009. Additionally, a significant amount of untapped financial liquidity continues to remain dormant within the banking system. The aggregate loan-to-deposit ratio – dropping to 53 per cent

Table 2.8 Egyptian banking system: key financial soundness indicators

	2001	2002	2003	2004	2005	2006	2007	2008	2009
Regulatory capital (as per cent of RWA)	10.2%	11.0%	11.1%	11.4%	13.7%	14.7%	14.8%	14.7%	15.1%
NPLs (as per cent of total loans)	15.6%	20.2%	24.2%	23.6%	26.5%	18.2%	19.3%	14.8%	13.4%
Provisions (as per cent of classified loans)	69.4%	62.3%	57.0%	60.2%	51.0%	76.2%	74.6%	92.1%	100.4%
Return on assets	0.8%	0.5%	0.5%	0.5%	0.6%	0.8%	0.9%	0.8%	0.8%
Return on equity	13.7%	8.9%	8.9%	9.8%	10.2%	14.3%	15.6%	14.1%	13.0%

Sources: IMF, Global Financial Stability Reports, 2005–2010.

in 2009 – points to a clear under-leveraging in the sector, which has become a more acute problem in recent years, especially after the recent set of reforms aimed at improving the banks' balance sheets. The remainder of the banking assets are held in safe and higher-yield government debt, with treasury bills held representing nearly one-third of total assets.

These points underscore the present trade-offs between the level of public debt, restrictiveness of prudential regulations, extent of information sharing, adequacy of corporate governance practices and credit availability. Although the government has pursued an ambitious reform agenda in some of these areas, a comprehensive assessment is necessary to ensure that the post-reform conditions are consistent with the country's long-term development strategy of facilitating endemic growth in the private-sector.

2.3.3 Morocco

Morocco has one of the largest banking sectors in the Southern Mediterranean, with the total assets of commercial banks representing over 120 per cent of the country's GDP. Commercial banks play a crucial role in the country's financial system and have increasingly developed links with other financial intermediaries in the rapidly expanding insurance, securities, leasing and factoring sectors. The banking system is relatively concentrated, with the market share of the top three banks remaining around two-thirds of the total bank assets. In 2009, the sector consisted of a total of 13 privately-owned banks, seven of which are majority-owned by foreign shareholders, and six publicly-owned banks. In addition to these depositary institutions, there are six offshore banks and 12 microfinance institutions, which are not included in the figures below.

The central bank, Bank Al-Maghrib (BAM), was created in 1959 (under its prior name, Banque du Maroc) to issue banknotes and coins, safeguard the stability of the currency and to preserve the soundness of the banking system. More specifically, the by-laws of BAM stipulate that the chief role of the body is "to ensure the well-functioning of the banking system and the implementation of the laws and regulations relating to the surveillance and control of the activities of credit institutions and related institutions". The head of the body, the Governor, is elected by the Sovereign; the head of the supervisory unit within BAM is named by the Governor of BAM, with an undefined tenure – possibly for life.

Macroeconomic conditions have improved in recent years, thanks to increased FDI and remittance inflows as well as tourism receipts. Fiscal conditions have also recovered due to structural reforms and fiscal consolidation efforts. Since Morocco has a pegged currency, fixed at a basket of currencies consisting of the euro and the US dollar, and a partially closed capital account, the capital inflows have contributed to the increase of domestic liquidity and, in parallel, of banks' liquid assets. The central bank, BAM, has increased the banks' required reserves and used its deposit facility regularly to absorb excess liquidity and to keep price stability under control.

The Moroccan banking sector has undergone significant changes following the reform process of the early 1990s. The process aimed to establish a financial sector that serves the market economy, mobilising savings and optimally allocating investments. The requirements for private banks to hold development bank bonds were largely abolished by the banking law of 1993. Interest rate subsidies and controls were completely eliminated in the years that followed, with the exception of sight deposits and small savings deposits, which continue to be non-remunerated. The more recent 2006 banking law has reinforced the autonomy and roles of the country's regulatory

Table 2.9 Structure of the Moroccan economy and banking system

	2001	2002	2003	2004	2005	2006	2007	2008	2009
GDP per capita ($)	1,308	1,385	1,688	1,905	1,967	2,142	2,427	2,827	2,865
GDP per capita Growth (per cent)	–	2.1%	5.1%	3.5%	1.7%	6.4%	1.5%	4.1%	4.3%
Inflation (per cent)	–	2.8%	1.2%	1.5%	1.0%	3.3%	2.0%	3.9%	1.0%
Deposit Rate	–	4.5%	3.8%	3.6%	3.5%	3.7%	3.7%	3.9%	3.8%
Lending Rate	–	13.1%	12.6%	11.5%	11.5%	–	–	–	–
Bank assets (per cent of GDP)	85%	86%	86%	88%	96%	102%	117%	120%	121%
Top-3 banks (per cent of total assets)	–	51%	54%	64%	64%	64%	63%	65%	66%
Number of banks	19	18	18	17	16	16	16	18	19
of which: public	7	7	6	6	5	5	5	5	6
of which: foreign	7	5	5	5	5	5	5	7	7
Public banks (per cent of total assets)	–	–	–	–	–	29%	27%	26%	25%
Foreign banks (per cent of total assets)	–	–	–	–	–	22%	22%	21%	21%
Branches	1,805	1,878	1,948	2,033	2,223	2,447	2,748	3,138	3,538
Inhabitants per branch	15,974	15,540	15,154	14,677	13,559	12,463	11,230	9,952	8,913

Note: Deposit rate is determined based on the 3-months TD rate and the lending rate is determined by the maximum export credit.

Sources: IMF and Bank al-Maghrib.

authority, BAM, enlarged its control to the entire banking sector, enhanced deposit insurance schemes and broadened its supervisory authority.

Despite the excess liquidity, credit to the private sector remained flat in the first half of the 2000s, remaining around 50 per cent of GDP (Figure 2.11). A number of underlying factors can be put forward to explain the unresponsiveness of credit conditions to the overall availability of liquidity. The Moroccan economy is made up of a large number of small firms operating in the informal sector with opaque information on creditworthiness. Additionally, the banks had a large portfolio of NPLs, which undermined their appetite for risk. Lastly, the handsome interest earnings from holding excess reserves also competed with any real lending activity that the banks might undertake.

Private credit growth picked up substantially in the second half of the decade, representing over 80 per cent of the GDP by the end of 2009. These developments are partly explained by dropping NPL ratios, which might have contributed to an increasing risk appetite for banks (Table 2.10). Moreover, BAM encouraged lending by strengthening credit information standards and risk management capacity of banks, most notably by setting up a credit bureau in 2009. The resources of public credit guarantee schemes have also been expanded substantially, reaching $370 million (0.4 per cent of GDP) in outstanding guarantees in 2009, compared to $251 million in 2007. Lastly, the rising asset prices, notably in the real estate markets

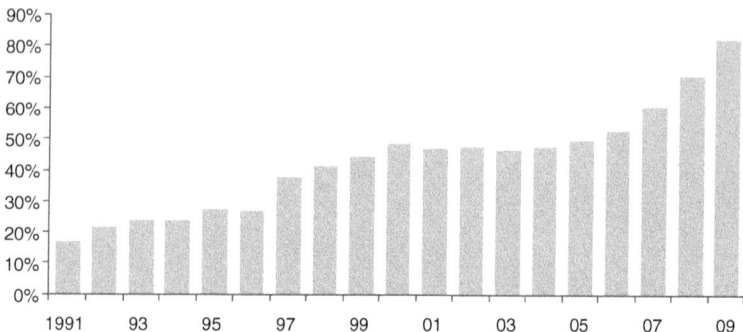

Figure 2.11   Private sector credit in Morocco (as per cent of GDP)
Source: Beck & Demirgüç-Kunt (2009).

Table 2.10 Moroccan banking system: Key financial soundness indicators, 2001–09

	2001	2002	2003	2004	2005	2006	2007	2008	2009
Regulatory capital (as per cent of RWA)	12.6	12.2	9.3	10.5	11.5	12.3	10.6	11.2	11.7
NPLs (as per cent of total loans)	17	17	18	19	16	11	8	6	6
Provisions (as per cent of NPL)	53	55	55	59	67	71	75	75	74
Return on equity	10.2	1.9	–2.1	10.9	6.3	17.4	20.6	16.7	17.0
Return on assets	0.9	0.3	–0.2	0.8	0.5	1.3	1.5	1.2	1.3

Source: Bank al-Maghrib.

(reaching 20 per cent in some cities in 2007), have created a wealth effect and increased collateral values, lifting both the demand and supply of credit (Allain and Oulidi, 2009).

The aggregate balance sheet for the Moroccan banking sector highlights some of the issues discussed (Table 2.11). Unlike their counterparts in Algeria and Egypt, public debt represents a small proportion of the portfolios of Moroccan banks. This is especially the case since 2008, when the ratio of public debt and public loans to total assets dipped below 10 per cent.

In fact, the total outstanding public debt has declined over the last eight years while the total assets have increased more than twofold. On the liability-side, the funding is mostly through customer deposits, which have represented roughly 60 per cent of the total liabilities. The banks increasingly use the money market for their funding, although their share in total liabilities remains small.

The 2000s have also witnessed the opening of a number of microfinance institutions. The 1999 microcredit law allowed these institutions to borrow funds from the domestic financial market and offer credit without being restricted by rate caps. Within several years, Morocco became a regional leader in the microfinance sector, currently supervised by BAM (after the introduction of the new banking law in 2006). By 2008, the Moroccan microfinance sector provided funding to over 1.2 million active borrowers and had a total loan portfolio of over $700 million, representing approximately 1 per cent of loans to the private sector.

Table 2.11 Assets and liabilities of Moroccan banks (millions of Moroccan Dirham)

	2003	2004	2005	2006	2007	2008	2009	2010*
Assets	409,576	442,487	507,702	591,284	720,313	828,100	888,566	925,571
Balances with non-residents	15,862	19,693	28,038	30,618	32,299	28,856	28,599	23,602
Balances with central bank	38,637	47,753	48,987	53,206	65,932	61,097	42,829	32,184
Loans	232,305	249,594	289,345	352,198	455,729	561,907	630,504	680,125
...of which: Government	4,451	4,984	6,723	6,549	6,177	12,252	16,108	16,175
...of which: Non-bank private	224,369	241,513	271,983	329,483	429,208	534,061	589,555	637,144
Negotiable debt securities	88,811	85,437	99,278	101,240	103,610	101,275	97,041	98,311
...of which: Government	78,568	73,752	83,558	88,838	89,344	78,875	69,990	68,906
...of which: Non-Bank Private	2,430	3,513	6,545	7,130	6,329	12,726	14,795	14,446
Money market funds	0	0	548	4,084	1,280	1,316	1,756	2,634
Shares and other equity	13,435	18,084	16,246	21,328	25,161	35,404	45,977	45,407
Fixed assets	11,494	12,736	13,485	13,727	14,795	15,770	16,806	17,853
Other assets	9,033	9,190	11,775	14,883	21,507	22,475	25,054	25,456
Liabilities	409,576	442,487	507,702	591,284	720,313	828,100	888,566	925,571
Liabilities to non-residents	13,785	11,430	12,022	12,847	12,372	13,472	12,282	19,290
Liabilities to public & fin. inst.	17,685	17,042	28,466	36,816	48,918	57,887	74,031	84,917
Non-bank private deposits	279,474	302,863	347,158	403,273	474,915	524,672	542,820	549,676
...of which: Sight deposits	151,868	170,767	199,490	233,667	291,721	306,617	323,302	326,329
...of which: Term & saving accounts	127,607	132,096	147,668	169,606	183,194	218,055	219,518	223,348
Money market funds	0	0	15,323	22,107	30,546	39,202	50,893	59,899
Negotiable debt securities	9,592	7,559	5,672	6,873	12,236	29,223	36,031	35,956
Shares and other equity	36,271	37,074	38,986	47,137	57,041	66,266	73,212	78,966
Other liabilities	34,263	42,256	41,824	37,006	45,865	38,766	39,553	40,299

Note: *October 2010 figures.
Source: Bank al-Maghrib.

The government's limited role in the banking sector is another aspect that sets Morocco apart from its neighbours. This has not always been the case as the Moroccan government maintained a substantial proportion of banking under its control in the late 1990s and early 2000s. In recent years, however, considerable progress has been made in restructuring public banks, sale of public shares and the full compliance of remaining public banks with regulatory requirements by 2007. The state-owned banks continue to represent a significant proportion of total activities, but their market shares have declined substantially, down to 25 per cent of total assets in 2009 from 40 per cent in 2002 (Table 2.9).

The government's involvement is not strictly restricted to its direct control over the banking sector. The Moroccan government, like its neighbours, has used the domestic banking sector to fund the public budget. In the 1980s and 1990s, all banks were required to hold a substantial proportion of their portfolio in treasury bonds. The banks were also required to hold bonds issued by the various development banks, which were publicly owned. By the late 1990s, most of these requirements were dropped. As a consequence, the government securities now account for a much smaller proportion of the banks' balance sheets, dropping from 20 per cent of total assets in 2003 to about 7 per cent in October 2010 (Table 2.11).

As noted in the IMF's (2008) revised assessment, Morocco's banking supervision complies with the majority of the Basel Core Principles for Effective Banking Supervision (BCP). Morocco has required all banks to apply the standardised approach to risk under Basel II since 2007, earlier than all other countries in the region. BAM has published several guidelines for the implementation of the second and third pillars of Basel II, in line with the Basel Committee's recommendations. Minimum capital adequacy levels have been shifted to 10 per cent of risk-weighted assets (RWA) in 2008 with an intention to raise them further to 12 per cent in the upcoming years.

Morocco is also a leader in other areas of regulation in the region. The country is one of the two South-MED countries covered in this study (apart from Algeria) to have an explicit deposit insurance scheme. Created in 2006, the scheme is funded by the banks and compensates depositors for lost funds up to 80,000 Moroccan Dirhams (DH) (approximately €7,200 as of end-2010) per depositor. If the fund is insufficient to pay out all eligible deposits, proportional haircuts are applied to the legal protection. The funds may also be used to provide emergency credit to problem banks, which has been identified as a potential source of conflict by the IMF in its most recent FSAP update, even though the fund has never been used for that purpose in practice (IMF, 2008).

As another regional "first", a private credit bureau became operational in October 2009. The bureau is developed and operated by Experian, which is a global leader in credit information services. The setup of private credit bureaus was heralded by a series of regulatory arrangements in 2007, delegating the credit information exchange functions to the private sector and effectively abolishing the similar functions of the public credit registers. According to the legal framework for private credit bureaus, BAM acts as an intermediary in the flow of information. All regulated credit institutions, including microcredit institutions, are required by law (that is, mandatory reporting) to provide positive and negative information about the creditors to BAM. The full data files are then passed over to the credit bureau.

Despite the absence of formal agreements (that is, MoUs) or participation (that is, observer in Committee of European Banking Supervisors (CEBS)), the Moroccan authorities have also been relatively eager to cooperate with their EU counterparts on select matters. Cooperation on assisting publicly-owned institutions was in place in the early 2000s. Moreover, BAM has shown its intention to engage in cooperation on the implementation of the internal ratings approach under Basel II and the upcoming Basel III agreements.

To summarise, Moroccan authorities have successfully implemented the reform programmes over the last decade to modernise the financial services sector. Today, the country is exemplary for its banking regulations, deposit guarantee scheme, information-sharing infrastructure and in the microfinance sector. The main challenge the country will face in the upcoming years will be the potential for instability from external markets as capital flows and exchange rate policies are liberalised, as intended by the authorities. Although the IMF's (2008) stress tests have revealed that the banking sector is resistant to credit, liquidity and interest risks, there are vulnerabilities arising from concentration risks and exposure to the real estate sector. More broadly, the authorities have to ensure that the recent jump in private credit does not lead to a resurgence of NPLs.

2.3.4 Tunisia

Following Morocco, Tunisia's banking system is the most developed in the region, with total assets representing nearly 97 per cent of GDP in 2009. The banking system dominates the financial markets, with the capital and insurance markets representing a very small proportion of the overall financial activities. The banking sector is comprised of 18 commercial banks, three of which remain publicly-controlled, that is, with majority state-ownership. The system is relatively dispersed, with the market share of the largest three banks accounting for about one-third of the total assets of commercial banks.

The banking system is supervised by an organ of the central bank, Banque Central de Tunisie (BCT), although the control over the state-owned institutions is exercised in part by the Ministry of Finance. The head of the supervisory body is appointed by the Governor of the central bank with an undetermined tenure.

The macroeconomic conditions have remained relatively stable in the past decade. Following structural reforms, fiscal and external vulnerabilities were significantly reduced. Real GDP growth in this period remained at around 5 per cent while inflation remained less than 6 per cent for most of the decade. Despite these positive aspects, unemployment remains high, at around 13 to 14 per cent. The conditions are particularly dire among the youth, with 30 per cent of those aged 15 to 24 remaining unemployed. Indeed, the high unemployment rates are blamed as one of the principal causes (in addition to low levels of accountability) of the protests and fall of the Ben Ali government at the beginning of 2011.

Starting in the late 1990s and early 2000s, the Tunisian authorities have embarked on an ambitious financial reform. In addition to attempts to strengthen the credit culture, the authorities have also revised the laws on the central bank and credit institutions in the 2000s. The prudential rules, first adopted in 1991, were revised in 2001, setting the standards on capital requirements, reserve requirements, liquidity requirements, risk management and relations with affiliates. In the same year, new laws were enacted to give the BCT a number of surveillance powers on monetary and on-site supervision.

Although recent privatisation efforts have reduced direct state-ownership, public banks continue to play a predominant role in the banking sector, representing just under one-third of total assets in 2009. The three banks that remain majority-owned by the state

Table 2.12 Structure of Tunisian economy and banking system

	2000	2004	2009
GDP per capita ($)	2,036	2,845	3,852
GDP per capita growth (per cent)	–	5.1%	1.9%
Inflation (per cent)3	–	3.6%	3.7%
Commercial bank assets (per cent of GDP)	89%	89%	97%
Top-3 banks (per cent of total assets)	–	–	34%
Number of commercial banks	13	16	18
...of which: public	5	3	3
Public banks (per cent of total assets)	49%	44%	32%
Branches	–	–	1,209
Inhabitants per branch	–	–	8,541

Sources: IMF and Banque Central de Tunisie (BCT).

are among the largest four banks in the country. The largest one, which also happens to be the second largest bank in Tunisia, Société Tunisienne de Banque (STB), accounts for around one-third of all loans to the tourism sectors. The second largest public bank, Banque National Agricole (BNA), provides more than half of the loans to the agriculture and fisheries sectors. The third public bank, Banque de l'Habitat (BH), provides nearly one-fifth of the real estate loans, which represent a substantial proportion of total outstanding credit.

One of the key characteristics of Tunisia's banking system is the persistently low quality of assets, emanating from problem loans. In 1997, the authorities launched a plan to tackle the problem though restructuring. As noted in IMF (2002, 2007c), in the early 2000s the authorities allowed banks to create asset management companies as their subsidiaries in order to purchase and pool NPLs. The problem loans to public enterprises were similarly restructured, this time backed with government guarantees. In 2001, reporting require-ments were toughened, requiring banks to obtain detailed financial statements certified by external auditors or rating agencies for large exposures. Starting in 2004, the BCT forced banks to allocate their net incomes and withhold dividends, if necessary, to cover any under-provisions. Two public banks with extensive problem loans were privatised in the same year, even though the government continues to hold significant minority stakes. Legal reforms to facilitate recovery were also implemented in recent years in an attempt to streamline sale of assets and restrict undue delays in recovery of claims. More recently, the authorities increased the provisioning requirements and expanded the tax deductibility of provisions.

Despite regulators' attempts and a generally good performance of the Tunisian economy in recent years, the NPLs have remained relatively high. As shown in Table 2.14, over the last decade the ratio of NPLs to gross loans has remained around 15 to 20 per cent for most years in both publicly-owned and privately-owned banks. The NPL ratios have declined in recent years in line with the objectives set by authorities to reduce them below 15 per cent by the end of 2009 (see Table 2.14). These developments are, at least in part, due to the improved risk assessment practices on the part of banks through the increased availability of borrower information, reforms to facilitate the sale of collateral, privatisation of public banks as well as the new tax and regulatory arrangements on provisioning. Nevertheless, the NPLs continue to be a problem in the country's banking sector, representing over 13 per cent of gross loans.

Aside from politically-connected lending, several reasons can be put forward to explain the persistence of problem loans in Tunisia's banking system.

First, some of the recent jumps in problem loans in the existing loan portfolio can be explained by the external economic environment and events. For example, the global slowdown and the recession in the tourism sector following the events of 11 September 2001 and the April 2002 terrorist attack in Djerba have severely affected the asset quality of the banking system. This pushed the NPL ratios up by 4 to 5 per cent between 2001 and 2003.

Second, NPL ratios often have a lagged policy response when the stock of older NPLs does not improve significantly over time. According to IMF (2009a), although the new NPLs remain low, the asset quality of the existing stock of loans has not improved over the last few years. This was largely due to the perverse incentives provided by the prior restructuring efforts, giving banks no incentives to opt for a deeper restructuring (that is, full write-offs) or a thorough assessment of the debt-repayment capacity of borrowers.

Third and last, most of the recent policies to address credit quality problems are backward-looking and do not have a direct impact on reducing NPLs before they arise. This includes a majority of the

Table 2.13 Assets and liabilities of Tunisian banks (millions of Tunisian Dinar – TD)

	2000	2001	2002	2003	2004	2005	2006	2007	2008	2009	2010*
Assets	23,745	26,278	27,015	28,185	31,138	33,954	36,470	41,377	46,682	51,892	53,840
Cash	146	144	139	139	138	136	201	241	235	259	276
Deposits at BCT	302	605	530	558	764	1,058	1,341	1,920	3,204	3,689	2,824
Foreign assets	928	808	957	853	906	1,281	1,393	1,996	1,755	2,160	2,258
Claims on state	1,620	1,487	1,559	1,664	2,145	2,271	2,609	2,817	2,501	3,060	3,014
Private credit	14,538	16,241	17,122	18,141	19,981	21,561	23,149	25,465	29,322	32,191	34,715
Securities	746	797	1,020	1,120	1,232	1,415	1,539	1,650	1,803	2,128	2,252
Other assets	5,465	6,195	5,688	5,711	5,972	6,232	6,237	7,287	7,863	8,404	8,501
Liabilities	23,745	26,278	27,015	28,185	31,138	33,954	36,470	41,377	46,682	51,892	53,840
Sight deposits	3,583	3,959	3,697	3,919	4,265	4,721	5,422	6,271	7,000	8,263	8,795
Other deposits	8,365	9,293	10,119	10,868	12,151	13,273	14,674	16,539	19,278	21,427	22,261
Foreign liabilities	2,783	2,886	3,280	3,180	3,695	4,194	4,331	4,899	5,147	5,819	5,804
Liab. to BCT	454	870	504	444	93	4	123	17	18	2	53
Special resources	849	945	1,080	993	1,033	1,105	1,135	1,092	1,139	1,163	1,177
Equity	2,841	2,881	3,076	3,431	4,014	4,486	4,928	5,471	6,258	7,064	7,225
Other liabilities	4,870	5,444	5,260	5,350	5,888	6,170	5,857	7,089	7,842	8,153	8,525

Note: *May 2010 figures.

Source: Banque Central de Tunisie (BCT).

Table 2.14 Tunisian banking system, financial soundness indicators (per cent)

	2000	2001	2002	2003	2004	2005	2006	2007	2008	2009
Reg. capital (as per cent of RWA)	11.3	11.1	10.2	9.3	11.6	12.4	11.8	11.6	11.7	12.4
Private banks	10.6	10.5	10.3	8.4	12.4	13.5	12.1	9.7	11.0	11.6
Public banks	11.8	11.8	10.1	10.8	10.1	10.0	9.3	9.9	9.6	10.9
NPLs (as per cent of total loans)	21.6	19.2	20.9	24.2	23.6	20.9	19.3	17.6	15.5	13.2
Private banks	15.4	16.1	18.1	21.6	20.4	20.0	19.0	18.1	15.3	12.5
Public banks	26.8	22.8	24.3	26.7	27.4	22.1	19.7	17.3	15.9	14.1
Provisions (as per cent of NPL)	49.2	47.4	43.9	44.1	45.1	46.8	49.0	53.2	56.8	58.3
Private banks	54.7	47.7	44.9	39.9	43.5	45.9	48.4	52.0	55.0	59.2
Public banks	46.6	47.1	42.9	46.2	47.6	49.1	50.2	55.0	58.1	57.1
RoA	1.3	1.1	0.7	0.5	0.5	0.6	0.7	0.9	1.0	1.0
RoE	14.5	13.2	7.6	4.6	4.8	5.9	7.0	10.1	11.2	11.7

Sources: IMF (2007, 2010d).

regulatory arsenal put forth by the authorities to address the high level of NPLs, such as the use of provisions or the legal reforms, which have only an *ex-post* impact. Indeed, these measures can only mitigate the transaction costs and legal uncertainties once the loans are deemed problematic. More forward-looking risk assessment measures are needed to minimise NPLs before they arise. These include the adoption of Basel II standards, more regular stress-testing, developing CAMEL-type regulatory assessment tools and enhancing the credit information environment by developing a private credit bureau (IMF, 2010d).

The (previous) presidential programme of 2010–14 identifies the strengthening of the financial sector as a key policy objective. Perhaps most importantly, the authorities have shown their willingness to implement the Basel II framework, although no clear timeline has been set for the adoption of the international standards. A deposit insurance scheme is also under preparation under the programme. Other aims include the consolidation of the banking institutions, increasing banks' impact on the economy, restructuring the public sector and promoting Tunisia as a regional banking services hub. The relevance of the programme in the aftermath of the events of January 2011 remains to be seen.

Despite the absence of formal arrangements with EU supervisors, the BCT will take part in a 'twinning project' with the Banque de France to put in place the monetary policy tools for supporting price stability and reinforcing institutional capacities, including transparency of monetary policy actions.

As the events in the beginning of 2011 amply demonstrate, political stability is a key challenge for the country and the region as a whole. It is therefore questionable to what extent these ambitious aims, especially those relating to the branding of Tunisia's banking sector as a regional centre, can materialise without stable and sustainable political conditions. In addition, the Tunisian authorities have to aim more at devising a forward-looking supervisory and regulatory regime, giving banks the proper incentives and ability to manage risks and limiting moral hazard.

2.4   Conclusions

The foregoing analysis reveals that the financial systems in the Southern Mediterranean are unable (or unwilling) to divert the financial resources available to them as funding opportunities to private enterprises. In recent years, in view of underdeveloped capital markets and in an effort to restructure their banking systems, the authorities of the four surveyed countries have engaged in a variety of reforms to modernise their banking systems. These include restructuring and privatisation of public banks, implementation of prudential regulation and risk management frameworks and enhancing supervisory responsibilities. Morocco and Egypt have improved the availability and sharing of credit information. These reforms have led to a persistent growth of credit to the private sector.

The discussion above shows that one potential explanation of financial underdevelopment is the heavy presence of the state, either directly in the form of publicly-owned banks or indirectly in the form of public debt in banks' portfolios. For the latest years for which data are available (2008–9), the market shares of public banks range from a low of one-quarter of total banking assets in Morocco and Tunisia to highs of 67 per cent to 90 per cent in Egypt and Algeria, respectively. These ownership structures and the underlying conditions, such as the high returns that government debt earns in Egypt, are likely to crowd out the credit to private enterprises. Indeed, public debt and loans, including loans to public enterprises, account for nearly one-third of the total balance sheets of the Algerian and Egyptian banks, surpassing the share of private credit.

Aside from crowding out private credit and constraining financial development, the state's dominant role in the banking sector appears to have a serious negative impact on credit quality. Indeed, the ratios of non-performing loans to gross loans for the Southern Mediterranean countries are among the highest globally. Owing to the relatively limited role of the state, Morocco is once again an exception, with the lowest NPL ratios among the four countries. Moreover, the four countries have implemented policies to improve the quality of loans, including privatisation improvements in credit information systems, loan repurchase programmes and other plans to clean balance sheets. Nevertheless, the banking systems of the four Southern Mediterranean countries have among the worst loan qualities in the region (Figure 2.12).

The persistence of the non-performing assets and underdeveloped financial systems remain leads to questions on the adequacy of the recent regulatory reforms in the banking sector in the four

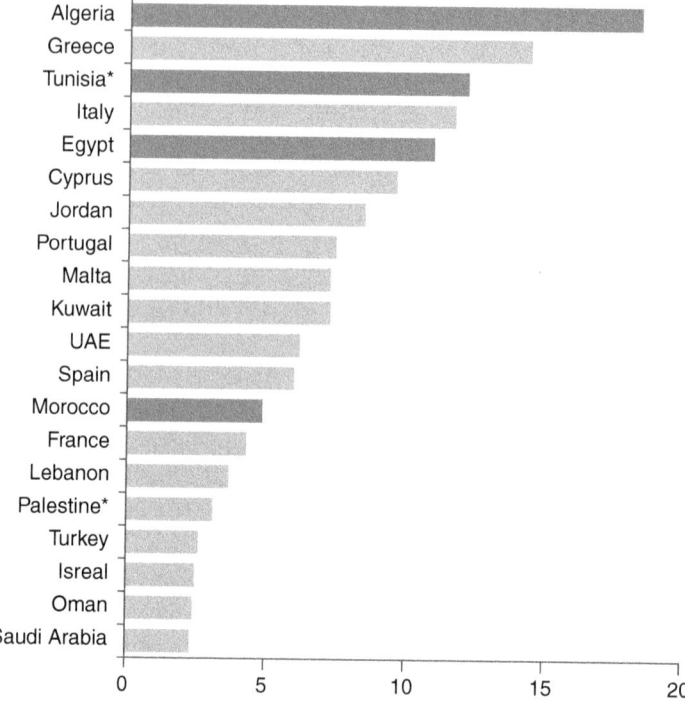

Figure 2.12   Non-performing bank loans in the Mediterranean and Middle East (per cent of total loans, 2011)

Notes: *2010 instead of 2011 data. The 2011 figures on NPLs do not reflect substantial worsening in loan qualities in most countries, with the exception of some of the EU-MED countries (that is, Cyprus, Greece, Italy, Portugal and Spain).

Sources: *IMF,* Global Financial Stability Report & Financial Soundness Indicators (FSIs), *2013.*

investigated countries. As noted above, the prevalence of the publicly-owned banks may be at the root of the problem (Case of Algeria). However, shortcomings in various legal, regulatory and supervisory frameworks may also matter. The next chapter provides a deeper analysis of the regulatory conditions over several dimensions, providing the analytical tools for making cross-country comparisons over time.

3
Convergence of Banking Sectors Regulations

Over the last years, Mediterranean countries have undertaken substantial reforms in their financial sectors. This chapter develops a number of indicators to track the evolution and assess the adequacy of banking regulations using publicly available and comparable surveys for a large sample of countries since the early 2000s. To allow comparability across the Mediterranean, this chapter develops the measures for ten South and East Mediterranean countries (SEMCs) (Algeria, Egypt, Israel, Jordan, Lebanon, Morocco, Palestine, Syria, Tunisia and Turkey) and seven EU Mediterranean countries (Cyprus, France, Greece, Italy, Malta, Portugal and Spain).

The aim is to develop quantitative measures of regulatory development to assess regulatory convergence on international norms. In line with Ayadi et al. (2011, 2013b), seven distinct regulatory areas are identified for assessing the various dimensions of regulatory adequacy. These cover the definition of banking, licensing requirements, capital requirements, the independence and power of the supervisor, the presence of safety nets, disclosure and the availability of credit information using distinct data sources. Although these provide a broad view of the extent of regulation, several potential areas (that is, payment and settlement systems, credit guarantee schemes and financial inclusion) have been excluded due to the unavailability of comparable information sources for the sampled countries.

The analysis shows some levels of convergence in banking regulations in the region. The region has improved credit information and capital requirements as well as reduced entry obstacles in recent years. Nevertheless, they still suffer from key weaknesses in deposit insurance, entry obstacles, political interference and the strength of legal rights.

The remainder of this chapter is structured as follows. The second section provides a description of the methods and data used to analyse the convergence of banks in the Euro–Mediterranean area. The third section presents and discusses the quantitative measures. Based on the results, conclusions and policy recommendations are drawn in the fourth section.

3.1   Methodology

The main source of information for the regulatory adequacy indices are the Bank Regulation and Supervision Surveys (BRSS) developed by Barth et al. (2001), later revised in 2003, 2007 and 2011. All four surveys are built on official responses to questionnaires that were sent to the national regulatory and supervisory agencies of over 120 countries, most of which were returned. The questions cover a wide variety of areas, including banking activity, entry, capital regulations, supervisory authority, private monitoring, deposit insurance and external governance.

One of the key advantages of the BRSS is that the questionnaires have remained relatively similar over the years, although the later versions cover more areas than the original survey. This particular feature of the datasets allows us to make comparisons by building composite indices based on specific answers over time to track the evolution of the different regulatory and supervisory elements.

A key disadvantage of the Barth et al. (2001) survey is that the number of questions responded to in the 2003, 2007 and 2011 revisions vary from one country to another. For the Mediterranean countries, the aggregate response rates are generally lower than for the entire sample. As noted in Figure 3.1, among the SEMCs, the Moroccan regulatory authorities were the most responsive to the survey, with an average response rate above 95 per cent. In contrast, three SEMCs – Algeria, Syria and Tunisia – had response rates of between 83 per cent and 90 per cent, which is well below the average rate for the Mediterranean countries.

Although the response rates appear high in general, the existence of a single partial or empty answer renders the construction of a relevant composite index dubious, since there is no clear way of scoring for missing responses. Moreover, some countries, such as Algeria, Palestine, Syria, Tunisia and Turkey, have not responded to all four surveys. Palestine (the 2011 survey) only responded to a single survey, Algeria (2003, 2007), Syria (2007, 2011) and Tunisia (2003, 2011) to two surveys and Turkey (2000, 2003, 2011) to three surveys. To avoid any inconsistencies, empty answers were scored as zero in the construction of the relevant indices. This approach is in line with Barth et al. (2006, 2012). Moreover, the assessment of regulatory convergence is based on the calculation of regional averages, weighted by the total banking assets of each country. These allow us to make a sounder judgment of whether the regulatory conditions on both coasts of the Mediterranean are converging.

A second disadvantage of Barth et al. (2001) and its revisions is that the questions did not cover all regulatory and supervisory areas. Two major areas where the surveys lacked depth were the details on deposit

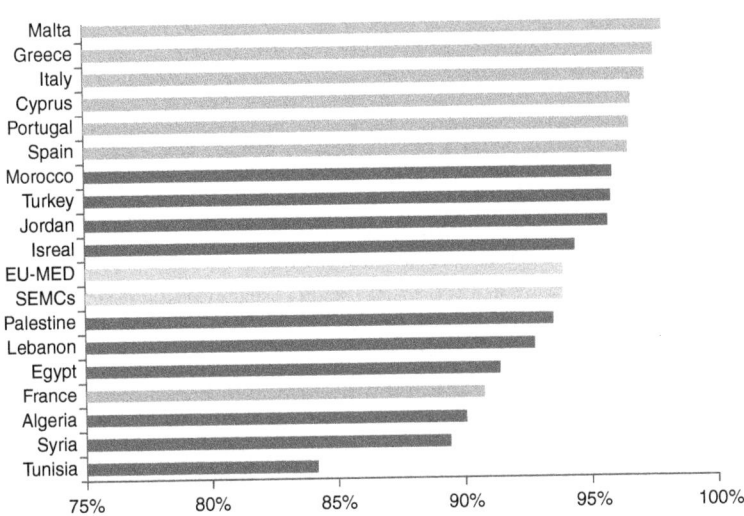

Figure 3.1   Average response rates to the BRSS of Barth et al.

Note: Response rates are averaged over the four surveys and correspond to the number of questions with complete (that is, excluding empty or partial) answers divided by the total number of questions used to compute the composite indices presented in this report.

Source: BRSS.

insurance guarantee schemes and institutional variables, such as the extent of credit information sharing and creditors' legal rights. To fill the gap, several additional sources were used to supplement the construction of the composite indices, including the deposit insurance database of Demirgüç-Kunt et al. (2005), the IMF and World Bank's Financial Sector Assessment reports, the World Bank's Doing Business Indicators and the websites of the national authorities.

3.2 Composite indices

Seven composite indices have been created using the various data sources identified above:

    I. Scope restrictions
   II. Entry obstacles
  III. Capital requirement stringency
  IV. Supervisory authority
   V. Deposit insurance
  VI. Private monitoring
 VII. Credit information and laws.

These areas provide relatively broad coverage of the quality and evolution of banking regulation and supervision. The composite indices have been calculated for each country and also for the SEMC and EU-MED countries included in our sample.

The following sections revise and compare the evolution of the regulatory conditions in each of the seven areas noted above.

3.2.1 Area I: Scope restrictions

As is evident from the differing business models of financial institutions across the world, financial institutions are becoming increasingly complex and offering a wider spectrum of products. Some countries restrict banking to a narrow range of activities, such as taking deposits and issuing credit with little flexibility in debt and asset management, while others provide more flexibility. The regulations typically restrict the extent to which banks may engage in the business of (i) securities underwriting, brokering, dealing and all aspects of the mutual fund industry; (ii) insurance underwriting and selling and (iii) real estate investment, development and management.

The composite indicator used in this area to assess the extent of restrictions imposed on banking activity is based on the Banking Activity Restrictiveness Index in the BRSS. The surveys provide measures of the degrees of restrictiveness for each of the above four categories, ranging from unrestricted (1 point), mostly permitted (2 points) and too restricted (3 points) to fully prohibited (4 points). The Banking Activity Restrictiveness Index sums up the scores for each category to come up with a measure of the extent to which restrictions are present for banks, with a maximum restrictiveness score of 12 points, where no activity other than narrow banking is allowed.

The country-specific results summarised in Figure 3.2 and Table 3.1 show that the regulators in the SEMCs impose more restrictions than the EU-MED countries in general. A deeper analysis of the survey results (not included here) shows that on both coasts of the Mediterranean, regulators impose some form of restriction on insurance activities. Israel and Jordan's banks face high restrictions among the sampled countries, where all real estate activities and some securities and insurance activities are prohibited. This is largely in line with Turkey's banks, although the latter have only to deal with a few restrictions in order to engage in securities activities, and Syria's banks, which are prohibited from engaging in both insurance and real estate activities, but on the other hand have complete freedom to engage in securities activities. Morocco's banks are similarly restricted in their activities, but are to a limited extent allowed to engage in insurance activities. Algerian banks are prohibited from engaging in insurance activities, but have complete freedom in engaging in securities and real estate activities. In contrast, Palestine's banks have complete freedom to engage in insurance activities and face fewer restrictions in both securities and real estate investment activities. Lebanon's banks are prohibited from engaging in real estate activities yet have a large degree of freedom to engage in insurance and securities activities. Egypt imposes some restrictions on insurance and real estate, largely comparable with the EU-MED countries. It is not possible to judge the changing conditions in Tunisia owing to the incompleteness of information. Turning to the EU-MED countries, the banks in general face fewer restrictions than most of their neighbours. All EU-MED banks have complete freedom in engaging in securities activities. Moreover, Spanish, Portuguese and Greek banks are also less restricted from engaging in insurance and real estate activities. Still, Cypriot and Maltese banks are prohibited from engaging in real estate activities and French banks in insurance activities.

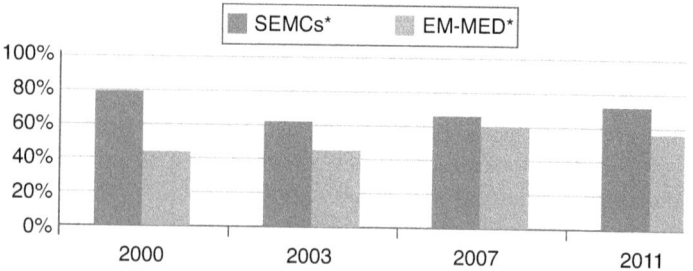

Figure 3.2   Banking activity restrictiveness, by region (% of maximum score)

Table 3.1   Banking activity restrictiveness, by country and region (% of maximum score)

	2000	2003	2007	2011
Algeria	–	42	50	–
Egypt	83	58	58	67
Israel	83	83	75	83
Jordan	67	50	67	83
Lebanon	75	67	75	58
Morocco	83	58	75	67
Palestine	–	–	–	42
Syria	–	–	67	75
Tunisia	–	67	–	50
Turkey	75	50	–	75
SEMCs*	80	63	67	73
Cyprus	42	67	67	58
France	33	33	58	67
Greece	58	67	50	50
Italy	58	67	75	58
Malta	58	67	67	67
Portugal	50	58	75	42
Spain	50	42	42	42
EU-MED*	44	46	59	58
AVG	47	47	59	59
STDEV	14	15	12	11

Notes: *Regional averages are weighted by total banking assets. Higher values represent more restrictive rules, with a maximum score of 12 points.

Source: BRSS.

The figures show that there is a convergence tendency when the regional weighted averages are considered. Indeed, while the EU-MED weighted averages have moved up gradually over time, the SEMCs averages have gone down, converging on the former. However, there are clear differences within each sub-region. For example, Israel and Jordan impose substantial restrictions while Palestine has the most flexible system. As for the EU-MED countries, Spain's system imposes the least restrictions while France and Malta have increasingly narrowed the scope of banking activities over the years. This EU-MED trend may change as a result of the new banking reforms that are moving towards more restrictions on banking activities as a result of the financial crisis.

3.2.2 Area II: Entry obstacles

The competitive conditions in a country depend crucially on the regulatory structures and conditions that might hinder or prevent entry into the banking sector by domestic or foreign banks. In some countries, the obstacles may take the form of excessive licensing or entry requirements, which are applicable to domestic and foreign banks alike. In others, the governments may restrict foreign entry as part of a conscientious policy choice, either explicitly by setting limits on ownership or more importantly by rejecting foreign applications in a disproportionate manner. Lastly, a banking sector that is predominantly state-owned may be disadvantageous for the development of privately owned banks.

Three indicators are utilised to construct the composite index assessing the impact of entry obstacles.

The first indicator that comes to mind for measuring how much the regulatory structure obstructs entry is legal licensing requirements, which may hamper entry by making the procedures unnecessarily cumbersome. The relevant measure is based on the set of requirements for the licensing application to be considered valid. The index is built on the total number of required documents, including (i) draft by-laws, (ii) an organisational chart, (iii) financial projections, (iv) financial information on potential shareholders, (v) the background of directors, (vi) the background of management, (vii) details of funding sources and (viii) market differentiation intended.

Figure 3.3 and Table 3.2 show that most SEMCs impose levels of stringency in terms of entry requirements that are similar to those

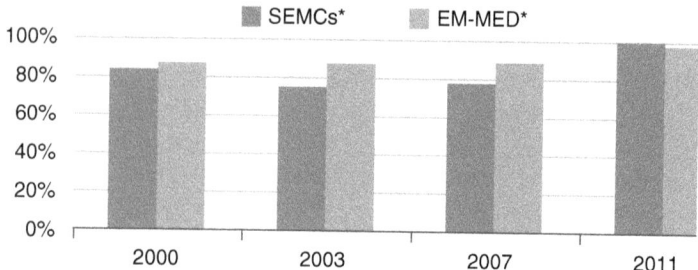

Figure 3.3 Requirements for entry into the banking sector, by region (% of maximum score)

Table 3.2 Requirements for entry into the banking sector, by country and region (% of maximum score)

	2000	2003	2007	2011
Algeria	–	88	100	–
Egypt	75	100	100	100
Israel	75	38	38	100
Jordan	100	88	100	100
Lebanon	100	100	100	100
Morocco	100	100	100	100
Palestine	–	–	–	100
Syria	–	–	100	100
Tunisia	–	100	–	100
Turkey	88	88	–	100
SEMCs*	83	77	79	100
Cyprus	100	75	38	100
France	75	75	88	100
Greece	100	88	88	88
Italy	100	100	100	100
Malta	100	100	100	100
Portugal	88	88	88	88
Spain	100	100	88	100
EU-MED*	87	87	90	99
AVG	87	86	90	99
STDEV	12	14	9	3

Notes: *Regional averages are weighted by total banking assets. Higher values represent more restrictive rules as a share of a maximum of 8 points.

Source: BRSS.

of EU-MED countries. In particular, all of the eight requirements named above are commonplace in all ten SEMCs for which the latest survey was completed. As for the EU-MED countries, almost all of them require all eight documents. Only Greece and Portugal do not legally require banks to provide information on the background of future managers.

These results show that most countries in the Mediterranean require similar documents for licensing. This means that these figures probably give at best an incomplete picture of the obstacles faced by potential entrants. More realistically, these requirements are most likely used on both sides of the Mediterranean to screen potential entrants, ensuring that they are "fit and proper" to run a banking business.

As noted above, the set of licensing requirements do not paint a complete picture of entry obstacles. The second index considers the more discretionary power that the authorities enjoy by granting or rejecting entry. More specifically, the index is based on the fraction of licensing applications for foreign banks that have been denied within the past five years from the day the survey was conducted.

Figure 3.4 and Table 3.3 clearly show that denials of foreign banking applications are more commonplace in the SEMCs, which is in stark contrast to the EU-MED countries, where such denials are very rare. In particular, all of the licensing applications for foreign banks for the years between 1995 and 2002 were denied in Egypt.

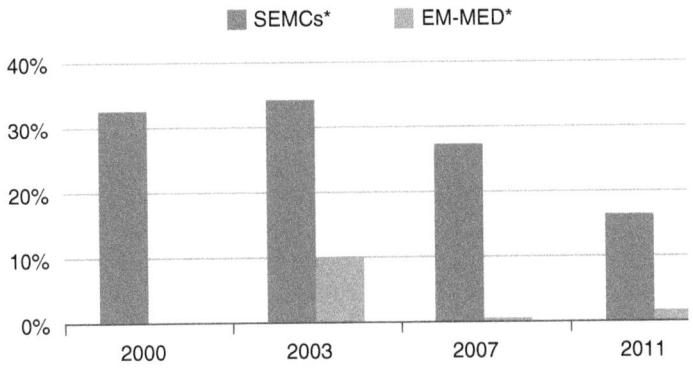

Figure 3.4 Share of foreign applications denied, by region (%)

Table 3.3   Share of foreign applications denied, by country and region (%)

	2000	2003	2007	2011
Algeria	–	0	–	–
Egypt	100	100	32	80
Israel	0	17	20	0
Jordan	–	80	90	50
Lebanon	0	0	0	0
Morocco	–	0	50	0
Palestine	–	–	–	0
Syria	–	–	0	0
Tunisia	–	0	–	0
Turkey	–	42	–	13
SEMCs*	33	34	28	18
Cyprus	0	0	0	20
France	0	–	0	0
Greece	0	14	0	0
Italy	0	13	3	9
Malta	0	0	0	0
Portugal	0	0	0	0
Spain	0	7	0	0
EU-MED*	0	10	1	2
AVG	2	13	2	3
STDEV	13	15	6	10

Note: *Regional averages are weighted by total banking assets.
Source: BRSS.

More recently, Egypt denied nearly 80 per cent of the foreign
licensing applications (four out of five) in the five years leading
to 2011. Jordan denied two of the four applications over the same
period. Turkey also refused two of the fifteen foreign applications.
Israel and Morocco denied several foreign banking applications in
the past, but none of the five applications was denied in the last
observation period of 2006 to 2010. Algeria, Lebanon, Palestine,
Syria and Tunisia do not appear to use foreign denials as an entry
obstacle. Overall, the percentage of foreign denials in the SEMCs has
decreased gradually since 1995. These results show signs of convergence between the SEMCs and EU-MED countries.

The third and last indicator on entry obstacles relates to the dominance of government-controlled banking. The index is a simple measure of the market power of banks that are majority-owned by the state, that is, the percentage of total banking assets controlled by the government-owned banks (for example, the government possesses more than 50 per cent of the bank's equity). The relevant data are available for the 2003, 2007 and 2011 surveys.

Figure 3.5 and Table 3.4 point at significant differences on the two sides of the Mediterranean. While the state has little control over banking in the EU-MED countries, except for Greece and Portugal, public banks represent a significant part of the banking activity in the SEMCs. This is particularly the case for Algeria, Egypt and Syria, where the state has control over a significant majority of the banking sector. State-owned banks in these countries often enjoy implicit or explicit state guarantees, with access to public funding, and are possibly subject to less strict or to flexible rules, which may represent a disadvantage for potential entrants and more generally undermine healthy competition (Barth et al., 2004).

Put together, the three indices provide a contrasting picture of the sampled countries in terms of entry obstacles. The set of documents needed for a valid licensing application are largely similar on both

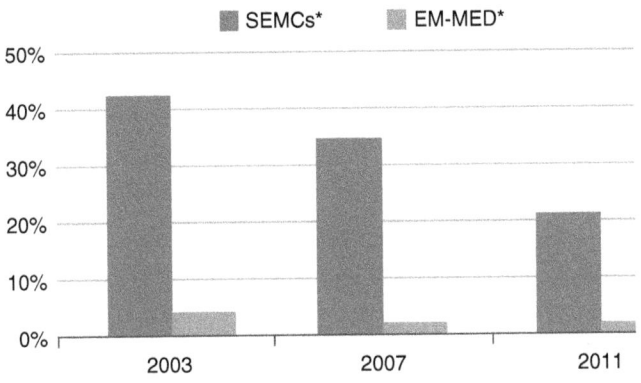

Figure 3.5 Market share of government-controlled banks, by region (% of total assets)

Table 3.4   Market share of government-controlled banks, by country and region (% of total assets)

	2003	2007	2011
Algeria	96	90	–
Egypt	65	67	–
Israel	46	0	0
Jordan	0	0	–
Lebanon	2	–	–
Morocco	35	29	–
Palestine	–	–	0
Syria	–	–	71
Tunisia	43	–	–
Turkey	32	–	32
SEMCs*	43	35	22
Cyprus	4	3	1
France	0	0	2
Greece	23	–	11
Italy	10	9	0
Malta	0	0	0
Portugal	23	25	23
Spain	0	0	0
EU-MED*	4	3	2
AVG	7	4	3
STDEV	13	10	8

Notes: *Regional averages are weighted by the total banking assets. Figures represent share of banks with at least 50% state ownership.

Source: BRSS.

sides of the Mediterranean. These requirements are most likely used to ensure that only "fit and proper" undertakings are allowed to operate as banks. Only two countries, Greece and Portugal, can be distinguished in this respect, with few licensing requirements. Turning to less official controls that the authorities exert on the banking sector, foreign entry denials are proportionally high in some of the SEMCs, particularly in Egypt and Jordan. The state also maintains substantial direct control over the banking sector in most of the countries in the region, with publicly owned banks accounting for more than two-thirds of the banking sector activities in Algeria, Egypt and Syria. In short, although the official entry conditions appear comparable, there are significant and persistent entry obstacles that can curtail competition in the SEMC banking sectors, possibly emanating from official authority in practice and political interference.

3.2.3   Area III: Capital requirement stringency

One of the common aims of regulating banks is to ensure that they operate soundly. Regulatory capital requirements are an important part of these rules, which determine the minimum amount of capital a bank should hold relative to its total assets (or risk-weighted assets).

Comparing the capital ratios represents a good first step towards understanding how sound the banking sector is. The capital ratios in the SEMCs are clearly higher than in the EU-MED, as depicted in Figure 3.6 and Table 3.5. For a start, with the exception of Greece, all the countries have maintained a total capital ratio of between 9 per cent and 15 per cent. Since 1998, the banks in the SEMC have become better capitalised, with the average capital ratios reaching 16.9 per cent towards the end of the period. In 2011, the capital ratios slightly decreased to 15.5 per cent; in particular, the capital ratios of fast-growing banking sectors, like that of Turkey, declined.

The SEMC banks appear to be at least as well capitalised as their northern counterparts, especially since the early 2000s. Does this result reflect the stringency of capital requirements or a lower appetite

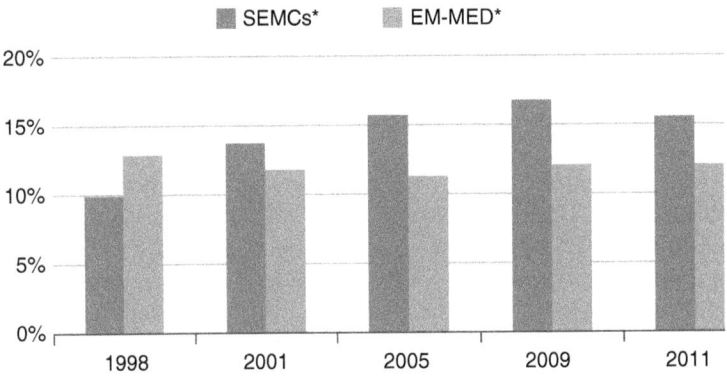

Figure 3.6   Regulatory capital ratios, by region (% of risk-weighted assets)

Table 3.5 Regulatory capital ratios, by country and region (% of risk-weighted assets)

	1998	2001	2005	2009	2011
Algeria	–	11.9	12.0	22.1	20.9
Egypt	10.2	9.8	14.1	15.1	15.6
Israel	9.2	9.5	10.7	12.6	14.0
Jordan	–	17.5	17.6	19.6	18.2
Lebanon	–	18.0	22.9	13.7	13.3
Morocco	13.1	12.6	11.5	11.8	11.7
Palestine	–	–	–	21.9	21.6
Syria	–	–	–	21.0	–
Tunisia	–	10.6	12.4	12.2	11.5
Turkey	–	20.8	22.8	20.6	16.6
SEMCs*	9.9	13.7	15.7	16.9	15.5
Cyprus	9.9	14.0	13.0	12.0	8.3
France	–	12.1	11.4	12.4	12.8
Greece	11.4	13.6	13.3	11.7	-1.7
Italy	13.4	10.4	10.6	12.1	12.7
Malta	–	–	–	13.5	13.5
Portugal	12.3	9.5	11.3	10.5	9.8
Spain	12.5	13.0	11.7	11.9	12.4
EU-MED*	12.9	11.7	11.3	12.1	12.1
AVG	12.6	11.9	11.6	12.4	12.4
STDEV	1.1	1.7	1.8	1.8	2.5

Notes: *Regional averages are weighted by total banking assets; Figures represent the share of total capital in risk-weighted assets using the 1988 Basel Accord definitions.

Sources: BRSS and IMF Global Financial Stability Reports.

for risk? In other words, is it the regulations that make the banks sounder or are the banks simply not willing to take too many risks? To answer this important question, it is necessary to look deeper into the rules.

There are different ways of measuring the stringency of capital requirements. The index that is used here gives consideration to the types of capital allowed, the risk weights applied and whether the minimum capital ratios vary with risk. More specifically, the capital stringency index aims at determining the extent to which capital requirements restrict leverage potential and risky behaviour, including questions on (i) whether the minimum capital-to-asset requirements are in line with 1988 Basel Accord definitions;

(ii) whether the minimum ratio varies with the bank's credit risk or (iii) market risk; and whether the value of (iv) unrealised loan losses, (v) unrealised security losses or (vi) foreign exchange losses are deducted from regulatory capital. Additionally, the index seeks to measure the restrictions imposed on the source of regulatory capital, such as (vii) whether these funds are verified by regulatory authorities; and whether (viii) cash and government securities, or more generally (ix) non-borrowed funds, are the only allowed forms of capital for initial disbursements and subsequent injections. A greater number of affirmative responses to these questions lead to a higher stringency score.

Figure 3.7 and Table 3.6 summarise the comparison of the stringency of capital requirements for the countries in our sample. A quick glance through the figures reveals that the capital requirements have become more stringent in most of the countries in the sample. More and more SEMCs are implementing legislation to align their capital requirements with the Basel II capital standards. Jordan, Lebanon, Morocco, Syria and Turkey, for instance, adopted legislation that allowed banks to vary their minimum capital requirements depending on banks' individual credit risk and market risk. The implementation of this legislation led to a jump in capital stringency between 2007 and 2011. Among the SEMCs, Tunisia is the only exception, with clearly less stringent capital requirements. The Tunisian authorities notably filled out fewer questions regarding capital stringency than seven years earlier.

Among the EU-MED countries, Cyprus has the most stringent capital requirements, with affirmative answers to six out of seven questions in 2011, followed by France and Spain. Like all other EU-MED countries, the Cypriot regulatory/supervisory authorities do not verify the sources of funds to be used as capital. For France and Spain, there was a clear tendency of a substantial strengthening of the rules. However, during the financial crisis, the capital requirements in these countries were relaxed a bit. Both countries allowed banks to increase capital with assets other than cash or government securities. The initial capital of banks in Greece, Italy and Malta can also include borrowed funds. Banks in Portugal are not obliged to deduct unrealised losses in securities portfolios from capital, but may fund capital contributions using assets other than government securities or cash.

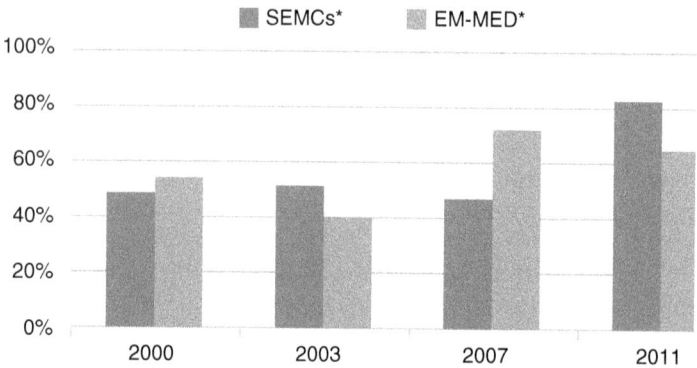

Figure 3.7 Stringency of capital requirements, by region (% of maximum score)

Table 3.6 Stringency of capital requirements, by country and region (% of maximum score)

	2000	2003	2007	2011
Algeria	–	44	78	–
Egypt	56	33	33	71
Israel	33	56	44	86
Jordan	67	67	56	86
Lebanon	56	67	56	71
Morocco	56	56	33	86
Palestine	–	–	–	86
Syria	–	–	33	71
Tunisia	–	67	–	57
Turkey	56	56	–	86
SEMCs*	48	53	46	81
Cyprus	11	44	67	86
France	56	22	89	71
Greece	33	56	33	57
Italy	44	33	33	57
Malta	67	56	56	57
Portugal	44	67	78	57
Spain	78	89	89	71
EU-MED*	55	40	73	68
AVG	54	41	72	69
STDEV	12	25	25	8

Notes: *Regional averages are weighted by total banking assets; Higher values represent more restrictive rules as a share of a maximum score of 9 points in 2000, 2003 and 2007 and 7 points in 2011.

Source: BRSS.

With these results in hand, it is easy to see that there is a pattern of convergence. EU members Greece, Italy, Malta and Portugal have rather flexible capital requirements, while the opposite is true for Cyprus, France and Spain. In contrast, the capital requirements of most of the SEMCs are in general more stringent than the EU-MED averages, especially regarding rules concerning the usage of non-cash or government securities and borrowed funds for capital.

3.2.4 Area IV: Supervisory authority

A key issue in the effectiveness of banking regulations is whether the supervisory authorities have the necessary powers to apply a variety of measures to discipline or, at the extreme, resolve banks that violate the rules or engage in imprudent activities. To that extent, in most countries, the supervisors take prompt corrective action against a bank if the capital falls below the minimally required level. If the deterioration of the bank continues, the supervisor must have the ability to find a resolution before the bank becomes insolvent, posing a systemic threat. To be effective, the supervisors need access to reliable and frequently updated information on the condition of the banks. The judicial systems often allow the courts to intervene, thereby diminishing, postponing or reversing illegitimate supervisory actions; however, these actions should not undermine the supervisor's chief responsibility of protecting and ensuring an orderly operation of the banking market. These aspects of supervisory system issues should be in line with the regulatory priorities and not subject to political patronage. In short, the supervisors should have the authority to discipline potentially troubled banks and resolve problems while remaining independent of political influence.

Two indices are used for measuring supervisory authority.

The first index measures the official power of the supervisor to take specific actions to correct or prevent problems. The relevant questions include the ability of supervisors to (i) meet external auditors without the approval of a bank; (ii) communicate directly with auditors on illicit activities undertaken by a bank's management or directors; (iii) receive disclosure of off-balance-sheet items; (iv) take legal action against negligent auditors; (v) change the organisational structure of troubled banks; (vi) order the management or directors to cover losses, and (vii) suspend dividend distributions, as well as (viii) bonuses and (ix) management fees. Additionally, for the 2003, 2007 and 2011 surveys, questions on troubled banks considered the supervisors' ability to (x) declare insolvency; (xi) suspend ownership rights; (xii) supersede shareholder rights; and (xiii) fire or hire management or (xiv) directors. An affirmative answer to any of these questions represents greater supervisory power. Some of these powers may only be exercisable by some supervisory-like institutions, such as the depository insurance agency or the bank restructuring agencies, which grant more moderate power to supervisors. In other cases, the courts or the government may be involved, which would serve to void the power of the supervisors in those actions.

Interestingly, Figure 3.8 and Table 3.7 show that the SEMCs and EU-MED countries grant more or less the same power to their supervisory authorities. Yet there are large differences among the individual countries. In Jordan and Palestine, the official supervisor is allowed to intervene directly in all the domains highlighted above. On the other hand, the official supervisor in Syria has mostly elementary tools. It has, for instance, the possibility to meet external auditors without the approval of the bank. But it is not allowed to communicate directly with auditors on illicit activities or take any legal action against these auditors. The official supervisor can further prevent dividends being paid out, but it cannot suspend bonuses for the management. Moreover, as in all the SEMCs excluding Jordan and Palestine, the Syrian official supervisor does not have the authority to declare a bank insolvent or supersede shareholder rights.

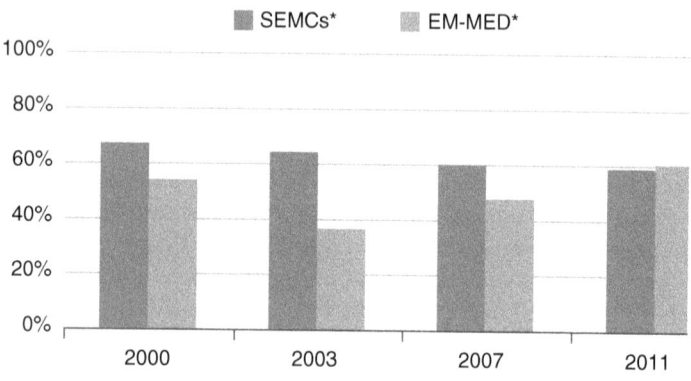

Figure 3.8 Official supervisory power, by region (% of maximum score)

Table 3.7 Official supervisory power, by country and region (% of maximum score)

	2000	2003	2007	2011
Algeria	–	76	58	–
Egypt	100	74	74	64
Israel	44	37	53	50
Jordan	67	74	47	79
Lebanon	100	53	53	50
Morocco	78	66	68	43
Palestine	–	–	–	79
Syria	–	–	68	36
Tunisia	–	68	–	57
Turkey	67	82	–	68
SEMCs*	69	63	60	59
Cyprus	100	42	63	64
France	67	37	45	57
Greece	56	63	53	39
Italy	33	26	37	71
Malta	67	74	74	71
Portugal	67	74	74	71
Spain	44	47	61	57
EU-MED*	54	38	48	60
AVG	56	40	48	60
STDEV	16	13	10	8

Notes: *Regional averages are weighted by total banking assets; Higher values represent more restrictive rules as a share of a maximum score of 9 points in 2000, 19 points in 2003 and 2007, and 14 points in 2011.

Source: BRSS.

Turning to the EU-MED countries, it is interesting to see that the new member state, Cyprus, grants increasing official power to their authorities. The same applies to France and Italy and, to a lesser extent, Portugal and Spain. Greece once again obtains the lowest score in official supervisory power: unlike other countries in our sample, the Greek supervisory authority has no right to meet the external auditor without prior approval of the bank, or to sue the auditors for negligence. The banks are also not obliged to publish information on off-balance-sheet positions. Furthermore, the supervisor does not have any power to suspend shareholder rights or replace management.

The second index for assessing supervisory authority turns more generally to the independence of the supervisor from political influence. For this index, three questions from the BRSS are considered: (i) Are supervisory bodies accountable *only* to a legislative body? (ii) Are supervisors legally liable for their actions committed in the exercise of their duties? (iii) Does the head of the agency have a fixed term? The level of independence is determined by points obtained from counting affirmative answers to questions (i) and (iii) and a negative answer to (ii).

The results depicted in Figure 3.9 and Table 3.8 show a clear divergence in terms of independence from political interference. While the banking supervisors of the EU-MED countries have become more independent, far less has changed in the SEMCs. The biggest concern remains the accountability of the supervisor directly to the executive arm, that is, president, prime minister or other cabinet members, which is the case in all of the SEMCs.

Of particular concern is Algeria, where none of the three criteria outlined above was satisfied in the last available survey, which implies an enormous potential for political interference. The same can also be said of other countries, such as Israel, Lebanon, Morocco and Syria. In comparison, the supervisor is only accountable to a legislative body (such as a parliament) in almost all EU member states except Greece and Italy, as well as in Egypt, Jordan, Palestine, Tunisia and Turkey. Once again, the Italian supervisory authority remains well below the EU standards in terms of independence from political interference due to its accountability to the central government and its legal liability for damages to a bank in the exercise of its duties. Another key distinguishing factor is the fixed term for the head of the regulatory authority, which is not available as an option in Algeria, Israel, Morocco or Syria, but has become increasingly popular among the EU members.

The results of the BRSS surveys reviewed in this section show that the powers granted have increased or remained constant in almost all of the countries. Moreover, the official powers granted to supervisors appear to be on the rise on both sides of the Mediterranean. Turning to operational independence, government officials have the ability to politically interfere in the work of the supervisors. Therefore, despite the fact that the supervisors are assigned almost full authority, it is possible that these powers remain notional due to government interference. Provided that some of the SEMCs have

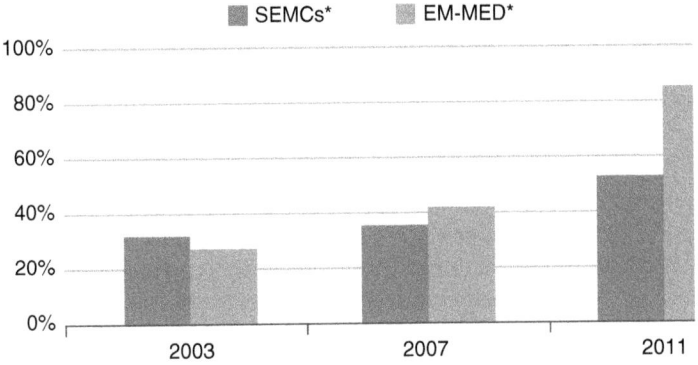

Figure 3.9 Independence from political interference, by region (% of maximum score)

Table 3.8 Independence from political interference, by country and region (% of maximum score)

	2003	2007	2011
Algeria	33	0	–
Egypt	67	67	67
Israel	0	33	33
Jordan	67	33	67
Lebanon	33	33	33
Morocco	33	33	33
Palestine	–	–	67
Syria	–	0	33
Tunisia	67	–	67
Turkey	33	–	67
SEMCs*	31	35	53
Cyprus	67	100	100
France	33	33	100
Greece	67	33	67
Italy	0	33	33
Malta	100	67	67
Portugal	67	67	100
Spain	33	67	100
EU-MED*	27	42	85
AVG	28	42	82
STDEV	19	15	28

Notes: *Regional averages are weighted by total banking assets; Higher values represent more independence as a share of a maximum score of 3 points.

Source: BRSS.

a substantial government presence in the banking sector (already noted above), operational independence should be a guiding principle to ensure that all banks – publicly or privately-owned – are treated equally.

3.2.5   Area V: Deposit insurance

Deposit insurance systems are among the key elements of a country's financial safety net, designed to prevent any disruptions to the financial markets and the economy. By protecting depositors, the deposit insurance schemes provide confidence to relatively small depositors and prevent bank runs. At the same time, they may introduce moral hazard, diminishing the depositors' incentives to monitor and screen the banks and amplifying the shareholders' incentives to engage in excessive risk. The moral hazard problem implies that banks have incentives to take on risk that can be shifted to a deposit insurance fund or, ultimately, the taxpayers.

Efforts are being taken across the world to mitigate moral hazard problems arising from deposit guarantee schemes. First, the amount of coverage matters. In some countries, aside from limits on the total amount, co-insurance is imposed to ensure that depositors bear some share of the costs. Second, the use of risk-adjusted premiums may also serve to better internalise the costs of the risks that they take. Third, the way that the deposit insurance schemes are funded also matters. For example, when the government is explicitly or implicitly involved in providing the necessary funds, moral hazard may be attenuated, especially in countries where the government has ample resources. In turn, when the system is backed with funds provided by banks, moral hazard can be limited by the understanding that the amount of guarantees is restricted by the pooled reserves.

Looking at the existing schemes, there are clear differences on the two coasts of the Mediterranean (Table 3.9). The revised EU Deposit Insurance Directive requires member states to maintain deposit insurance with a coverage limit of at least €100,000, raised from a minimum of €20,000 in the aftermath of the 2007–9 financial crisis. Most of the countries in the EU-MED have chosen to set this base amount as their coverage limit, representing between four and six times the average figures for annual income per capita. The 2009 amendment also abolished the co-insurance system, which allowed up to 10 per cent of losses to be shared with covered depositors. Risk-based premiums exist in about half of the countries, including France, Greece, Italy and Portugal. Setting itself clearly apart from the other countries in the region, Italy has an *ex-post* funding structure, where the banks are required to contribute after the deposit guarantee scheme is activated. Cyprus, France and Malta have hybrid systems in which substantial amounts of supplementary (*ex-post*) funding may be activated if the funds' resources fall below pre-set levels. The levels of *ex-ante* funds display substantial variation, wherever they exist, with a low of 0.1 per cent of eligible deposits in France and a high of 1.69 per cent in Greece.

Turning to the SEMCs, Egypt, Israel, Palestine, Syria and Tunisia have no schemes in place. In Algeria, Morocco and Turkey, the coverage limits represent one to two times the average annual income, pointing at a much lower level of protection afforded than in the EU. As in the EU-MED, the deposit guarantee schemes do not have a co-insurance option. Turkey is the only country that uses risk-based premiums.

The deposit insurance scheme index identifies the level of observance of standards that are thought to mitigate the moral hazard problem. Since recent information is available, the index is constructed for the years 2003, 2007 and 2011. For countries with an explicit system, three issues are relevant: (i) whether a co-insurance discount is applicable to pay-outs; (ii) whether premiums are risk-adjusted; and iii) whether only banks take a primary role. An additional point is scored for an affirmative answer to each one of these questions. A score of zero is assigned to countries where no explicit system exists, since in those cases the government is assumed to provide implicit guarantees, implying a greater incentive for banks to take risks.

The scores in Figure 3.10 and Table 3.10 show that moral hazard issues stemming from implicit guarantees are more of a threat in the SEMCs. For the most part, this is owing to the absence of explicit deposit guarantee schemes in Egypt, Israel, Palestine, Syria and Tunisia. The Algerian system was equivalent to an implicit guarantee in 2003, as the government had a direct funding role. Looking at

Table 3.9 Deposit guarantee schemes in the Mediterranean, latest available figures

		Coverage limit		Funding (public or banks)	Co-insurance	Risk-based premiums	Ex post/ex ante	Coverage ratio**
	Est. date	€ (current)	(% of GDP per capita in 2012, PPP)					
SEMCs								
Algeria	1997	6,000	108	Banks	No	No	Ex ante	n.a.
Egypt	–	–	–	–	–	–	–	–
Israel	–,	–	–	–	–	–	–	–
Jordan	2000	52,500	1,142	Banks	No	No	Ex ante	1.87
Lebanon	1967	2,500	19	Banks	No	No	Ex ante	n.a.
Morocco	1993	7,000	177	Banks	No	No	Ex ante	n.a.
Palestine	–	–	–	–	–	–	–	–
Syria	–	–	–	–	–	–	–	–
Tunisia	–	–	–	–	–	–	–	–
Turkey	1983	21,000	182	Banks	No	Yes	Ex ante	6.05
EU-MED								
Cyprus	2000	100,000	479	Banks	No*	No	Hybrid	0.31
France	1999	100,000	363	Banks	No*	Yes	Hybrid	0.10
Greece	1995	100,000	515	Banks	No*	Yes	Ex ante	1.69
Italy	1987	103,291	428	Banks	No*	Yes	Ex post	0.00
Malta	2003	100,000	494	Banks	No*	No	Ex ante	0.40
Portugal	1992	100,000	561	Banks	No*	Yes	Ex ante	1.06
Spain	1977	100,000	424	Banks	No*	No	Hybrid	0.65

Notes: *Co-insurance has been abandoned by the amending Directive 2009/14/EC; **The actual EU-MED coverage ratio is calculated as the ratio of *ex-ante* funds and eligible deposits using published figures for 2007–8. For Turkey and Jordan, the end of 2011 total reserves of the deposit insurance schemes are divided by the total insured deposits.

Sources: European Commission (2010), IMF (2008), Bank Al-Maghrib and Banque d'Algérie.

countries with explicit systems, some similarities emerge. Out of the three issues outlined above, Algeria, Cyprus, Spain, Greece, Jordan, Lebanon, Malta and Morocco only satisfied the requirement that the banks (and not the government) take the primary role of funding the scheme in 2011. The French, Greek, Italian and Portuguese systems, in contrast, include risk-adjusted premiums, significantly impacting the EU-MED averages. Lastly, the EU-MED averages display a downward trend, which is entirely due to the gradual abandonment of the co-insurance payouts. On the other hand, in 2010 the European Commission published a proposal to harmonise the deposit guarantee schemes in the EU, which would oblige the EU member states to implement a risk-based deposit guarantee scheme that is bank-funded. However, the proposal has not been adopted, since the European Parliament and Council have not yet agreed on the final terms.

Many of the SEMCs do not have an active deposit insurance scheme, albeit some countries, such as Israel, Palestine, Syria and Tunisia, are studying or considering implementing one. A badly designed scheme can invite additional risks and may not be better than a system with no scheme at all. The results show that the schemes in Jordan, Lebanon and Morocco (as well as in some EU-MED countries) may indeed amplify the moral hazard risks. Still, these conclusions should be interpreted with care. As the recent financial crisis has shown, when a run on a bank has the potential to spur broader panic, the governments are likely to step in to

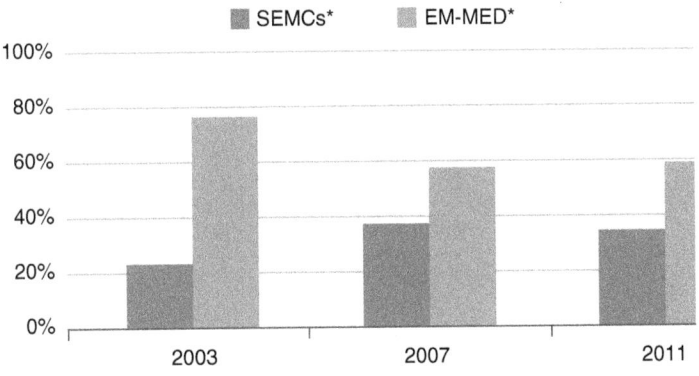

Figure 3.10   Deposit insurance index, by region (% of maximum score)

stop a potential bank run, notwithstanding the types of explicit arrangements in place. One may wonder, quite justifiably, whether the named arrangements really do mitigate moral hazard when they may be so easily replaced with limitless state support. Yet, it should not be forgotten that such blanket guarantees are not viable in most of the SEMCs with limited public resources. Therefore, the explicit schemes, wherever they exist, are the only viable insurance for depositors, highlighting the importance of the design issues in resource-poor countries.

Table 3.10 Deposit insurance index, by country and region (% of maximum score)

	2003	2007	2011
Algeria**	67	100	100
Egypt	0	0	0
Israel	0	0	0
Jordan	67	67	33
Lebanon	33	33	0
Morocco	67	67	33
Palestine	0	0	0
Syria	0	0	0
Tunisia	0	0	0
Turkey	33	67	67
SEMCs*	22	40	35
Cyprus	67	33	33
France	100	67	67
Greece	33	33	67
Italy	67	67	67
Malta	67	33	33
Portugal	100	100	67
Spain	33	33	33
EU-MED*	77	59	59
AVG	74	58	57
STDEV	30	18	18

Notes: *Regional averages are weighted by total banking assets; **The Algerian deposit guarantee system, which has existed since 1997, was partly funded by the government in 2003. Higher values represent more restrictive rules as a share of a maximum score of 3 points.

Sources: BRSS, Demirgüç-Kunt et al. (2005), European Commission (2010), Federal Deposit Insurance Corporation, Bank Al-Maghrib and Banque d'Algérie.

3.2.6   Area VI: Private monitoring

Most of the regulatory factors considered in this study relate to the rules and standards set forth by the regulators, which are used to distinguish between acceptable and unsound behaviour. In this manner, the regulatory principles are often well defined, calling for compliance with specific rules or standards. There are other hard-wired forces that also influence banks, however. Market forces and investors may additionally be crucial in shaping decisions and, in particular, restraining risky behaviour. For example, block-holders can, at least in theory, exercise their voting power to influence managerial actions. More realistically, debtors or stockholders use available information to assess the bank's conditions and indirectly influence the management by withdrawing funds, which has an impact on the borrowing costs of the banks. As far as depositors and other debt-holders are concerned, private monitoring could be seriously undermined when an explicit and over-generous scheme for deposit insurance exists.

The availability of reliable and timely information for investors is at the core of market discipline. The index is therefore based on the survey responses to a number of questions on disclosure rules and standards. These concern whether (i) a certified audit is required; and whether all of the top ten banks are rated by (ii) domestic or (iii) international credit rating agencies. They also consider whether: income standards include accrued but unpaid interest on (iv) performing or (v) non-performing loans; (vi) banks are required to produce consolidated accounts; (vii) directors are liable for erroneous or misleading reporting; (viii) subordinated debt is allowable or required as part of capital; (ix) off-balance-sheet items are disclosed to the public; (x) banks are required to disclose risk-management procedures; and (xi) supervisors are required to make enforcement actions public. The private monitoring score increases with affirmative answers to the previous set of questions.

The comparisons point at a small but growing disparity between the two coasts of the Mediterranean in Figure 3.11 and Table 3.11. Although most countries fulfil a majority of the requirements, the continual progress of the European countries is not paralleled in the SEMCs.

The most striking difference between the SEMCs and EU-MED countries is the share of the top ten banks that are rated by (international

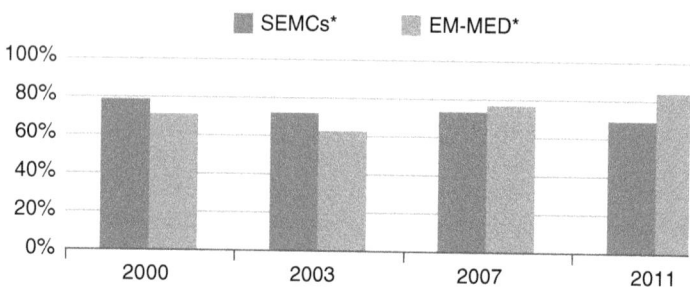

Figure 3.11 Private monitoring, by region (% of maximum score)

Table 3.11 Private monitoring, by country and region (% of maximum score)

	2000	2003	2007	2011
Algeria	–	64	55	–
Egypt	78	73	73	73
Israel	89	82	82	73
Jordan	78	64	64	73
Lebanon	100	64	64	36
Morocco	67	73	64	73
Palestine	–	–	–	82
Syria	–	–	82	73
Tunisia	–	55	–	55
Turkey	67	73	–	73
SEMCs*	79	73	71	69
Cyprus	67	73	73	82
France	67	55	73	91
Greece	67	64	82	73
Italy	67	73	73	73
Malta	89	73	73	73
Portugal	89	55	64	55
Spain	89	73	82	82
EU-MED*	71	63	75	83
AVG	72	64	74	82
STDEV	9	9	5	10

Notes: *Regional averages are weighted by total banking assets. Higher values represent more restrictive rules as a share of a maximum score of 9 points in 2000 and 11 points in 2003, 2007 and 2011.

Source: BRSS.

or domestic) credit rating agencies, which has widened substantially according to the 2011 survey. In particular, almost all of the top ten banks are rated by credit rating agencies in the EU, except Cyprus and Malta. In the SEMCs, most banks are not rated. In some cases, this is due to the inherent structure of the market. For example, Algeria's largest banks are state-owned and as of 2007 they were not subject to ratings. In other countries, there are clear problems with disclosure. In three of the most developed markets in the region, Israel, Lebanon and Morocco, only half of the top ten banks are rated.

Another common issue, especially more recently, is the exclusion of accrued (though unpaid) interest from income statements, which allows banks undue flexibility in determining their earnings. Lastly, according to the 2011 BRSS, the banks in Tunisia are not required to make public their risk-management procedures, despite this requirement having become standard in the region in recent years.

These results show that the regulatory structures of the SEMCs have not matched the progress made in the EU-MED countries in enhancing disclosure rules. Still, it is true that there are broad similarities on both sides of the Mediterranean. For example, a certified audit is compulsory in all of the sample countries and the accounting rules exhibit similarities in most of the countries. Even so, the proportion of banks subject to independent ratings has not changed much in the SEMCs over the past few years.

3.2.7   Area VII: Credit information and laws

Access to information and laws on creditor protection are crucial for ensuring the smooth operation of credit markets. Economic theory suggests two critical limits to the amount of credit that financial institutions can grant to potential borrowers. On the one hand, credit conditions are clearly bound by the ability of creditors to enforce contracts, require repayment, claim collateral and possibly gain control over the receivables. The easier these actions are, the more likely it is that lenders will grant the loans. On the other hand, lenders would like to have access to accurate information on the potential borrowers, such as credit histories, other lenders and other banking transactions.

Theoretical models suggest that an operational information-sharing infrastructure can reduce adverse selection in credit markets and facilitate access to credit, especially among more opaque borrowers, such as SMEs (Pagano and Jappelli, 1993). When such information is available, the creditors can make a better judgement of the creditworthiness of the borrowers. Other studies have documented the importance of creditors' rights for the availability of credit (La Porta et al., 1998; Levine, 1998). Recent studies have confirmed these views with increasingly convincing evidence that both credit information mechanisms and creditors' rights have a nontrivial impact on the flow of credit and financial development (Jappelli and Pagano, 2002; Djankov et al., 2007; Haselmann et al., 2010).

The indices on credit information and laws developed in this section are based on the "Getting Credit" methodology developed in the World Bank's Doing Business surveys. The relevant area covers the legal rights of borrowers and lenders with respect to secured transactions and the extent of credit information sharing. Two sets of indicators are used for these purposes.

The first set describes how well the collateral and bankruptcy laws facilitate lending, covering (i) the ability to use moveable assets while keeping possession of assets and the ability to obtain non-possessory security rights in (ii) a single or (iii) all moveable asset classes without requiring a specific description of the collateral. It also covers (iv) the extension of security rights to future or after-acquired assets; (v) the ability to secure all types of debts and obligations through a general description; and (vi) the availability of a collateral registry. In addition, it looks at the ability of secured creditors to obtain priority without exceptions in the case of (vii) defaults (viii) liquidations and (ix) restructuring; and (x) the possibility of out-of-court agreements on collateral enforcement. An affirmative answer to any one of these questions enhances the relevant scores.

Figure 3.12 and Table 3.12 show that fewer legal rights are granted to creditors in the SEMCs. Israel does exceptionally well, better than almost all countries, by satisfying all but one criterion on the availability of out-of-court agreements on collateral enforcement. Among the EU-MED countries, Cyprus does equivalently well, complying with all but one criterion, namely regarding the secured creditors' claims during reorganisation. France and Spain also perform well. Other countries, including those in the SEMCs, do relatively badly, complying only with the criteria on the use of movable assets as collateral, the ability to grant non-possessory rights for a group of assets and the use of debts in collateral agreements.

The second index measures the availability, coverage and depth of credit information, either through public credit registries or private

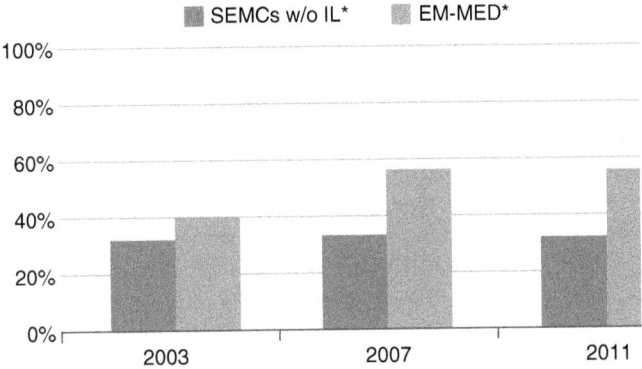

Figure 3.12 Strength of legal rights, by region (% of maximum score)

Table 3.12 Strength of legal rights, by country and region (% of maximum score)

	2003	2007	2011
Algeria	30	30	30
Egypt	30	30	30
Israel	90	90	90
Jordan	20	20	20
Lebanon	30	30	30
Morocco	30	30	30
Palestine**	10	10	10
Syria	10	10	10
Tunisia	30	30	30
Turkey	40	40	40
SEMCs*	48	45	45
Cyprus	–	90	90
France	40	70	70
Greece	40	40	40
Italy	30	30	30
Malta	–	–	30
Portugal	30	30	30
Spain	60	60	60
EU-MED*	41	56	57
AVG	41	56	56
STDEV	12	18	18
SEMCs w/o IL*	32	33	33

Notes: *Regional averages are weighted by total banking assets; **Data for West Bank and Gaza. Higher values represent more independence as a share of a maximum score of 10 points.

Source: World Bank Doing Business.

credit bureaus. The relevant questions relate to (i) the collection of both positive and negative information; (ii) the collection of data on firms and information; (iii) the collection of data from retailers and utility companies; (iv) the availability of credit history for at least two years; (v) the availability of data on small loans (that is, less than 1 per cent of annual incomes); and (vi) the ability of borrowers to access their credit history. As above, an affirmative answer to any one of these questions leads to an additional score for the credit information index.

Figure 3.13 and Table 3.13 clearly show that the SEMCs have progressively closed the gap with the EU-MED in terms of the depth of credit information. The average score of the SEMCs in the last survey was even higher than the score of their EU-MED counterparts. In recent years, the credit bureaus in Algeria, Egypt, Morocco, Palestine and Tunisia have improved their information provisioning substantially. In the more recent Doing Business survey, Egypt even satisfied all of the six criteria. The credit bureaus in Lebanon, Morocco, Tunisia and Turkey only failed to satisfy the criteria to also collect data from retailers and utility companies. Similarly, the credit bureau in Israel also met five of the criteria, but it did not report both positive and negative credit information. Jordan and Syria are clearly outliers in the SEMC; exceptionally, both countries have credit bureaus that only met two of the criteria.

Turning to the EU-MED countries, Cyprus and Malta are exceptions with low scores. In Cyprus, the private credit bureau only meets two

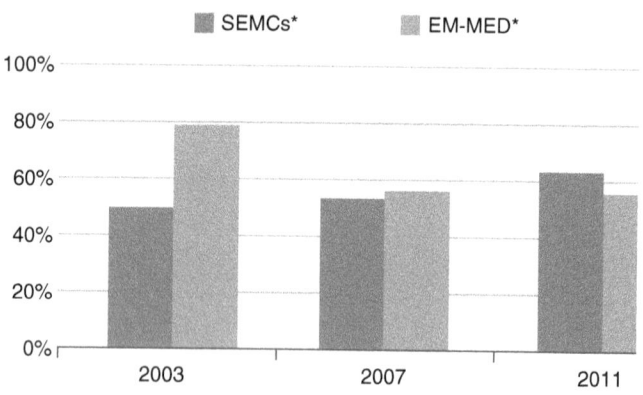

Figure 3.13   Depth of credit information, by region (% of maximum score)

Table 3.13 Depth of credit information, by country and region (% of maximum score)

	2003	2007	2011
Algeria	17	33	67
Egypt	33	83	100
Israel	50	83	83
Jordan	33	33	33
Lebanon	67	83	83
Morocco	17	33	83
Palestine**	0	50	67
Syria	0	0	33
Tunisia	33	83	83
Turkey	83	83	83
SEMCs*	49	72	81
Cyprus	–	0	33
France	67	67	67
Greece	67	67	83
Italy	100	83	83
Malta	–	–	0
Portugal	83	83	83
Spain	83	83	83
EU-MED*	79	74	74
AVG	77	74	75
STDEV	17	11	11

Notes: *Regional averages are weighted by total banking assets; **Data for West Bank and Gaza. Higher values represent greater independence as a share of a maximum score of 6 points.

Source: World Bank Doing Business.

criteria and in Malta there is no credit bureau at all. More broadly, the other EU-MED countries comply with almost all of the criteria. Like many of their SEMC counterparts, French, Greek, Italian and Portuguese credit registries do not collect information from retailers or utility companies. Moreover, the French credit bureau does not provide both positive and negative information. The Spanish credit bureaus do not distribute historical credit information of more than two years, but meet all the other criteria.

In summing up, the figures above show that substantial reforms in recent years have helped the SEMCs to clearly close the gap with the EU-MED countries in terms of the use of credit information. The same cannot be said concerning the strength of legal rights; the EU-MED countries' average is clearly higher than that of the SEMCs.

3.3   Conclusions

The previous section reviewed the quality and the level of convergence of the regulatory and supervisory structures of the SEMCs and EU-MED countries. The assessment included seven dimensions, including the scope of banking, entry obstacles, the stringency of capital requirements, the power and independence of the supervisory authority, the incentives provided by the deposit insurance scheme, private monitoring, and creditors' rights and access to information. This section provides a summary of these areas, offering a comparative analysis of the seven composite indicators that aggregate the relevant indices.

The diagrams in Figure 3.14 and the summary in Table 3.14 show the key remaining weaknesses that distinguish the SEMCs from their counterparts in the EU-MED.

The collective assessment of the convergence of the regulatory and supervisory structures of the SEMCs with the EU-MED standards

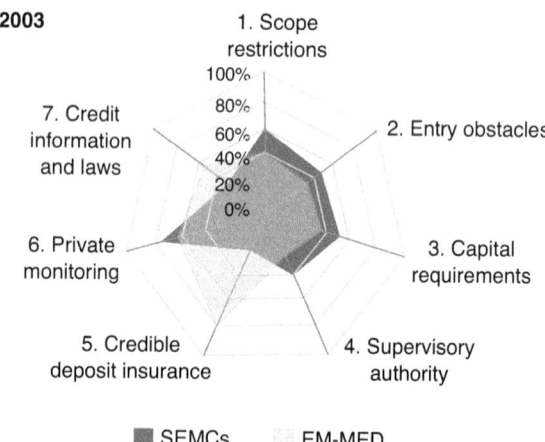

Figure 3.14   Regulatory standards in the SEMCs and EU-MED regions

Note: The figures above sum up the SEMC and EU-MED weighted averages for the regulatory indices in each of the seven areas discussed in Sections 3.2.1–3.2.7.

gives a mixed picture (Figure 3.14 and Table 3.14). Despite some improvements, key weaknesses remain in deposit insurance, entry obstacles and the strength of legal rights. Moreover, some disparities have also become more apparent, especially in the potential for political interference and private monitoring.

The deposit insurance index has failed to improve in recent years, because the Egyptian, Israeli, Palestinian, Syrian and Tunisian authorities have chosen not to put in place an explicit insurance scheme. As discussed in Section 3.2.5, implicit schemes may enhance risk-taking through a blanket government guarantee for the leading institutions. In addition, in Algeria, Jordan, Lebanon and Morocco, no effort has been made to align the banks' incentives by implementing risk-based premiums or co-insurance schemes, which would help internalise some of the costs to the deposit guarantee schemes that stem from excessive risk-taking.

Another major issue, the presence of entry obstacles, continues to be a key weakness in the regulatory structures of the region. Although the licensing requirements exhibit similarities on both shores of the Mediterranean, other indicators point at substantial barriers to entry. Government ownership, which is widespread in the region, gives undue advantages to incumbent banks and restricts entry incentives. In Algeria, Egypt and Syria, as well as to some extent Morocco, Tunisia and Turkey, government ownership remains significant. Although government ownership may have some benefits, the authorities have to ensure that such roles are well defined within a national strategy with clear objectives and instruments, and that they do not represent an obstacle to the development of the financial system. The rates of foreign denials are also very high, further supporting the idea of substantial entry barriers and competitive advantages enjoyed by domestic incumbent banks.

In addition to the two key weaknesses summarised above, the 2011 survey points at three new concerns. Poor accounting practices have contributed to an increasing disparity in private monitoring indices. Furthermore, political interference has become a significant possibility, potentially undermining supervisory authority and reinforcing the governments' direct control – an additional concern for the competitiveness and efficiency of the banking sector (Casu and Ferrari, 2013). As the eruption of public discontent in Tunisia and Egypt in early 2011 clearly attests, the region's governments have

Table 3.14 Summary of key regulatory weaknesses in the SEMCs

	Description	General remarks	Algeria	Egypt	Israel	Jordan
AREA I: Scope restrictions	Restrictions on or prohibition of various activities	Slightly more stringent than EU-MED standards	Some restrictions on real estate; insurance activities prohibited	Some restrictions on insurance and real estate	Some restrictions on securities trading and insurance; real estate activities prohibited	Some restrictions on securities trading and insurance; real estate activities prohibited
AREA II: Entry obstacles	Licensing, foreign entry and presence of public banks	Below EU-MED standards due to foreign denials and the role of government	Public banks represent >90% of bank activity	Foreign denials; public banks represent > 60% of bank activity		Foreign denials
AREA III: Capital requirements	Extent to which capital requirements restrict risks	More stringent capital requirements than the EU-MED		Market risks not considered		
AREA IV: Supervisory authority	Ability of supervisors to prevent and correct problems	Below EU-MED standards due to potential for political interference	High potential for political interference	Some potential for interference	High potential for political interference	Some potential for interference
AREA V: Deposit insurance	Presence of an explicit scheme and mitigation of moral hazard	Below EU-MED standards due to the implicit insurance and adverse incentives	No co-insurance or risk-adjusted premiums	No explicit deposit insurance scheme	No explicit deposit insurance scheme	No co-insurance or risk-adjusted premiums
AREA VI: Private monitoring	Availability of reliable and timely information to investors	Increasing disparity due to limited rated banks and flexibility in accounting	Top banks not rated; flexibility in accounting	Several top banks not rated	Several top banks not rated	Several top banks not rated

AREA VII: Credit info. and laws	Ability of legal and information systems to facilitate lending	Below EU-MED standards due to deficient legal rights	No private credit registry; limited legal rights for creditors	Limited legal rights for creditors		No private credit registry; limited legal rights for creditors
AREA I: Scope restrictions	Real estate activities prohibited	Some restrictions on insurance; real estate activities prohibited		Insurance and real estate activities prohibited	Some restrictions on securities and insurance	Some restrictions on insurance; real estate activities prohibited
AREA II: Entry obstacles	Public bank activity	Foreign denials		Public banks represent >70% of bank activity	Public banks have a diminishing role	Foreign denials; Public banks represent >30% of bank activity
AREA III: Capital requirements	Broad definition of capital			Broad definition of capital		
AREA IV: Supervisory authority	High potential for political interference	Some potential for interference	Some potential for interference	High potential for political interference	Some potential for interference	Some potential for interference
AREA V: Deposit insurance	No co-insurance or risk-adjusted premiums	No co-insurance or risk-adjusted premiums	No explicit deposit insurance scheme	No explicit deposit insurance scheme	No explicit deposit insurance scheme	No co-insurance
AREA VI: Private monitoring	Several top banks not rated	Several top banks not rated; flexibility in accounting	Several top banks not rated	Several top banks not rated	Flexibility in accounting rules; no risk management disclosure	Flexibility in accounting
AREA VII: Credit info. and laws	No private credit registry; limited legal rights for creditors	Limited legal rights for creditors	No private credit registry; barely any legal rights for creditors	No private credit registry; barely any legal rights for creditors	No private credit registry; limited legal rights for creditors	Limited legal rights for creditors

Source: Authors' compilation.

attempted to maintain (perhaps for far too long) a tight grip on their countries' political and economic systems. It is exactly such forms of interference that may conflict with the objectives of the financial and competition authorities.

In contrast, the SEMCs have implemented a number of reforms to improve the availability and use of credit information by financial institutions. Egypt, and more recently Morocco, established private credit bureaus in 2006 and 2009, respectively. The SEMC–EU gap has been bridged. The SEMCs' average is now above the EU-MED average. Algeria, Israel, Jordan, Lebanon and Tunisia continue to rely solely on public registries, three of them meeting all the criteria except collecting credit information on retail stores or utility companies. The same applies to Turkey, which has both public and private credit bureaus. Although the literature provides little guidance, private credit bureaus have better access to new technologies and know-how to ensure that information-sharing mechanisms work effectively. The countries in the region should continue to monitor developments and spearhead innovative systems to use the stock of information and infrastructure already set up by the public systems.

4
Analysis of Banking Efficiency and Convergence

The process of financial reform undertaken by both developed and developing countries aimed to establish a market-based financial sector, to boost bank competition through improved mobilisation of savings, to enhance market-based allocation of resources and to foster more efficient risk-management capabilities. However, the conventional wisdom relating to the positive effect of reforms on financial sector performance is not always validated by empirical studies (Berger et al., 2000). Despite a vast literature on the effects of deregulation on the efficiency and productivity of banks (see Berger and Mester, 2003; Mukherjee et al., 2001; Isik and Hassan, 2003; Zhao et al., 2010; among others) deregulation seems to have had a positive effect in some countries but not in others. Indeed, the outcome of deregulation policies seems to reflect several country-specific demand and supply conditions of the banking industry prior to deregulation.

This chapter attempts to shed light on these issues by examining the effect of financial reform on the efficiency of the banking sector in 11 countries in the Mediterranean region: Cyprus (CY), Algeria (DZ), Egypt (EG), Spain (ES), Greece (GR), Israel (IL), Italy (IT), Malta (MT), Morocco (MA), Portugal (PT) and Tunisia (TN) over the period 1995–2008. The second part of the analysis aims to contribute to the current debate on fostering integration in the Mediterranean region. Following Casu and Girardone (2010), we use the concepts of β-convergence and σ-convergence and employ a dynamic panel data analysis to assess the speed at which financial markets are integrating.

Our results indicate an improvement in bank efficiency across the region, particularly in the latter part of the sample period. The overall mean efficiency in the region is increasing, driven by technological improvements by the best practice banks. Spanish banks dominate the region in terms of both overall efficiency and meta-technology ratios. Nonetheless, during the sample period, the average meta-technology ratio for the region is also increasing, thus indicating an ability of banks in all countries to appropriate the best available technology.

These results are supported by the estimation of β-convergence and σ-convergence. The β coefficient is always negative and statistically significant, thus indicating that convergence in efficiency scores has occurred across countries in the MED-11 area. Furthermore, results for the σ-convergence suggest an increase in the speed of convergence, as the σ coefficient is always negative and statistically significant. This indicates that, whereas the technological gap is still wide, it is narrowing at a faster speed.

4.1 Literature review

There is a vast literature on the use of frontier techniques to evaluate bank efficiency, using both parametric and non-parametric methodologies. While earlier studies focused on one methodological approach and on individual countries (mainly the US, or EU countries) (Berger and Humphrey, 1997; Goddard et al., 2001), in recent years both the number of cross-country studies and the number of studies focusing on developing countries has increased, mainly due to the unprecedented economic reforms implemented in such countries (for a review of recent literature see, among others, Berger, 2007; Goddard et al., 2007; Hughes and Mester, 2010).

Most cross-country studies assume that banks in different countries can access the same banking production technology. In other words, they assume a common production frontier for all countries in order to be able to compare efficiency results across borders. The interpretation of the resulting efficiency scores relies significantly on the validity of this assumption. In some cases this is a major drawback, as the production technology is substantially different among countries, particularly if countries are at different levels of financial development. Bank efficiency estimates may be influenced by factors not generally included in the efficiency analysis, such as differences in bank type, ownership and other bank specific conditions. In such cases, the assumption of a common frontier may be misleading. Further, such an assumption can lead to biased efficiency results of banks from different countries as it ignores differences in regulatory, competitive and economic conditions that are beyond a bank's control (Dietsch and Lozano-Vivas, 2000; Chaffai et al., 2001). The Bos and Kool (2006) study indicates that if environmental factors are not appropriately controlled, efficiency estimates may be biased. Recent empirical studies have attempted to overcome this problem by integrating country-specific environmental variables into the efficiency estimation.

The influence of environmental variables on cross-country efficiency levels has been of interest for many researchers. Bikker (2004) investigates the differences in X-efficiency levels of European banks and concludes that X-efficiency estimates from single-country studies, as often found in the literature, can be very misleading. He documents significant differences in cost-efficiency scores across countries and sizes of banks and bank specialisation, as well as institutional conditions (supervisory rules, government interference, customer preferences and level of development). Bos et al. (2005) analyse the effects of accounting for heterogeneity on the German bank efficiency scores for the period 1993–2003. They find that banks of different sizes, geographic origins and types (cooperative and savings) have significantly different cost efficiency scores. Dietsch and Lozano-Vivas (2000) investigated the influence of the environmental conditions on the cost-efficiency of the French and Spanish banking sector over the period 1992–98. They showed that the specific environmental conditions of each country occupy an important role in the definition and specification of the common frontier of different countries.

In fact, when environmental variables are incorporated in the model, the differences between both banking industries are reduced substantially and the cost-efficiency scores improved. The Chaffai et al. (2001) study, on a sample of European countries over the period 1993–97, report similar findings. They conclude that controlling for environmental conditions reduces the differences in average operational inefficiency scores among countries. Grigorian and Manole (2006) use a Data Envelopment Analysis (DEA) approach to estimate the efficiency levels of transition countries between 1993 and 1995, and a two-step approach to explain the differences in efficiency across countries. They find that foreign ownership and enterprise restructuring enhance commercial bank efficiency. Bos and Kool (2006), on the other hand, find that market specific factors and regional macroeconomic factors are of limited importance in explaining operational efficiency of the Dutch cooperative banking sector. Battese et al. (2004) have recently proposed a so-called 'meta-frontier' as the method to estimate country or regional-specific frontiers, and end up with efficiency scores that can be compared in an absolute sense. The meta-frontier results from the envelopment of regional specific frontiers. Bos and Schmiedel (2007) apply the meta-frontier methodology to eight European banking markets for the period 1993–2000. The authors conclude that for most countries included in the study, profit efficiency in particular improves significantly when estimated using a meta-frontier instead of a common-frontier, arguing that this may be evidence of the importance of local market circumstances. Ben Naceur et al. (2011) examine the effect of financial-sector reform on bank performance in selected Middle Eastern and North African (MENA) countries in the period 1994–2008 using DEA and employ a meta-frontier approach to calculate efficiency scores in a cross-country setting. They then employ a second-stage regression to investigate the impact of institutional, financial and bank-specific variables on bank efficiency. Overall, their results show that the observed efficiency levels of banks vary substantially across markets, with differences in technology explaining most of the efficiency differentials.

Several studies investigate the existence and implications of financial convergence, especially in relation to the deregulation processes.[1] Only a few studies, however, directly address the issue of the relationship between financial integration and bank efficiency. Tortosa-Ausina (2002) examines the convergence in efficiency of Spanish banks following deregulation through a model of distribution dynamics and finds evidence of decreased dispersion of efficiency scores at the end of the deregulation period. Murinde et al. (2004) investigate the convergence of the banking systems in Europe following the launch of the single market programme in 1993. They find weak evidence of convergence and only for specific products. Weill (2009) attempts to provide evidence of financial integration by estimating the convergence of cost efficiency derived from the application of Stochastic Frontier Analysis (SFA) methodology. His results indicate an on-going process of convergence at the EU level. More recently, Casu and Girardone (2010) evaluate the dynamics of EU banks' cost efficiency by means of DEA and then assess their convergence both towards an EU-wide frontier and towards best practice. Their results seem to provide supporting evidence of convergence of efficiency levels towards an EU average. Nevertheless, the potential gains brought about by increased integration seem to have been offset by a decrease in the overall efficiency levels of EU banks.

4.2 Methodology

4.2.1 Data envelopment analysis

DEA is a mathematical linear programming technique developed by Charnes et al. (1978), which identifies the efficient frontier from the linear combination of those units/observations that (in a production space) use comparatively fewer inputs to produce comparatively more outputs. The original (or Charnes, Cooper and Rhoades – CCR model) assumes constant returns to scale (CRS), which is the optimal scale in the long run. Banker, Charnes and Cooper (1984) (or the BCC model) include an additional convexity constraint (λ) to allow for variable returns to scale (VRS). In particular, if at any time t there are N firms that use a vector of inputs to produce a vector of outputs, the input-oriented BCC measure of efficiency of a particular firm is calculated as:

$$\min_{u,l} \theta_i$$
$$s.t. \sum_{r=1}^{N} y_{mr}^t \lambda_r^t \geq y_{mi}^t, \ \sum_{r=1}^{N} x_{kr}^t \lambda_r^t \leq \theta_i x_{ki}^t, \ \lambda_r^t \geq 0, \tag{1}$$
$$\sum_{r=1}^{N} \lambda = 1$$

where $\theta_i \leq 1$ is the scalar efficiency score for the i-th unit. If $\theta_I = 1$ the i-th firm is efficient as it lies on the frontier, whereas if $\theta_i < 1$ the firm is inefficient and needs a $(1-\theta_i)$ reduction in the inputs levels to reach the frontier.

The choice of using a DEA is based on several considerations: it works well even with a small sample size and it does not require any assumption about the functional form of the frontier or of the inefficiency component. We adopt an input-minimisation orientation, based on the assumption that during periods of regulatory changes and increased competition, market participants strategically focus on cutting costs. Therefore we would expect changes in inputs used to be closely associated with the changes in market structure.

4.2.2   Meta-frontier analysis

There are various ways to incorporate environmental variables in the estimation of bank efficiency; the most commonly used are the one-step and the two-step approach. In the one-step approach, environmental variables are included directly in the estimation of efficiency whereas in the two-step approach, efficiency scores obtained in the first stage of analysis are then regressed on a number of country-specific environmental variables. Both approaches are employed in the literature: the one-step approach seems to be the preferred choice if using a parametric approach to the efficiency evaluation, following the maximum likelihood procedure of Battese and Coelli (1995). On the other hand, the two-step approach seems to be the favoured approach if efficiency is estimated by means of DEA. In a typical two-stage study, the relative efficiency of each institution is evaluated in the first stage based and then regressed (as the dependent variable in an ordinary least squares or a Tobit regression) on various explanatory variables in the second stage to identify the factors whose impact on efficiency is statistically significant. A theoretical justification for the use of a two-stage method that uses DEA in the first stage is provided by Banker and Natarajan (2008).

Departing from the standard two stage approach, Battese et al. (2004) and O'Donnell et al. (2008) recently proposed a so-called 'meta-frontier' method to estimate country- or regional-specific frontiers and obtain comparable efficiency scores, as the meta-frontier results from the envelopment of regional specific frontiers.

In this study, to accommodate the potential country variation of available banking technology and to obtain comparable technical efficiencies for the countries in our sample, we follow the meta-frontier approach. If we consider the available technology to be a state of knowledge in existence at a given point in time, we can define the meta-technology as the totality of the regional-/country-specific technologies. The meta-frontier production function is therefore a frontier function that envelops all frontiers of individual countries/ groups.

To apply the meta-frontier approach with DEA, it is necessary to solve separate models (equation (1)) for each country in order to specify the country-specific frontiers and one for the joint data set for solving the meta-frontier. The efficiencies measured relative to the meta-frontier can be decomposed into two components: a component that measures the distance from an input-output point to the group frontier (the common measure of technical efficiency) and a component that measures the distance between the group frontier and the meta-frontier (representing the restrictive nature of the production environment).

The meta-technology ratio (DEA-MTR), that is the relative productivity of technologies, can be obtained as the ratio between meta-frontier (in)efficiency (DEA-M) and the country-specific (in)efficiency (DEA-C). The higher the ratio, the closer a country's production technology is to the 'best practice' in the region. Vice versa, the lower the ratio, the bigger is the technology gap.

4.2.3 Modelling convergence

To investigate the convergence of bank efficiency levels across the 11 countries in the Mediterranean region (MED-11) over the period 1994–2008, we follow Casu and Girardone (2010) and employ the concepts of β-convergence and σ-convergence (Barro and Sala-i-Martin, 1991, 1992, 1995; Quah, 1996).

To estimate unconditional β-convergence or the 'catch-up effect', we employ the following equation:

$$\Delta_{yi,t} = \alpha + \beta \left(\ln y_{i,t-1} \right) + \rho \Delta y_{i,t-1} + \epsilon_{i,t} \tag{2}$$

where $i = 1, \ldots, 11$ and $t = 1, \ldots, 14$; $y_{i,t}$ = the mean efficiency of the banking sector of country i at time t; $y_{i,t-1}$ = the mean efficiency of the banking sector of country i at time $t-1$; $\Delta_{yi,t} = \ln(y_{i,t}) - \ln(y_{i,t-1})$; α, β and ρ are the parameters to be estimated and $\epsilon_{i,t}$ = error term. A negative value for the parameter β implies convergence; the higher the coefficient in relative terms the greater the tendency for convergence. Equation (2) is first estimated without including the lagged dependent variable ($\Delta y_{i,t-1}$), as in the conventional growth theory models. The β-convergence equations are estimated by pooled OLS regression and Generalised Method of Moments (GMM) to introduce dynamic behaviour in the time series and cross-sectional variation (Blundell and Bond, 1998).

To estimate cross sectional dispersion or σ-convergence, that is to estimate how quickly each country's efficiency levels are converging to the average, we adopt the following autoregressive distributed lag model specification[2]:

$$\Delta E_{it} = \alpha + \sigma E_{i,t-1} + \rho \Delta E_{i,t-1} + \epsilon_{i,t} \tag{3}$$

where $E_{i,t} = \ln(y_{i,t}) - \ln(\bar{y}_t)$; $E_{i,t-1} = \ln(y_{i,t-1}) - \ln(\bar{y}_{t-1})$; $y_{i,t}$ and $y_{i,t-1}$ are defined as before; $\bar{y}_t$ = the mean efficiency of the MED-11 banking sectors at time t; $\bar{y}_{t-1}$ = the mean efficiency of the MED-11 banking sectors at time $t-1$; $\Delta E_{it} = E_{i,t} - E_{i,t-1}$; α, σ and ρ are parameters to be calculated and $y_{1,t}$ is the error term; $\sigma < 0$ represents the rate of convergence of $y_{i,t}$ towards $\bar{y}_t$; the larger is σ in absolute value, the faster the rate of convergence. The model in equation (3) is estimated initially without the inclusion of the lagged dependent variable (ΔE_{it-1}) , as we did for the β-convergence in equation (2).

4.3 Descriptive statistics

The sample relates to a balanced sample of commercial and savings banks in the following 11 countries in the Mediterranean region: Cyprus (CY), Algeria (DZ), Egypt (EG), Spain (ES), Greece (GR), Israel (IL), Italy (IT), Malta (MT), Morocco (MA), Portugal (PT) and Tunisia (TN) over the period 1995–2008.

Table 4.1 below provides some descriptive statistics of the total number of observations in the sample and the average total assets by year and country.

As is apparent from Table 4.1, Italy and Spain dominate the sample, while the number of observations for Algeria, Israel, Morocco and Malta is particularly low. Data availability improves in the final years of the sample period, probably due to better reporting of accounting data; however, for the purpose of the present analysis, we concentrate on continuously operating institutions over the time period.

Substantial differences in the average size of banks are apparent, with Spanish banks being the largest. The average size (total assets) of all institutions in the sample increases from €4,056 million in 1995

Table 4.1 Number of observations and average total assets (€ million)

	N. of obs.	1995	1996	1997	1998	1999	2000	2001	2002	2003	2004	2005	2006	2007	2008	Change 1995–2008 (%)
CY	4	2,369	2,895	3,371	3,653	4,505	5,435	6,585	7,053	7,652	8,653	10,489	14,221	18,209	21,300	899
DZ	2	2,851	2,739	2,440	2,477	2,574	2,547	2,642	2,354	2,297	2,266	2,716	2,848	3,002	4,021	141
EG	14	1,459	1,571	1,803	1,962	2,403	2,777	3,114	2,784	2,169	2,229	3,129	3,511	4,146	4,321	296
ES	65	10,264	11,275	12,658	13,605	15,184	18,663	19,919	19,818	21,749	30,402	36,931	41,634	47,559	51,800	505
GR	8	7,812	8,690	10,035	10,972	13,497	15,804	16,956	17,248	17,723	18,848	22,279	27,218	33,131	38,674	495
IL	5	3,489	3,655	3,666	3,579	4,798	5,771	6,346	4,615	4,074	4,072	4,765	5,305	5,631	6,462	185
IT	80	3,049	3,347	3,592	3,926	4,078	4,386	4,693	5,057	5,113	5,694	6,232	6,795	7,246	8,429	276
MA	4	2,320	2,334	2,318	2,634	2,973	3,274	3,390	3,509	3,685	4,965	6,095	7,444	8,658	10,537	454
MT	4	1,008	1,162	1,314	1,474	1,670	1,837	1,975	2,137	2,203	2,281	2,395	2,692	2,904	3,161	314
PT	10	8,910	9,617	10,845	12,500	14,495	18,857	20,559	20,928	22,458	23,646	26,185	28,842	31,887	34,340	385
TN	10	1,088	1,121	1,078	989	1,163	1,379	1,544	1,453	1,404	1,435	1,575	1,633	1,733	1,941	178
Mean	206	4,056	4,401	4,829	5,252	6,122	7,339	7,975	7,905	8,230	9,499	11,163	12,922	14,919	16,817	375

to €16,817 million in 2008. It is necessary to point out, however, that in some countries the high number of small- and medium-sized institutions has an impact on the overall country averages (for example, Italy), whereas in other countries there is only a small number of large banks present in the sample (for example, Israel).

4.3.1   Input and output variables

There are two main approaches to the definition of inputs and outputs of financial institutions: the production approach and the intermediation approach. Both approaches are widely used in the literature and there is no consensus on the superiority of one or the other. In this study we follow a variation of the intermediation approach (Sealey and Lindley, 1977). This approach views financial institutions as mediators between the supply and the demand of funds. As a consequence, deposits are considered as inputs, and interest on deposits as a component of total costs, together with labour and capital.

In the cross-country setting of the present study, the need for comparable data from different countries imposes strong restrictions on the variables one is able to use, not least because of the various accounting criteria used in the four countries under investigation. To minimise possible bias arising from different accounting practices, the broad definition of variables as presented by Bankscope was chosen.

Specifically, the input variable used in this study is Total Costs (Interest Expenses + Overheads), whereas the output variables capture both the traditional lending activity of banks (total loans) and the growing non-lending activities (other earning assets).

We aggregate the cost expenditure[3] into a single input to minimise the well-known dimensionality problem associated with DEA. In small samples, if we have a high number of variables relative to the number of observations, units can be wrongly identified as efficient because too many constraints have been specified. Observations tend to become incomparable and hence figure on the frontier owing to the inability of DEA to identify peers. One way around this, commonly used in the literature, is to aggregate the input variables in a single monetary value. Tables 4.2, 4.3 and 4.4 report the descriptive statistics of the input variable (total costs) and the two output variables (total loans and total other earning assets), respectively.

Table 4.2 Total costs (average, € million)

	1995	1996	1997	1998	1999	2000	2001	2002	2003	2004	2005	2006	2007	2008	Change 1995–2008 (%)
CY	179	221	254	288	320	392	418	464	465	494	547	615	913	1,130	630
DZ	149	163	141	124	104	137	127	81	65	65	106	72	102	92	62
EG	116	133	150	159	195	240	252	193	138	135	208	247	275	354	305
ES	909	940	885	913	894	1,216	1,312	1,131	961	1,020	1,397	1,706	2,277	2,852	314
GR	899	987	1,026	1,165	1,282	1,386	1,118	992	903	940	980	1,297	1,867	2,496	278
IL	209	171	275	306	361	428	564	242	246	240	314	230	244	278	133
IT	297	306	283	267	231	261	276	267	258	252	261	307	376	463	156
MA	129	137	135	147	155	179	178	186	178	261	277	269	326	397	307
MT	55	66	76	86	109	110	115	106	99	92	96	105	120	132	238
PT	815	799	781	919	883	1,123	1,276	1,130	1,105	1,176	1,215	1,408	1,793	2,247	276
TN	68	73	56	64	69	84	96	93	85	87	102	108	120	122	180
Mean	348	363	369	404	418	505	521	444	409	433	500	579	765	960	276

Table 4.3 Total loans (average, € million)

	1995	1996	1997	1998	1999	2000	2001	2002	2003	2004	2005	2006	2007	2008	Change 1995–2008 (%)
CY	1,334	1,639	1,903	2,185	2,610	3,155	3,592	4,019	4,360	4,841	5,484	7,474	10,327	13,413	1005
DZ	863	792	602	429	539	690	842	734	763	784	939	893	994	1,358	157
EG	656	740	865	971	1,270	1,506	1,604	1,309	902	884	1,160	1,233	1,430	1,658	253
ES	4,619	5,183	6,169	7,021	8,072	9,967	11,027	11,622	13,112	18,454	22,804	28,097	32,289	34,605	749
GR	2,734	3,110	3,516	4,224	5,437	6,679	7,926	9,427	10,569	11,477	13,410	17,193	22,395	28,460	1041
IL	2,481	2,535	2,422	2,434	3,167	3,938	4,504	3,386	2,885	2,707	2,978	3,237	3,373	3,907	158
IT	1,480	1,522	1,678	1,902	2,178	2,506	2,713	2,972	3,219	3,501	3,916	4,381	4,946	5,938	401
MA	1,233	1,259	1,217	1,420	1,624	1,718	1,724	1,690	1,759	2,390	3,270	3,926	4,956	6,365	516
MT	500	656	711	775	851	918	961	997	1,034	1,106	1,141	1,312	1,454	1,648	330
PT	3,629	4,125	5,161	6,948	8,791	11,937	13,462	14,291	14,657	15,632	16,757	18,706	21,665	24,134	665
TN	722	711	672	700	782	979	1,103	1,076	1,037	1,027	1,110	1,142	1,167	1,325	183
Mean	1,841	2,025	2,265	2,637	3,211	3,999	4,496	4,684	4,936	5,709	6,634	7,963	9,545	11,165	606

Table 4.4 Total other earning assets (average, € million)

	1995	1996	1997	1998	1999	2000	2001	2002	2003	2004	2005	2006	2007	2008	Change 1995–2008 (%)
CY	685	878	1,094	1,038	1,238	1,545	2,221	2,072	2,416	2,963	4,117	5,220	6,242	6,009	877
DZ	1,577	1,620	1,508	1,707	1,655	1,476	1,217	1,017	916	865	1,102	1,329	1,303	1,780	113
EG	693	724	824	863	962	1,089	1,305	1,296	1,156	1,242	1,810	2,104	2,483	2,346	338
ES	4,731	5,105	5,383	5,320	5,503	6,425	6,383	6,045	6,485	9,888	11,731	11,049	12,163	13,258	280
GR	4,559	4,993	5,742	6,061	7,029	7,994	7,736	6,773	6,115	5,456	6,640	6,988	6,853	6,334	139
IL	818	851	669	655	985	1,044	999	653	633	860	1,388	1,732	1,997	1,646	201
IT	1,298	1,536	1,593	1,673	1,500	1,462	1,467	1,507	1,325	1,596	1,897	2,000	1,829	1,822	140
MA	600	601	609	683	962	1,229	1,436	1,369	1,394	1,687	1,849	2,341	2,465	2,891	482
MT	411	408	487	571	660	744	827	942	973	1,010	1,074	1,171	1,187	1,330	323
PT	4,285	4,447	4,509	4,281	4,034	5,108	5,008	4,613	4,902	5,939	7,549	7,997	8,091	7,625	178
TN	104	139	135	189	238	274	294	260	250	293	329	345	412	386	371
Mean	1,797	1,937	2,050	2,095	2,251	2,581	2,627	2,413	2,415	2,891	3,590	3,843	4,093	4,130	230

Total costs increase steadily (+276 per cent) over the sample period; costs increase in all countries. The largest increase is displayed by banks in Cyprus (+630 per cent) and the smallest by banks in Algeria (+ 62 per cent).

Tables 4.3 and 4.4 show the averages for the two output variables, total loans and total other earning assets.

Total loans are steadily increasing in all countries, with the highest percentage change displayed by Greek and Cypriot banks. This might be a consequence of increased lending following EU membership. Other earning assets are also increasing steadily, but not at the same rate as loans (percentage change 230 per cent versus 606 per cent).

Figure 4.1 illustrates the trend of the input and output variables, both as averages and as percentage change (1995 as base year). Bank growth in these countries has been mainly driven by development of the traditional lending function, and the increase in total costs seems to be mirrored by the steady growth of bank loans. Cypriot and Moroccan banks display the most remarkable increase in other earning assets; this is possibly due to the entry of foreign banks.

4.4   Results

4.4.1   Efficiency results

This section presents the results of the application of the DEA metafrontier analysis to evaluate the efficiency of banks in selected countries in the Mediterranean region.

Table 4.5 reports descriptive statistics of efficiency scores for the countries under observation as well as estimates for all countries combined (meta-frontier). Technical efficiencies and meta-technology ratios are estimated for each country in each of 14 years of analysis, relative to a balanced panel data set rather than relative to yearly frontiers, which makes analysis of the evolution of efficiency over time meaningful.

The average annual efficiency scores of banks of each country relative to each country's frontier (DEA-C) reveal a general steady trend. The results relative to the country frontiers are reported only for completeness of the analysis. Recall that these efficiencies are calculated relative to each country's frontier; the boundaries of these frontiers are restricted technology sets, where the restrictions derive from the available economic infrastructure and other characteristics of the production environment, as discussed above. Also recall the small number of observations in some countries, which causes dimensionality problems

We now move to the crucial part of this analysis, the measurement of efficiency relative to a meta-frontier, defined as the boundary of an unrestricted technology set. It is interesting to note that in most countries, the country-specific frontiers were at least partially tangent to the meta-frontier. This is the case when at least one observation from each country lies both on the country and on the meta-frontier and it is therefore positioned in the point of tangency between the country and the meta-frontier. This indicates that the meta-frontier closely envelops the country-specific frontiers and that the value of the technological gap ratio equals the maximum value of one for at least one observation in each of the sample countries.

Looking at the efficiency scores derived from the estimation of the meta-frontier as displayed in Table 4.6, Spanish banks dominate the region, with average efficiency scores of 80.4 per cent. Cypriot, Egyptian and Tunisian banks are lagging behind with average efficiency scores of 55.6 per cent, 49.5 per cent and 58.1 per cent over the period. The region's average efficiency score is 63.5 per cent, which indicates that Mediterranean banks could, on average, reduce costs (inputs) by 36.5 per cent and still produce the same outputs.

Figure 4.2 illustrates the trend of efficiency levels over the period 1995–2008. For all countries, it is possible to note an improvement in efficiency levels in the later stages of the analysis, from 2005 onwards (with the exception of Egypt). This improvement is particularly remarkable for Algerian and Moroccan banks. The overall mean efficiency in the region is improving, once again driven by improvements in the best practice. Minimum average efficiency scores also seem to be increasing, following a drop in 2008.

Table 4.7 illustrates the meta-technology ratios. The meta-technology ratio (DEA-MTR) or technological gap, is calculated as the ratio between meta-frontier (in)efficiency (DEA-M) and the country-specific (in)efficiency (DEA-C) and it indicates the relative productivity of technologies. The higher the ratio, the closer a country's production technology is to the 'best practice' in the region. Vice versa, the lower the ratio, the bigger is the technology gap. An

Table 4.5 Country-specific DEA efficiency scores (DEA-C)

	1995	1996	1997	1998	1999	2000	2001	2002	2003	2004	2005	2006	2007	2008	Mean
CY	96.9	97.2	96.6	97.9	100.0	98.2	99.8	100.0	97.3	95.2	95.6	95.1	92.9	99.3	97.3
DZ	100.0	94.4	93.1	95.7	100.0	100.0	100.0	100.0	94.7	90.4	91.3	90.2	91.4	98.6	95.7
EG	89.4	88.7	91.3	88.6	86.1	86.6	85.1	83.9	80.8	89.5	90.4	89.5	83.7	79.0	86.6
ES	90.4	90.3	87.4	86.2	83.1	87.4	87.3	86.4	87.1	84.1	83.0	85.2	86.1	87.5	86.5
GR	96.0	94.0	94.9	88.1	94.8	96.5	97.5	96.9	94.0	91.5	94.2	89.6	93.2	93.4	93.9
IL	94.9	93.0	98.2	93.4	96.5	96.5	99.0	96.6	89.7	98.6	99.1	93.8	95.3	88.9	95.2
IT	81.2	83.2	86.8	85.6	83.5	81.6	83.2	80.8	68.4	79.4	80.8	80.5	84.0	82.3	81.5
MA	100.0	97.3	98.0	96.6	99.2	96.7	100.0	100.0	100.0	98.2	100.0	100.0	100.0	100.0	99.0
MT	100.0	100.0	100.0	100.0	100.0	100.0	100.0	100.0	100.0	100.0	100.0	99.2	100.0	100.0	99.9
PT	89.8	89.4	91.6	95.4	95.1	91.2	93.7	93.5	90.3	89.1	93.4	92.7	93.5	95.3	92.4
TN	80.3	86.1	92.5	92.5	91.3	96.9	94.9	89.3	92.8	93.0	93.0	96.4	87.8	94.9	91.6
Mean	92.6	92.2	93.7	92.7	93.6	93.8	94.6	93.4	90.5	91.7	92.8	92.0	91.6	92.7	92.7

Table 4.6 Mean meta-frontier DEA efficiency scores

	1995	1996	1997	1998	1999	2000	2001	2002	2003	2004	2005	2006	2007	2008	Mean
CY	47.7	52.2	70.0	57.9	46.1	53.1	61.6	53.7	46.1	42.5	48.2	60.8	69.9	69.2	55.6
DZ	74.2	78.3	82.9	94.3	87.8	71.2	70.0	73.2	64.3	57.2	52.1	73.7	72.6	93.7	74.7
EG	51.7	51.4	60.1	56.1	43.2	45.3	49.3	49.8	44.5	45.7	45.4	53.3	52.0	45.7	49.5
ES	59.3	65.7	84.0	85.3	82.3	87.2	85.5	85.7	75.7	83.0	82.9	84.2	85.0	79.2	80.4
GR	45.4	43.5	52.7	48.4	41.0	48.4	65.3	62.4	56.6	50.4	52.9	54.2	63.9	68.1	53.8
IL	74.6	92.3	69.9	56.7	46.2	52.2	48.5	67.1	43.2	42.4	37.5	66.6	74.2	77.9	60.7
IT	44.5	47.9	58.6	65.6	63.9	69.8	71.8	71.8	57.6	63.2	62.0	64.0	70.3	73.5	63.2
MA	57.8	55.9	74.4	69.2	58.8	65.1	71.8	60.3	49.1	45.4	49.7	65.0	85.5	93.9	64.4
MT	76.1	79.5	87.3	81.5	63.4	65.2	67.7	57.3	63.8	56.2	59.7	62.9	62.7	70.4	68.1
PT	59.8	62.9	80.8	73.0	68.1	76.3	78.2	78.0	65.5	67.6	70.3	66.7	68.5	64.2	70.0
TN	43.3	46.9	82.5	76.3	62.9	70.1	72.3	63.4	47.8	48.2	44.1	45.2	49.9	60.6	58.1
Mean	57.7	61.5	73.0	69.5	60.3	64.0	67.4	65.7	55.8	54.7	55.0	63.3	68.6	72.4	63.5

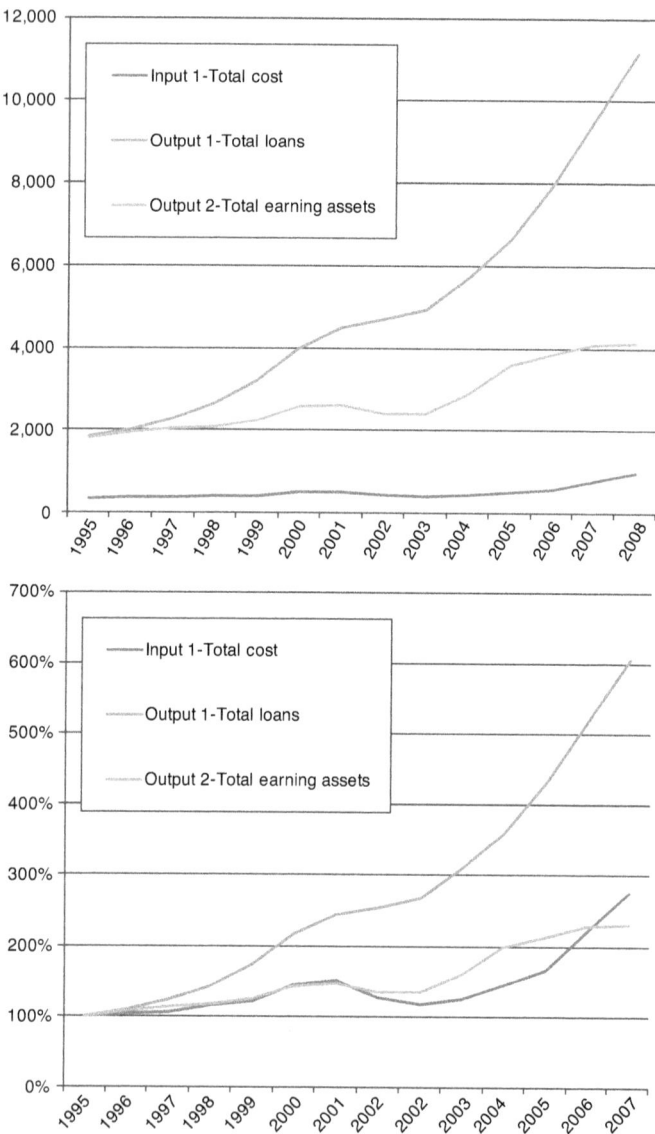

Figure 4.1   Average and percentage change – input and output variables

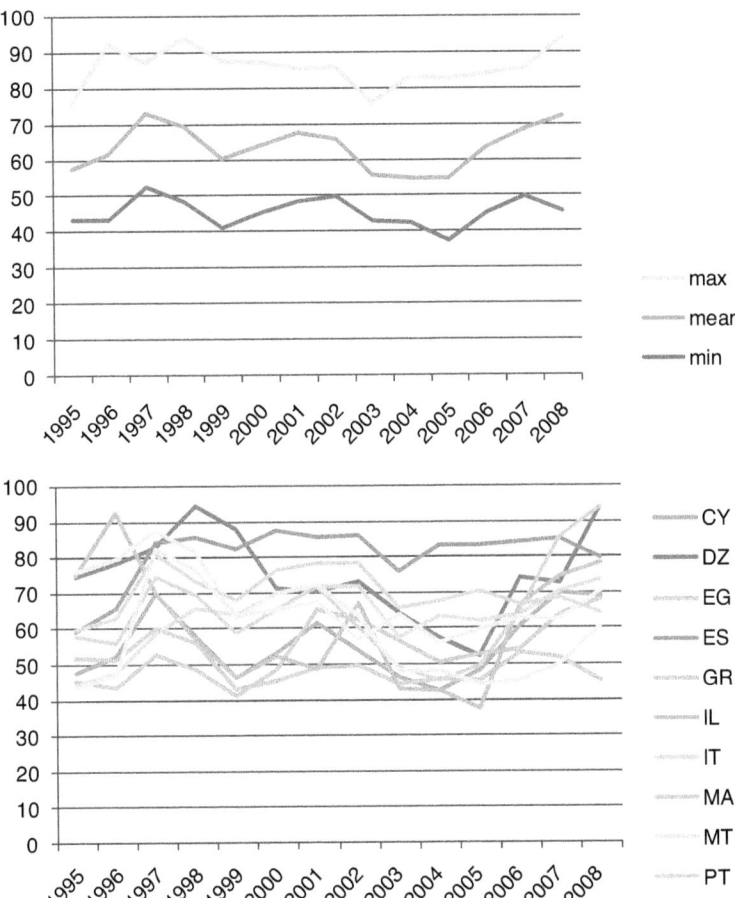

Figure 4.2 Average meta-frontier DEA scores

increase in the meta-technology ratio can be seen as convergence towards the best practice.

During this period of analysis, the average meta-technology ratio is increasing, indicating an ability of banks in all countries to appropriate the best available technology. Spanish banks exhibit the highest meta-technology ratio; the ratios also display an increasing trend over time. This indicates that Spanish banks consistently improved their performance and their technology became best

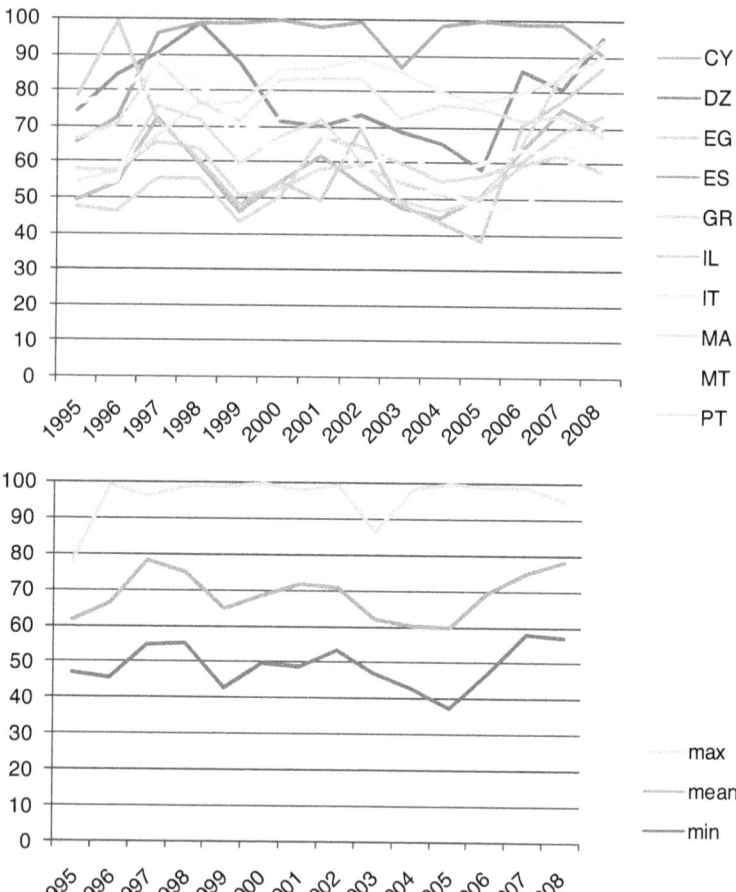

Figure 4.3   Average meta-technology ratios

practice. The dominance of Spanish banks is clearly illustrated in Figure 4.3. Moroccan and Algerian banks seem to catch up with best practice.

There is overall some indication of catching up with the best available technology. However, the institutions comprising the sample are often the largest banks in some countries and are for the majority

Table 4.7 Average meta-technology ratios

	1995	1996	1997	1998	1999	2000	2001	2002	2003	2004	2005	2006	2007	2008	Mean
CY	48.9	53.5	72.5	59.1	46.1	54.0	61.7	53.7	47.1	44.6	50.3	63.6	75.2	69.6	57.1
DZ	74.2	84.6	90.4	98.7	87.8	71.2	70.0	73.2	68.8	65.2	57.7	85.9	80.8	95.1	78.8
EG	57.6	57.3	65.5	63.3	50.4	52.6	58.1	59.0	54.0	50.8	50.1	59.1	62.0	57.3	56.9
ES	65.3	72.3	96.0	99.0	98.9	99.8	97.7	99.1	86.5	98.4	99.8	98.7	98.8	90.4	92.9
GR	47.0	46.1	55.0	55.2	42.9	49.9	66.8	64.4	60.0	54.8	56.0	60.2	68.5	73.1	57.1
IL	78.2	99.2	71.2	60.3	47.8	54.1	49.1	69.6	48.1	43.1	37.8	70.4	77.6	86.8	63.8
IT	54.2	56.9	67.3	76.5	76.6	85.6	86.3	89.0	85.1	79.6	76.7	79.6	84.0	89.7	77.6
MA	57.8	57.2	75.8	71.6	59.2	67.1	71.8	60.3	49.1	46.2	49.7	65.0	85.5	93.9	65.0
MT	76.1	79.5	87.3	81.5	63.4	65.2	67.7	57.3	63.8	56.2	59.7	63.3	62.7	70.4	68.1
PT	66.2	70.6	87.8	76.4	71.2	82.9	83.3	83.3	72.3	75.8	75.0	71.7	73.4	67.5	75.5
TN	52.5	54.0	89.5	82.6	68.7	72.4	76.3	70.8	51.4	52.1	47.8	47.0	58.3	64.4	63.4
Mean	61.6	66.5	78.0	74.9	64.8	68.6	71.7	70.9	62.4	60.6	60.1	69.5	75.2	78.0	68.7

foreign-owned in the MENA region. As a result, the indication of catching up must be treated with caution.

4.4.2 Convergence results

To evaluate β-convergence for our cross-section of Mediterranean countries, we estimate equation (2) by OLS and GMM. Table 4.8 shows regression estimates of the convergence coefficient β for the period 1995–2008. The results from equation (2) that exclude the lagged dependent variable are reported in the first column. The beta coefficient is always negative and statistically significant, thus indicating that convergence in efficiency scores has occurred across countries in the MED-11 area. The results are confirmed in all three models although the goodness of fit for the SYS-GMM (last column) shows that the p-value for AR(1) is greater than 5 per cent.

Table 4.8   Beta convergence

Coefficients	Equation (2) without lagged dependent variable	Equation (2)	
	Pooled OLS Robust	Pooled OLS robust	SYS-GMM two step robust
β	−0.2502***	−0.3174***	−0.3952***
	(0.0588)	(0.0679)	(0.1816)
ρ		−0.1682*	+0.1516
		(0.8813)	(0.1801)
α	1.0481***	1.321***	1.6448**
	(0.2461)	(0.2843)	(0.7520)
Goodness of fit:			
R^2	0.1227	0.1626	
m1 p-value			0.245
m2 p-value			0.720
Sargan/Hansen			1.000

Notes: OLS = Ordinary Least Squares; SYS-GMM = System GMM;
*,**,*** indicates significance at the 10%, 5% and 1% levels. Asymptotic standard error in parentheses. Two-step estimates are Windmeijer corrected (Windmeijer, 2005); m1 and m2 are tests for first-order and second-order serial correlation. Sargan/Hansen is a test of the over-identifying restrictions for the GMM estimators.

Table 4.9   Sigma convergence (dependent variable ΔE)

Coefficients	Equation (3) without lagged dependent variable		Equation (3)		
	Pooled OLS robust	Fixed effects	Pooled OLS robust	Fixed effects	SYS-GMM two step robust
σ	–0.1874***	–0.4131***	–0.2129***	–0.5645***	–0.1791***
	(0.0607)	(0.0687)	(0.0641)	(0.0805)	(0.4521)
ρ			–0.0151	–0.1271	–0.1359
			(0.0972)	(0.0864)	(0.4760)
μ	–0.00032	–0.0074	–0.0029	–0.0095	–0.0019
	(0.0093)	(0.0100)	(0.0097)	(0.0092)	(0.0198)
Goodness of fit:					
R^2	0.0961		0.1194		
F-test		39.09***		26.08***	
m1 *p*-value					0.342
m2 *p*-value					0.843
Sargan/ Hansen					1.000

Notes: OLS= Ordinary Least Squares; SYS-GMM= System GMM;
*,**,*** indicates significance at the 10%, 5% and 1% levels. Asymptotic standard error in parentheses. Two-step estimates are Windmeijeier corrected (Windmeijer, 2005). m1 and m2 are tests for first-order and second-order serial correlation. Sargan/Hansen is a test of the over-identifying restrictions for the GMM estimators.

Table 4.9 reports the results for the σ-convergence. In our case, σ-convergence indicates how quickly each country's efficiency levels are converging to the average. Recall that σ<0 represents the rate of convergence of $y_{i,t}$ towards $\bar{y}_t$; the larger is σ in absolute value, the faster the rate of convergence. We firstly estimated the model with pooled OLS and fixed effects (the Hausman test allows us to reject random effects). Potential problems with these two models are addressed by the estimation of a dynamic GMM model. The last column of Table 4.9 reports the SYS-GMM estimations results (equation (3)). Following Arellano and Bover (1995) and Blundell and Bond (1998), the use of a GMM estimator should help mitigate possible endogeneity problems and omitted variable bias. Results for all the estimations suggest an increase in the speed of convergence as the σ coefficient is always negative and statistically significant. Further, the SYS-GMM results satisfy the three additional conditions: a significant AR(1) serial correlation, lack of AR(2) serial correlation and a high Sargan/Hansen test.

4.5   Conclusions

This chapter examines the dynamics of cost efficiency in 11 Mediterranean countries over the period 1994–2008. For all countries, the results indicate an improvement in efficiency levels in the later stages of the analysis, from 2005 onwards (with the exception of Egypt). This improvement is particularly remarkable for Algerian and Moroccan banks. The overall mean efficiency in the region is improving, once more driven by improvements in the best practice. Spanish banks dominate the region, with average efficiency scores of 80.4 per cent against the region's average of 63.5 per cent. Spanish banks also exhibit the highest meta-technology ratio, and the ratios increase over time. This indicates that Spanish banks consistently improved their performance and their banking technology became best practice. Nonetheless, during this period of analysis, the average meta-technology ratio is increasing, indicating an ability of banks in all countries to appropriate the best available technology.

These results are supported by the estimation of β-convergence. The β coefficient is always negative and statistically significant, thus indicating that convergence in efficiency scores has occurred across countries in the MED-11 area. Furthermore, results for the σ-convergence suggest an increase in the speed of convergence, as the σ coefficient is always negative and statistically significant. This indicates that, whereas the technological gap is still wide, the gap is narrowing at a faster speed.

5
Impact of Monetary Policy and Bank Regulations on Efficiency

Although the quality and adequacy of banking regulation and supervision are often touted as the essential factors contributing to a sound and well-performing banking sector, few studies have produced empirical evidence to back these assertions. A common finding is that certain specific regulatory elements may have a positive impact, while others may do the opposite or invite instability. Moreover, an adequate and well-functioning regulatory system appears to improve various performance or stability measures as long as they are complemented by other institutional and macroeconomic conditions.

This chapter focuses on a very specific question: Are the banks in the Mediterranean more cost efficient in countries with sounder regulatory and supervisory conditions? The results echo the recent findings in the literature. Certain regulatory aspects, such as disclosure requirements, credit information availability and entry obstacles, are highly important. The presence of an explicit deposit insurance scheme also improves efficiency, drawing attention to the importance of enhancing confidence for depositors. Other findings are less clear and require further investigation. For example, although restrictions on activities lower efficiency, it is possible that they could lead to increased risks.

The next section provides an overview of the literature. Then, Section 5.2 summarises the data sources and gives an extensive summary of the variables used and their hypothesised impacts. Section 5.3 discusses the empirical results and Section 5.4 summarises the main findings.

5.1   Literature review

The literature on the regulatory and supervisory determinants of bank efficiency is still in its infancy. Most studies use relatively broad measures of regulatory and institutional conditions. For example, Dietsch and Lozano-Vivas (2000) and Bos and Kool (2006) draw attention to the importance of a number of "environmental factors", including those relating to bank structure and regulation, such as concentration ratios, capital strength and intermediation ratios. The authors find that banks that operate in less concentrated markets, with greater capital and higher intermediation ratios, tend to have lower costs. Similarly, Fries and Taci (2005) focus on transition economies using a broad measure of banking sector reforms, developed by the European Bank for Reconstruction and Development (EBRD), to find that banks in countries with an active agenda tend to perform better and have higher profitability.

Our study is similar to several recent studies that empirically assess the impact of regulations on different measures of bank efficiency. Barth et al. (2006) use the BRSS database for the years 2000 and 2003 to identify the regulatory and institutional determinants of net interest margins and cost efficiency in 68 countries. The authors' results provide partial support for the importance of capital regulations and supervisory power. More specifically, aside from private monitoring, most of the variance in interest margins and overhead costs are explained by institutional and macroeconomic factors. The stringency of capital requirements and the power bestowed on supervisory authorities are at best weakly associated with greater efficiency. These findings provide a broad support for the third pillar of Basel II.

More recently, Pasiouras (2008) also uses the BRSS databases and a large sample of banks from 95 countries, but develops cost and scale efficiency measures. Although the results support all three pillars of Basel II, the results are especially strong for the market discipline mechanisms (that is, the third pillar). In addition, the role of bank-specific factors, such as bank liquidity and capitalisation, as well as market-specific factors, such as access to banking and presence of government-owned banks, are reaffirmed in the study.

In a later study, Pasiouras et al. (2009) assess the impact of regulatory conditions on profit and cost efficiency of banks using similar data. The authors find that regulations that improve supervisory power and market discipline tend to have a positive impact on both of the measures. In turn, capital requirements tend to improve only cost efficiency while reducing profit efficiency. In addition, the results show that restricting banks' activities may improve their profit efficiencies and worsen their cost efficiencies.

5.2 Methodology and data

The model for assessing the impact of regulatory and institutional factors on bank efficiency is as follows:

$$MTR_{it} = f(B_{it}, C_{it}, R_{it}) + \varepsilon_{it}$$

where B stands for bank-specific factors that relate to bank i at time t while C and R stand for country-specific and regulatory factors and MTR is the meta-technology ratio as derived in Chapter 4, which is the bank-specific meta-frontier efficiency divided by the country-specific efficiency.

The Barth et al. database provides up to three observations for each country, based on the 2000, 2003 and 2007 surveys. Due to different completion times, the surveys give a glimpse of the regulatory conditions between the publication year and one (or even two) years prior. For example, the 2000 survey was sent to the authorities in 1998, with most results arriving in 1999–2000. In order to minimise potential errors from misalignments between regulatory and non-regulatory factors, the later ones were averaged over a relevant time period. Moreover, the time spans were chosen to ensure that the current explanatory variables are used to explain future efficiency scores. Table 5.1 details the correspondence between the regulatory and non-regulatory variables.

The level of coverage of the sampled banks is depicted Table 5.2. When the entire sample is considered, the database covers just over half of the entire banking assets. The coverage in the SEMC is significantly more partial, with the total assets of the banks in the sample representing between one-quarter to one-third of the total assets of the banks in the region. Moreover, the total activities of the SEMC account for a small proportion of the entire sample. More

Table 5.1   Sample correspondence for survey years

Survey year	Meta-tech. efficiency (MTR)	Other variables (B, I, M)
2000	Avg. of 1999–2001	Avg. of 1998–2000
2003	Avg. of 2002–4	Avg. of 2001–3
2007	Avg. of 2006–8	Avg. of 2005–7

Note: For all non-regulatory variables (that is, *MTR, B, I, M*), the averages for the given periods were used.

Table 5.2   Coverage of sample

	Banks in sample (number of banks)			Coverage (% of bank assets in country)			Share in sample (% of entire sample assets)		
	2000	2003	2007	2000	2003	2007	2000	2003	2007
Algeria	2	2	2	27.6	10.3	8.8	0.48	0.97	0.89
Egypt	14	14	14	32.4	34.5	47.8	3.10	1.91	1.58
Israel	5	5	5	13.6	12.6	15.6	5.05	3.35	2.33
Morocco	4	4	4	35.1	38.7	54.0	0.96	0.83	0.83
Tunisia	10	10	10	73.1	72.2	74.3	0.49	0.42	0.31
SEMC	35	35	35	24.5	23.9	31.5	10.51	7.65	5.96
Cyprus	4	4	4	51.4	73.1	79.9	1.09	0.91	1.19
Spain	65	65	65	97.8	94.1	95.0	29.08	32.66	38.31
Greece	8	8	8	65.9	66.5	69.2	4.96	4.63	4.99
Italy	80	80	80	19.8	19.2	17.4	45.79	46.19	43.34
Malta	4	4	4	46.6	49.2	30.7	0.41	0.39	0.49
Portugal	10	10	10	59.8	64.4	72.4	8.16	7.58	5.73
EU-MED	171	171	171	55.1	52.4	60.0	89.49	92.35	94.04
ENTIRE SAMPLE	206	206	206	51.9	50.3	58.3	100.00	100.00	100.00

Sources: Bankscope, national central banks and the ECB.

specifically, the total assets of the SEMC banks within the sample represented are between 5 to 10 per cent of the total assets of all banks in the sample. This is simply an outcome of the size of the EU's banking market. In order to ensure a balanced database, Italy's larger banks were excluded.

Among the 11 countries in the sample, Algeria has the lowest coverage. This is entirely due to the fact that most of the Algerian banks are publicly-owned, and little information exists. All of the covered banks in Algeria are owned privately. For Israel, the detailed balance sheet information was available for only a small share of the banks. In other SEMC countries, the coverage is more complete. This is particularly the case in Tunisia, where the total assets of the sampled banks represent nearly three-quarters of the total assets of all banks in Tunisia.

5.2.1 Bank-specific variables

Four bank-specific variables are used to control for the market power, size, liquidity and capital strength.

The natural logarithm of a bank's assets, defined as the **bank assets** variable, serves as an indicator of the bank's size. Size could be a determinant of costs if there are increasing returns to scale. For example, larger banks may be able to reduce their operating costs by cutting back on personnel and administrative costs. Moreover, if a fixed cost is associated with financial transactions, larger banks may also be able to recue such costs. Lastly, larger banks may be in a better position to diversify their risks and thus reduce their borrowing costs.[1]

Market power is measured by the *bank market share*, that is, the share of a bank's assets in total banking assets for the relevant years. According to the traditional "quiet life hypothesis", banks that are in a dominant position are unlikely to occupy themselves with cost reduction and are likely to behave inefficiently (Hicks, 1935). Alternatively, managers of banks with extensive market power may have other incentives than being efficient, such as "building empires" (Hughes et al., 2003). These theories would suggest that market share would be negatively correlated with efficiency.

Bank liquidity will be measured by the ratio of cash and due from central bank and other banks (that is, demand and time deposits maintained in other banks) to customer deposits. Capital strength is measured by share of *bank equity* in total assets. Well-capitalised and liquid banks tend to face lower default risks and are thus likely to face lower funding costs. On the other hand, in the MENA region, such banks tend to hold significant amounts of government debt, possibly under direct or indirect government control and with extensive market power, both of which could lead to inefficiencies. Thus, there is no clear relationship between these two variables and bank efficiency.

5.2.2 Country-specific variables

Three country-specific variables are considered.

Inflation is often thought to increase instability and decrease bank efficiency, since it makes price discovery harder and makes interest rates less informative about the underlying conditions. High inflation may increase labour costs and, by increasing the number of transactions, lead to an increased competition in excessive branching and other operational costs. Additionally, inflation exacerbates information asymmetries, increasing the costs of state verification (Huybens and Smith, 1999). Economic growth, or more specifically real GDP growth, is included to control for business cycles.

The third indicator, *institutional quality*, is built by aggregating eight dimensions of the quality of political institutions. These dimensions are: (i) polity, which measures the relative strength of democratic (or conversely autocratic) institutions, determining the extent to which the executive arm is controlled by regular checks and balances, guarantee of civil liberties, freedom of political expression and participation; (ii) executive openness, which measures the openness of the executive recruitment; (iii) executive competitiveness, which controls for the competitiveness of the election procedures; (iv) executive constraints, measuring the extent of authority that can be practiced by the executive arm; (v) political competitiveness, which measures the competitiveness of the political arena; (vi) control of corruption, concerning the perception that public authorities can exercise their power without obtaining private gain; (vii) voice and accountability, which measure the degree to which citizens can voice their opinions and desires in the political system; and (viii) rule of law, capturing the perceptions on the quality of contract enforcement, property rights, police, courts and likelihood of crime and violence. The *institutional quality* variable is the first principal component of the seven variables identified above. By using a single variable to account for the various dimensions, the principal component analysis effectively addresses the potential multi-collinearity concerns that would arise from including the variables collectively.

Institutional and political conditions are likely to be very important in determining bank behaviour, stability and performance. For example, giving authorities extensive powers in countries where political freedoms and checks and balances are limited could lead to a misuse of authority. Indeed, Barth et al. (1999) and La Porta et al. (2002), among others, find that prevalence of state is associated with poorly operating financial systems. Public interference may also be an instrument for politicians to expand or maintain their power (Shleifer and Vishny, 1994). Another interesting question is whether banking stability closely reflects the ambitions of politicians who are in power[2].

A number of studies find that institutional conditions matter in the determination of bank efficiency. Pasiouras (2008) finds that the degree to which a country's laws protect private rights matters substantially, such that banks in better-governed countries are much more efficient. Using a sample that is similar to the present study, Ben Naceur et al. (2009) show that several institutional factors, most notably the quality of the judicial system and a better legal system, are crucial in explaining cross-country differences in bank efficiency across four Middle East and North Africa countries: Egypt, Jordan, Morocco and Tunisia.

5.2.3 Regulatory variables

The regulatory factors are mostly based on the Barth et al. surveys (BRSS) and, for the case of credit information, on World Bank's Doing Business Surveys. The variables used and a brief description of their construction methodology, already detailed in Chapter 3 , are presented below.

The index *scope restrictions* measure the degree of restrictions on what a bank can do, including prohibitions on key non-traditional activities, such as securities and insurance underwriting, brokering, dealing, real estate development and so forth.[3] In theory, restricting the range of activities may have opposing effects on efficiency. On the one hand, allowing banks to take equity positions can exacerbate the moral hazard problems between a borrower and a lender, adversely affecting the optimality of investment decisions and the overall bank efficiency (Boyd et al., 1998). On the other hand, when banks engage in a broader set of activities, their ability to diversify risks is also enhanced. A more stable income stream can serve to reduce borrowing costs, which will increase efficiency.

Entry obstacles are measured by aggregating the degree of licensing restrictions, the rate of foreign denials (share of denials in total applications over the past five years) and the total market share of the government-owned banks in terms of total assets. A regulatory structure that is more amenable to entry is likely to enhance competitive conditions, possibly undermining market power and the potential for a "quiet life" (see above). Several studies find that foreign entry is associated with more competitive conditions, translating into lower costs and profits for domestic banks, (Claessens et al., 2001; Claessens and Laeven, 2004). Highly predominant state-ownership of the banking sector may also undermine the competitive conditions.[4]

The *capital requirement stringency* considers whether there are explicit requirements on the amount and type of capital allowed, risk adjustments and initial capital.[5] Although stricter rules on capital and an autonomous supervisor may make the system as a whole sounder, the impact on efficiency is less than clear. More and better capital held by one bank could translate into lower borrowing costs and may signal operational efficiency. However, when the conditions apply to all the banks, the informational benefits do not materialise. Moreover, more stringent rules may increase compliance costs, undermining efficiency.

The index of *supervisory independence* measures the autonomy of the supervisor from political influence, considering whether the supervisor is ultimately accountable to a minister, could be sued for his/her actions committed in exercise of his/her duties, and whether the head of the agency has an undetermined (that is, non-fixed) term.[6] Under the "private interest view" to regulation, politically-oriented regulators fail to maximise social welfare and may thus undermine private-sector efficiency (Shleifer and Vishny, 1994; Barth et al., 2006).

The *deposit insurance* variable is a dummy that identifies the existence of an explicit deposit insurance scheme. Considering the index's impact on bank efficiency, there may be opposing forces at play. Several studies have noted that excessive guarantees may result in moral hazard and may encourage excessive risk-taking and increase the likelihood of crises (Merton, 1977; Bhattacharya and Thakor, 1993; Demirgüç-Kunt and Detragiache, 2002; Demirgüç-

Kunt and Kane, 2002). These risks could increase borrowing costs, thereby lowering efficiency. However, having a safety net could also enhance efficiency, especially in the context of developing countries where the (shadow) cost of funds is often high since many potential depositors may not open an account, or due to the risks of bank runs (Diamond and Dybvig, 1983). By reinforcing the soundness of deposits, the schemes may thus lower costs and enhance efficiency.

The *private monitoring* variable is an indicator for the disclosure of information, which is at the core of market discipline.[7] The disclosure of reliable and timely information allows investors and depositors to better understand and monitor the underlying risks and inefficiencies and can serve as a disciplining tool on the bank's management.[8] There are some questions, however, on whether disclosure requirements and practices can really function in countries with poor accounting standards and underdeveloped capital markets, which tend to be the primary customers of such information. In responding to these concerns, Caprio and Honohan (2004) note that despite these shortcomings, market discipline could work to discipline banks, especially in countries with no credible deposit guarantees – explicit or implicit – where market participants have strong incentives to engage in monitoring.

Credit information is an indicator for the availability, coverage and depth of credit information.[9] Information-sharing can impact efficiency levels through various channels. First, it can reduce market power by breaking the information monopolies developed by existing banks (Vives, 1990). In this manner, making information more available can work against the "quiet life" that the incumbent banks enjoy. Second, it improves the accuracy of credit-worthiness assessments of banks, thereby reducing credit risks and the efficiency in the allocation of credit (Pagano and Jappelli, 1993).

5.2.4 Data sources

Perhaps the most important challenge that researchers face in attempting to assess the impact of regulations is the availability of reliable data on regulatory conditions. Presently, the standard dataset that quantifies the quality and adequacy of banking regulations for a large set of countries over time is based on the detailed results of the Financial Sector Assessment Program (FSAP). Undertaken jointly by the IMF and the World Bank since 1999, the FSAP regularly evaluates the regulatory structures of its members by assessing their compliance with international standards. For the banking regulations, the assessors use the so-called "Basel Core Principles" (BCPs) of the Basel Committee on Bank Supervision, which were issued in 1997 as a basis for their evaluations.[10] These assessments are conducted according to standardised methods developed by the Basel Committee and result in a score of compliance on each one of the 25 BCPs.[11] The IMF has compiled an in-house database that provides the level of compliance in each one of BCPs for all the evaluated countries since 1999.[12]

As the earliest study of its kind, Sundararajan et al. (2001) have used the BCP database to show that it does a poor job in explaining interest spreads and credit risk. Attempting to explain this counterintuitive result, Das et al. (2005) find that regulatory quality leads to a more sound banking sector with less liquidity stresses as long as cross-country differences in institutional quality are accounted for. Pointing at a stronger degree of conditionality, Podpiera (2006) finds that a greater compliance with the BCPs has enhanced asset quality and bank performance when various financial, macroeconomic and structural factors are controlled for. More recently, Demirgüç-Kunt and Detragiache (2010) fail to find a relationship between BCP compliance and systemic risk measures.

Taking a different route, Barth et al. (2004) have compiled an alternative dataset on banking laws and regulations, also used in this study. The authors' dataset (referred to henceforth as the Barth et al. regulatory and supervisory survey or the "BRSS") is based on the results of a worldwide survey, collected from national regulatory authorities in over 150 countries in the years 2000, 2003 and 2007.[13] Analysing the data, the authors find regulatory systems that facilitate adequate private monitoring (that is, disclosure requirements) tend to have a beneficial effect across almost all the indicators they consider. Other regulatory variables, such as the official supervisory power or capital requirements, have no or little impact. In later work, Barth et al. (2006) show that several institutional factors, such as the absence of corruption and the presence of voice and accountability, also have a strong positive impact on net interest margins and overhead costs. Using the BRSS, Laeven & Levine (2008) find that the impact of regulations on risk depends crucially on a bank's ownership structure. In particular, banks with more powerful shareholders tend to take more risks, making the link between regulatory environment and risk-taking ambiguous (even negative) when ownership is not accounted for.

Comparing the different approaches to measuring regulatory adequacy and quality, one of the main questions is whether the BRSS and the IMF's BCP assessments are measuring the same things. In theory, there should be substantial correlation between the two databases since both are based on comparable principles. However, Čihák and Tieman (2008) note that the correlation between the two databases is exceptionally low. The differences can arise due to a variety of reasons. Neither measure is perfect in fully implementing the laws as "countries may change the regulatory framework to appear better on paper but not on ground"(Barth et al., 2006, pp. 81–2). The BCP assessments are likely to be more illuminating in this manner, as they depend on independent assessments and not on self-evaluations. The BRSS, which relies on answers to standardised questions, is less likely to contain potential "grading biases" that are more likely in the BCP assessments.

Table 5.3 details the data sources and provides a descriptive summary of the variables used in the regressions in this section. The institutional quality and the regulatory factors exhibit substantial variance, which could make them helpful in explaining the variability in the bank efficiency scores.

5.3 Empirical results

This section investigates the impact of complying with the regulatory standards developed in earlier chapters on efficiencies of banks. Since the efficiency scores developed in Chapter 4 are always positive and almost always fall within the unit range, the dependent variable (that is, the MTR) is a limited dependent variable. The empirical estimations in this section use the Tobit model. Two specifications were used to ensure that the results are robust. First, Table 5.4 gives the results of a pooled regression. Second, Table 5.5 provides results for random-effects panel regressions. The effects of each of the regulatory variables were estimated separately in order to reduce the potential multi-collinearity that exists between these variables.

Starting with the bank-specific variables, the results are mostly in line with prior literature. Bank size, or the natural log of bank assets, has a significant and robust impact on efficiency. Larger banks are

Table 5.3   Data sources and descriptive statistics

Variable name	Source	Obs.	Mean	St. dev.	Min	Max
Bank efficiency (MTR)	Own calculations and Bankscope	618	0.817	0.160	0.310	1.074
Bank assets	Bankscope	618	8.165	1.523	3.456	13.724
Bank market share	Bankscope	618	0.047	0.111	0.000	0.780
Bank liquidity	Bankscope	618	0.033	0.044	0.000	0.443
Bank equity	Bankscope	618	0.088	0.045	-0.037	0.364
Inflation	WDI	618	2.754	0.874	1.317	7.278
Growth	WDI	618	2.944	1.579	0.230	6.134
Institutional quality	Polity IV & Kaufmann et al. (2009)	606	9.777	3.726	-0.060	11.699
Scope restrictions	Barth et al. surveys	596	7.065	1.528	5.000	10.000
Entry obstacles	Barth et al. surveys	596	8.155	11.556	0.292	55.233
Cap. req. stringency	Barth et al. surveys	596	5.045	2.863	1.000	9.000
Supervisory indep.	Barth et al. surveys	596	1.099	1.027	0.000	3.000
Deposit insurance	Barth et al. surveys	596	0.904	0.294	0.000	1.000
Private monitoring	Barth et al. surveys	596	8.440	0.995	6.000	10.000
Credit information	Doing Business surveys	400	4.705	1.256	0.000	6.000

Note: The Bankscope database is compiled and distributed by Bureau van Dijk; World Development Indicators (WDI) and Doing Business surveys are both distributed by the World Bank; Polity IV is developed and distributed by the Center for Systemic Peace and Colorado State University.

more efficient, which would confirm the presence of scale economies, in line with the findings of Olson and Zoubi (2010). In turn, market power, as measured by the market share, generally has a negative impact on efficiency. This result confirms the "quiet life" hypothesis, which suggests that the market power that banks enjoy leads them to forego revenues or cost-saving opportunities. Several studies have found evidence for such a relationship with a variety of efficiency and performance measures, including Berger and Hannan (1998) for the US banks and Maudos and de Guevara (2007) for the EU banks.[14]

Banks that are more liquid are significantly less efficient. As noted repeatedly in earlier sections, the SEMC banks are more liquid because they hold more government assets. Since the opportunity costs of holding liquid assets are low, such banks are also more likely to hold more cash and cash-like deposits in the central bank and other banks. The relative inefficiency of these banks appears to confirm the "lazy banks" view, which suggests that banks in developing countries that invest in public assets develop more slowly and are substantially less efficient (Hauner, 2008; Hauner, 2009).

The results on the impact of capitalisation on efficiency are less conclusive for the strength of capitalisation. According to the pooled regression results (Table 5.4), well-capitalised banks have a slightly higher efficiency than other banks; however, these results are not robust and disappear completely in the panel regressions (Table 5.5). It is entirely possible that the positive impact of the strength of capitalisation is offset by the business models of such banks, which, much like the highly-liquid institutions, invest more in government assets.

Among the two macroeconomic factors, inflation clearly has the more robust impact. More specifically, a lower rate of inflation contributes substantially to greater bank efficiency, which is in line with the literature, (Demirgüç-Kunt et al., 2004; Kasman and Yildirim, 2006). In turn, economic growth is generally positively related to efficiency, pointing to economic spillovers and potential opportunities for banks to reduce costs during bursts of growth.

The institutional quality variable, which is an aggregation of a number of institutional factors, including the strength of democratic processes, political openness, power exercised by the executive arm, election procedures, control of corruption, voice and accountability, and the rule of law. The coefficient estimates are highly significant in all of the specifications and point to a strong positive correlation between the quality of institutions and efficiency. These findings are in line with recent findings and highlight the fact that bank regulations cannot be viewed in isolation from the overall institutional framework (Demirgüç-Kunt et al., 2004; Barth et al., 2006).

Table 5.4 Determinants of bank efficiency, pooled regressions

	I	II	III	IV	V	VI	VII
Bank assets	0.028***	0.027***	0.023***	0.032***	0.031***	0.027***	0.022***
	(0.004)	(0.005)	(0.004)	(0.004)	(0.004)	(0.004)	(0.005)
Bank market share	-0.408***	-0.460***	-0.385***	-0.486***	-0.502***	-0.424***	-0.188**
	(0.053)	(0.063)	(0.055)	(0.058)	(0.054)	(0.058)	(0.080)
Bank liquidity	-0.410***	-0.151	-0.486***	-0.416***	-0.398***	-0.475***	0.138
	(0.104)	(0.119)	(0.107)	(0.115)	(0.107)	(0.112)	(0.122)
Bank equity	0.191*	0.224	0.210*	0.326***	0.262**	0.331***	0.168
	(0.116)	(0.138)	(0.119)	(0.126)	(0.120)	(0.123)	(0.135)
Inflation	-0.041***	-0.004	-0.029***	-0.025***	-0.034***	-0.026***	-0.030***
	(0.006)	(0.007)	(0.006)	(0.006)	(0.006)	(0.006)	(0.007)
Growth	-0.001	0.010*	-0.002	0.024***	0.023***	0.013***	0.031***
	(0.004)	(0.005)	(0.004)	(0.004)	(0.004)	(0.004)	(0.005)
Inst. quality	0.012***	0.005	0.016***	0.022***	0.013***	0.018***	0.015***
	(0.002)	(0.004)	(0.002)	(0.002)	(0.002)	(0.002)	(0.003)
Scope restrictions	-0.042***	–	–	–	–	–	–
	(0.004)						
Entry obstacles	–	-0.006***	–	–	–	–	–
		(0.001)					
Cap. req. stringency	–	–	0.020***	–	–	–	–
			(0.002)				

Supervisory indep.	–	–	–	0.010*	–	–	–
				(0.005)			
Deposit insurance	–	–	–	–	0.173***	–	–
					(0.020)		
Private monitoring	–	–	–	–	–	0.032***	–
						(0.006)	
Credit information	–	–	–	–	–	–	0.049***
							(0.009)
Constant	0.899***	0.591***	0.473***	0.329***	0.317***	0.191***	0.254***
	(0.064)	(0.063)	(0.042)	(0.042)	(0.039)	(0.049)	(0.047)
Observations	584	380	584	584	584	584	400
Wald χ^2 (8)	465.4	284.5	437.3	360.3	424.4	386.0	299.9
Log likelihood	482.9	335.2	468.9	430.4	462.5	443.3	337.0

Notes: Standard errors in parentheses. The regressions use the Tobit estimation procedures to account for the limited dependent variable, the meta-technology ratio (MTR), or the ratio of bank-specific meta-frontier efficiency and the country efficiency. ***, **, * represent statistical significance at the 1%, 5%, and 10% levels (p-values), respectively.

Table 5.5 Determinants of bank efficiency, random-effects panel regressions

	I	II	III	IV	V	VI	VII
Bank assets	0.028***	0.022***	0.024***	0.026***	0.027***	0.020***	0.023***
	(0.005)	(0.006)	(0.005)	(0.005)	(0.005)	(0.006)	(0.005)
Bank market share	-0.274***	-0.273***	-0.263***	-0.245***	-0.268***	-0.201**	-0.120
	(0.077)	(0.085)	(0.077)	(0.080)	(0.077)	(0.081)	(0.085)
Bank liquidity	-0.306***	-0.184*	-0.317***	-0.325***	-0.325***	-0.338***	-0.022
	(0.095)	(0.097)	(0.095)	(0.096)	(0.093)	(0.095)	(0.106)
Bank equity	-0.079	0.204	-0.108	-0.086	-0.070	-0.074	0.157
	(0.127)	(0.144)	(0.128)	(0.128)	(0.125)	(0.128)	(0.132)
Inflation	-0.016***	-0.012**	-0.012***	-0.012***	-0.030***	-0.011***	-0.021***
	(0.004)	(0.005)	(0.004)	(0.004)	(0.005)	(0.004)	(0.006)
Growth	0.009***	0.011**	0.010***	0.013***	0.008***	0.011***	0.016***
	(0.003)	(0.005)	(0.003)	(0.003)	(0.003)	(0.003)	(0.005)
Inst. quality	0.021***	0.013***	0.022***	0.023***	0.013***	0.023***	0.016***
	(0.002)	(0.004)	(0.002)	(0.002)	(0.003)	(0.002)	(0.003)
Scope restrictions	-0.010***	–	–	–	–	–	–
	(0.003)						
Entry obstacles	–	-0.003***	–	–	–	–	–
		(0.001)					
Cap. req. stringency	–	–	0.006**	–	–	–	–
			(0.002)				
Supervisory indep.	–	–	–	0.003	–	–	–

	(1)	(2)	(3)	(4)	(5)	(6)	(7)
Deposit insurance	—	—	—	(0.003)	0.140*** (0.025)	—	—
Private monitoring	—	—	—	—	—	0.012*** (0.004)	—
Credit information	—	—	—	—	—	—	0.035*** (0.008)
Constant	0.505*** (0.059)	0.544*** (0.072)	0.408*** (0.047)	0.400*** (0.048)	0.436*** (0.047)	0.358*** (0.050)	0.320*** (0.048)
Observations	584	380	584	584	584	584	400
Wald χ^2 (8)	258.2	226.9	252.8	229.8	282.5	243.6	278.8
Log likelihood	570.4	370.6	568.7	566.4	580.6	570.3	387.0

Notes: Standard errors in parentheses. The regressions use the Tobit estimation procedures to account for the limited dependent variable, the meta-technology ratio (MTR), or the ratio of bank-specific meta-frontier efficiency and the country efficiency. ***, **, * represent statistical significance at the 1%, 5%, and 10% levels (*p*-values), respectively.

Turning to the regulatory factors, it is notable that several variables have robust and significant impact. The presence of explicit deposit schemes, greater disclosure practices for better private monitoring, and the availability and use of credit information all contribute strongly to greater efficiency. The same can also be said for the stringency of capital requirements, although the impact is less significant in the panel regression (column II) in Table 5.5. Restrictions placed on banking activities and entry obstacles adversely affect bank efficiency. Prohibiting security and insurance transactions may indeed reduce the banks' ability to diversify risks and activities, which is by and large compatible with the literature on the higher profitability of banking conglomerates and universal banking, (Vander Vennet, 2002). Supervisory independence has only a weak impact on efficiency in the pooled regression (column III of Table 5.4), possibly due to the fact that other political factors, that is, power of executive arm, are readily controlled.

The positive impact of the availability of information on bank efficiency is in line with the literature. In particular, the idea that disclosure laws and practices that facilitate private monitoring tend to reduce costs is echoed in several studies, including most notably Barth et al. (2006), Pasiouras (2008) and Pasiouras et al. (2009). Moreover, Brown et al. (2009) and Djankov et al. (2007) show that availability of credit information is associated with lower transaction costs and moderation of credit risks, enhancing the access of credit of opaque borrowers such as SMEs.

A more surprising result is the pro-efficiency impact of the presence of deposit insurance schemes. The results reviewed in this section show that Mediterranean banks operating under deposit insurance schemes are significantly more efficient than those without such schemes. There is some weak support for these findings in recent literature. For example, Pasiouras (2008) finds that deposit insurance schemes improve efficiency (albeit at a marginal level of significance) when other regulatory aspects are considered alongside. In other cases, the availability of such schemes seems to have no or negative impact on efficiency. The results obtained here would seem to support the idea that having a safety net probably enhances efficiency by lowering the (shadow) cost of funds, especially in the MENA region where the level of access to banking is particularly low.

5.4 Conclusions

The results of this section clearly show that the banks in countries with a stable monetary policy and a sound regulatory structure are significantly more efficient. In particular, lower inflation, the presence of deposit insurance schemes, disclosure standards that facilitate private monitoring and the availability of and access to credit information all enhance the cost efficiencies of banks. The stringency of capital requirements also has a positive impact on bank efficiency, albeit to a less extent. In turn, according to our findings, there is a case for allowing banks to engage in a wider scope of activities and dismantling entry obstacles. Supervisory independence seems to have no impact on cost efficiency, most likely due to the offsetting impact of increased risks arising from concentrated political power.

In short, our results support mainly the third pillar of Basel II with weaker support for the capital requirements. The rapid deployment of private credit bureaus, possibly modelled after the regional best-practice as evidenced by Morocco's brand new system, is also important in enhancing efficiency. However, none of these factors should be treated in a vacuum. Institutional quality, measured here by an aggregation of a number of political and governance-related factors, is a substantially important factor. Lastly, macroeconomic stability is also an important contributor to the efficiencies of banks.

It should be highlighted that the results of this section have assessed the importance of regulatory and supervisory practices for achieving bank efficiency. Other issues should also be considered for making a broad assessment of the suitability and adequacy of certain rules and standards. For example, while certain regulatory conditions may improve banks' cost efficiencies, they may undermine profits (for example, systemic stability).

6
Impact of Bank Regulations on Growth

The key justification for introducing financial regulations is based on the idea that financial markets are imperfect and that regulations can effectively correct these shortcomings. The various areas of regulations considered in this chapter have all sprung into existence due to these considerations. Since customers often have asymmetric information regarding the operations of the banks, licensing and disclosure requirements are put forward to restrict the possibility of improper activities while providing the investors with adequate information. Capital requirements are an attempt to contain the risk-taking incentives of the owners of banks. The powers granted to the supervisors ensure that they have access to adequate information on the financial intermediaries and can act in a timely and efficient manner when troubles arise. Deposit insurance schemes are put forward to mitigate the likelihood that imperfectly informed depositors lead to a bank run. Credit information availability is crucial to overcome credit rationing, which arises when the financial intermediaries have limited information on borrowers.

If the regulations and supervisory practices serve to respond to market imperfections in practice, they should have a clear pro-growth impact. A better functioning financial market that properly treats the information asymmetries that exist between the banks, their clients and the supervisors should indeed help allocate financial resources more efficiently. However, the impact of regulations may be more insidious if the authorities choose to use their powers for their own good and not for the common welfare. Under this so-called 'private interest view', politicians may attempt to orient the industry to lend to their politically connected clients and banks may capture the regulators to act in their own interests. In short, the political imperfections may pose a greater risk to growth than the market imperfections.[1]

This chapter turns to a broader investigation of the economic benefits of monetary policy and regulatory and supervisory practices. The main question is whether banking regulations and practices have an impact on growth. Several channels through which the relationship may operate are considered, including the impact of regulations on cost efficiency, issuance of credit to the private sector and capital market activity. The empirical analysis also controls for the presence of other intermediate channels that are not accounted for.

The results show that regulations impact economic growth through their impact on bank efficiency and financial development. The role of government in the banking sector has a clear negative impact on growth, even beyond its impact on the identified intermediate variables. Thus, governments that are heavily present in the banking sector also engage in other activities that are less favourable to growth. Moreover, the impact of disclosure requirements, scope restrictions and capital requirements are mostly indirect, operating through the financial development variables.

6.1 Literature review

One of the key links between financial regulations and growth is the presence of entry obstacles as a key impediment to a competitive market. There are several conduits through which financial regulations may exert an impact on economic growth. A well-functioning regulatory framework can reinforce financial development and, in doing so, facilitate the flow of funding to the real sectors. The predominant view in economic literature is that a developed financial system can generate significant benefits for the economy. Although the idea that the development of the financial services sector is essential for economic development goes at least as far back as Schumpeter (1934), it was King and Levine (1993) who first empirically demonstrated a strong and robust relationship. Since then, several studies have confirmed that financial development enhances growth through the availability of external funds, higher employment, firm creation, and so on.[2]

Economic theory identifies two main channels through which the positive impact of financial development on growth operates. On the one hand, a sound financial system increases the availability of resources for investment by mobilising idle savings, facilitating transactions and attracting foreign investments. On the other hand, such a system can improve the allocation of funding by enhancing risk management, transparency and corporate governance practices; reinforcing property and creditor rights; and so forth. A well-functioning financial system is especially important for the development of the private sector, particularly small- and medium-sized enterprises, which represent a significant proportion of economic activity but lack the internal sources to grow.[3]

Despite its wide recognition, several studies have challenged the validity of the so-called "finance-growth" view. Most of these doubts rest on the direction of causality.[4] In particular, using a panel of less developed countries, Demetriades and Hussein (1996) find evidence of bi-directionality – and in some cases inverse correlation – for a panel of 16 developing countries.[5] Allowing for a non-linear relationship, Deidda and Fattouh (2002) fail to confirm the results of King and Levine (1993) for less developed countries included in their dataset. Similarly, Rioja and Valev (2004) verify that the relationship depends on the level of economic development, with little or uncertain impact on low or high extremes of the income levels. Using a dataset of 11 MENA countries over the 1979–2003 period, Ben Naceur and Ghazouani (2007) find that the development of banking and the stock market has no – or even a negative – impact on growth in the MENA region.

One explanation of these contrasting results is that some factors that are unaccounted for in the empirical analysis may explain why a financial system functions well and economic growth occurs (possibly simultaneously). The omission of these variables may then lead to an incorrect assessment of the direction and strength of the causal relationship.[6] In response to these criticisms, the literature has turned on these deeper structural conditions. Indeed, the emerging academic consensus is that financial development could be beneficial as long as certain conditions are present to ensure that the system develops adequately to serve the financial needs of the citizens and the private sector.

Development of financial regulations can also impact economic growth through their effect on efficiency and competitive conditions in the financial sector. The previous section has also given some evidence of the impact of financial regulations on cost efficiencies of the banks in the Mediterranean region. Although the literature on the impact of regulations on bank efficiency is currently in its infancy, several studies have reached similar conclusions. In particular, Barth et al. (2006) uses the results of their own regulatory and supervisory surveys (BRSS) to provide partial support for the positive impact of disclosure requirements on net interest margins and cost efficiency. Pasiouras (2008) and Pasiouras et al. (2009) also use same data source to confirm the results of Barth et al. (2006) while showing that certain bank- and market-specific factors also matter.[7]

A number of studies have also noted how regulatory conditions may impact entry and more broadly the competitive conditions in financial markets. Focusing on entry into banking markets, Cetorelli and Strahan (2006) find that state-level restrictions on bank entry reduce the share of smaller enterprises, effectively reducing the growth potential of the state. Larger firms are less affected by entry obstacles, as they can use alternative funding sources and have an easier access to capital markets. Restricted entry tends to support the market power of the incumbent firms, which could reduce the credit available to the economy as a whole and thereby have a negative impact on growth, (Cetorelli and Gambera, 2001).[8] Using a large sample of banks from the Middle East and North African countries, Turk-Ariss (2009) shows that the degree of competition, measured by the so-called 'H-statistic' first developed by Panzar and Rosse (1987), is positively correlated with foreign bank entry but is a decreasing function of activity restrictions.[9]

6.2 Methodology and data

The basic regression used in this section takes the following functional form:

$$Growth_{it} = g(F_{it}, C_{it}, R_{it}) + \varepsilon_{it}$$

where *Growth* is the real per capita growth for country i at year t. The variables F, C and R represent financial development, macroeconomic and regulatory factors. In order to capture non-linear relationships, the natural logarithm forms were used for most economic and financial variables.

The use of financial development variables as explanatory variables may pose a bias in our estimations, since economic growth and financial development may be determined simultaneously. To control for these potential problems, an instrumental variables approach has been used in this section. As in La Porta et al. (1997), legal origin (that is, French, English or mixed) is assumed to shape financial development. The use of legal origins as an instrument for financial development has been a popular tool since these institutional conditions can be safely treated as a purely exogenous (that is, unchanging) determinant of economic growth. Moreover, several studies have shown evidence that legal origins influence financial development through their impact on the treatment of shareholders, rights of creditors, effectiveness of contract enforcement and the use of international accounting standards. More specifically, La Porta et al. (1998) show that French civil law countries are relatively low performing in terms of shareholder and creditor rights, with less comprehensive accounting standards.[10] Two dummy variables, English or mixed legal origin, are included to account for different types of systems. Additionally, a dummy variable for Muslim countries is also included.

Assuming that legal origin indicators serve as appropriate instruments of financial development variables, F is equivalent to a set of orthogonality conditions for the instrumental variables on the instrument variables Z and the error term, $E[Z'\varepsilon] = 0$. Two-staged GMM techniques are used to estimate the models with the relevant orthogonality conditions.

Since the number of moment conditions may exceed the number of coefficients to be estimated, tests of over-identifying restrictions are carried out. These tests determine whether or not the instrumental variables are associated with growth beyond their ability to explain any variation in financial sector development. More specifically, the Hansen-Sargan test ('J-test') has a null hypothesis of correct model specification, which has an asymptotic χ^2 distribution with degrees of freedom of the number of over-identifying restrictions (Hansen, 1982). Failure to reject the test supports the validity of the model.

A second set of tests is also carried out to check the weakness or strength of the instruments. The so-called "Cragg-Donald test" is simply an F-statistic on the hypothesis that the instruments do not enter the first stage regression of the two-stage estimations. A failure to reject the null hypothesis calls into question the validity of the instrumental variable estimates and hypothesis tests. The critical values of the test are given in Stock and Yogo (2001). As a simple rule of thumb, specifications with a Cragg-Donald F-value that exceeds 9.08 will be considered to be appropriately defined.[11]

The regulatory variables, R, are only available for the years 2000, 2003 and 2007. Nevertheless, changes in regulations are relatively slow over time, as the results in Chapter 3 amply demonstrated. It is therefore reasonable to assume that the regulatory factors remain constant in the periods prior to the observed outcomes, that is, in 1995–2000, 2001–3 and 2004–7.

The sources and descriptive statistics for the data used in this section are summarised in Table 6.1. A number of country-specific time variant variables are used to control for macroeconomic factors. Real *initial GDP per capita* is included to account for fast growth in poorer countries. The expected sign for the coefficient is negative, implying a significant catch-up effect. *Openness to trade*, which is calculated as the imports and exports divided by GDP, accounts for the positive spillovers from an open current account. *Inflation* rate is included to account for the impact of economic instability or inflationary policies on growth. Lastly, *lack of corruption* assesses the level of corruption within the political system and the bureaucracy.

Three financial variables are used to assess the impact on growth. First, *bank efficiency*, which is the country average for the meta-technology ratio scores for the banks (developed in Chapter 3). Second, *private credit* measures the share of private credits to the GDP. Lastly, the *stock turnover* measures the ratio of stocks traded divided by the average market capitalisation for the period.

In addition to these variables, the regulatory variables already revised in Chapter 5 are included, including scope restrictions, government-owned banks, capital requirements stringency, supervisor independence, deposit insurance, private monitoring and credit information. Entry obstacles were not included in the tests as government-ownership due to a lack of observations for foreign denials. Instead, the market share of state-owned banks is used as an

Table 6.1 Data sources and descriptive statistics

Variable name	Source	Obs.	Mean	St. dev.	Min	Max
Real GDP per capita growth	World Dev. Ind. (WDI)	142	2.424	2.081	-3.607	10.577
Initial GDP per capita (log)	WDI	154	8.603	1.064	7.028	9.776
Trade openness (log)	WDI	153	-0.343	0.381	-0.958	0.700
Inflation (log)	WDI	154	0.037	0.031	-0.004	0.261
Lack of corruption (log)	PRS Group	154	1.116	0.343	0.405	1.609
Bank efficiency (log)	Own calc. and Bankscope	154	0.519	0.091	0.321	0.692
Private credit (log)	WDI	153	-0.389	0.829	-3.242	0.945
Stock market turnover (log)	WDI	140	-1.215	1.165	-4.143	0.947
Scope restrictions	Barth et al. surveys (BRSS)	137	7.526	1.595	5.000	10.000
Government ownership	Barth et al. surveys (BRSS)	78	0.275	0.303	0.000	0.958
Cap. req. stringency	Barth et al. surveys (BRSS)	137	4.869	2.141	1.000	9.000
Supervisory independence	Barth et al. surveys (BRSS)	154	1.760	0.893	0.000	3.000
Deposit insurance	Barth et al. surveys (BRSS)	137	0.766	0.425	0.000	1.000
Private monitoring	Barth et al. surveys (BRSS)	137	8.212	0.958	6.000	10.000
Credit information	Doing Business surveys	140	8.000	2.921	4.000	14.000

Notes: Bankscope database is compiled and distributed by Bureau van Dijk; World Development Indicators (WDI) and Doing Business surveys are both distributed by the World Bank.

indicator of the entry conditions, including foreign denials and the number of licensing requirements.[12]

6.3   Results

The results of the regressions are summarised in Table 6.2. The Hansen J-tests fail to reject the null hypotheses for the 24 specifications, implying that the instruments are properly used and are not correlated with the residuals of the (second-stage) regressions. An additional statistic, the Cragg-Donald test for weak identification, is also included. These results point at potential problems due to weak instruments in Table 6.3, which endogenously account for private credit except for the last column (VIII), which controls for the level of credit information available.

The results show that some of the country-specific variables do not matter while others have a significant impact on growth. In particular, our results reveal that inflation is not a significant determinant of growth in any of the specifications, despite a consistently positive coefficient estimate. Openness to trade has a weak positive impact on growth when stock market turnover is considered in Table 6.4, that is, columns I and VIII. In turn, initial GDP per capita also has a persistently and significantly negative impact on growth, which implies that poorer countries tend to grow more quickly than richer ones, as in Barro (1991).

There is broad evidence that lack of corruption has a relatively consistent and positive impact on growth. This is in line with the findings in the growth literature.[13] Corruption could lead to a number of inefficiencies, such as rent-seeking and avoidance behaviour, which may lead to substantial deadweight losses (Rose-Ackerman, 1975; Shleifer and Vishny, 1993). Mauro (1995) shows that corruption affects growth by lowering returns from private investment.

The results show that the three financial development variables have a relatively limited impact on growth. In particular, private credit (Table 6.3) does not have a significant impact (although all of the coefficient estimates are negative) when it is allowed to be the endogenously determined financial development variable. In turn, both bank efficiency (Table 6.2) and stock market turnover (Table 6.4) have positive impacts on growth.

Table 6.2 Impact of regulations on growth controlling for efficiency

	I	II	III	IV	V	VI	VII	VIII
Bank efficiency	6.118*	0.700	0.038	3.623	6.584	2.824	2.749	1.880
	(2.956)	(3.288)	(3.707)	(3.782)	(4.004)	(3.316)	(3.080)	(3.150)
Initial GDP per capita (real)	-0.920***	-0.977***	-1.328***	-0.928***	-0.878***	-0.876***	-0.974***	-0.907***
	(0.269)	(0.271)	(0.313)	(0.319)	(0.275)	(0.279)	(0.285)	(0.305)
Openness to trade	0.659	0.089	-0.172	0.268	0.661	0.104	0.148	0.993
	(0.490)	(0.472)	(0.828)	(0.500)	(0.461)	(0.456)	(0.472)	(0.621)
Inflation	3.883	6.885	6.599	5.979	4.119	5.696	7.364	2.991
	(6.866)	(7.168)	(8.575)	(7.678)	(6.596)	(7.668)	(7.244)	(6.313)
Lack of corruption	1.130	1.626**	0.169	1.635**	0.961	1.490**	1.412**	1.118*
	(0.722)	(0.637)	(0.946)	(0.702)	(0.853)	(0.654)	(0.673)	(0.678)
Scope restrictions	–	-0.242*	–	–	–	–	–	–
		(0.134)						
Government-ownership	–	–	-0.023*	–	–	–	–	–
			(0.013)					
Cap. req. stringency	–	–	–	-0.160	–	–	–	–
				(0.097)				
Supervisory independence	–	–	–	–	0.068	–	–	–
					(0.223)			
Deposit insurance	–	–	–	–	–	-0.358	–	–
						(0.427)		

	(1)	(2)	(3)	(4)	(5)	(6)	(7)	(8)
Private monitoring	–	–	–	–	–	–	0.301	–
							(0.189)	
Credit information	–	–	–	–	–	–	–	0.037
								(0.092)
Constant	5.922**	10.219***	13.522***	7.290***	5.362*	6.911***	5.096*	7.968***
	(2.688)	(2.384)	(3.306)	(2.531)	(2.872)	(2.392)	(2.750)	(2.525)
Observations	142	127	77	127	142	127	127	130
F-test (second-stage)	4.068	4.907	4.555	2.303	3.599	2.712	2.928	4.253
...p-value	0.002	0.000	0.001	0.0-p439	0.002	0.017	0.011	0.001
Hansen J-test for overidentification	2.057	2.955	2.178	2.824	1.961	0.704	0.448	3.075
...p-value	0.358	0.228	0.337	0.244	0.375	0.703	0.799	0.215
Cragg-Donald test for weak id.(>9.08)	10.01	13.62	13.71	13.56	9.92	15.70	19.91	16.34

Notes: ***, **, * represent statistical significance at 1%, 5%, and 10% levels (p-values), respectively.

Table 6.3 Impact of regulations on growth controlling for private credit

	I	II	III	IV	V	VI	VII	VIII
Private credit	-0.631	-0.839	-1.125	-0.953	-3.856	-0.433	-1.034	-0.196
	(0.984)	(0.780)	(1.194)	(0.780)	(3.105)	(0.761)	(0.957)	(0.475)
Initial GDP per capita (real)	-0.769**	-0.753**	-1.299***	-0.656*	0.402	-0.780**	-0.796**	-0.923***
	(0.382)	(0.335)	(0.286)	(0.336)	(1.103)	(0.307)	(0.318)	(0.300)
Openness to trade	0.671	0.431	-0.083	0.475	1.518	0.139	0.448	0.966
	(0.679)	(0.568)	(0.667)	(0.559)	(1.151)	(0.517)	(0.599)	(0.664)
Inflation	-0.181	5.856	13.660	4.545	-15.272	3.945	5.817	0.952
	(7.568)	(7.393)	(9.036)	(7.867)	(19.562)	(7.503)	(7.115)	(6.685)
Lack of corruption	1.947**	2.100***	0.977	2.292***	1.922*	1.912**	2.180***	1.295*
	(0.867)	(0.754)	(1.175)	(0.849)	(1.027)	(0.841)	(0.828)	(0.690)
Scope restrictions	–	-0.200	–	–	–	–	–	–
		(0.136)						
Government-ownership	–	–	-0.042*	–	–	–	–	–
			(0.024)					
Cap. req. stringency	–	–	–	-0.102	–	–	–	–
				(0.072)				
Supervisory independence	–	–	–	–	1.498	–	–	–
					(1.254)			

	(1)	(2)	(3)	(4)	(5)	(6)	(7)	(8)
Deposit insurance	—	—	−0.306 (0.418)	—	—	—	—	—
Private monitoring	—	0.514** (0.250)	—	—	—	—	—	—
Credit information	0.074 (0.109)	—	—	—	—	—	—	—
Constant	8.609*** (2.030)	2.297 (4.276)	7.024*** (2.639)	−6.144 (12.352)	5.691* (3.024)	12.530*** (2.822)	7.739** (3.220)	6.897* (3.652)
Observations	130	127	127	142	127	77	127	142
F-test (second-stage)	4.284	3.055	2.747	2.470	2.318	5.713	5.087	3.986
...p-value	0.001	0.008	0.016	0.027	0.038	0.000	0.000	0.002
Hansen J-test for overidentification	3.264	0.107	1.151	0.659	2.400	2.053	1.975	4.367
...p-value	0.196	0.948	0.562	0.719	0.301	0.358	0.372	0.113
Cragg-Donald test for weak id.(> 9.08)	15.80	4.779	7.127	4.475	6.148	3.556	8.163	3.457

Notes: ***, **, * represent statistical significance at 1%, 5%, and 10% levels (p-values), respectively.

Table 6.4 Impact of regulations on growth controlling for stock market turnover

	I	II	III	IV	V	VI	VII	VIII
Stock turnover	0.784**	0.393	0.312	0.577	0.779**	0.393	0.394	0.657
	(0.363)	(0.400)	(0.356)	(0.415)	(0.363)	(0.398)	(0.385)	(0.463)
Initial GDP per capita	−1.306***	−1.179***	−1.712***	−1.225***	−1.297***	−1.103***	−1.155***	−0.971***
(real)	(0.289)	(0.334)	(0.376)	(0.398)	(0.296)	(0.346)	(0.332)	(0.300)
Openness to trade	1.715**	0.854	0.360	1.194	1.868**	0.694	0.774	1.610*
	(0.805)	(0.902)	(1.227)	(0.938)	(0.774)	(0.862)	(0.885)	(0.840)
Inflation	4.864	5.737	12.913	5.510	6.756	4.806	7.024	9.622
	(6.482)	(6.762)	(9.510)	(7.437)	(5.957)	(6.830)	(6.928)	(7.145)
Lack of corruption	1.156*	1.320*	0.302	1.933***	1.303*	1.731***	1.554**	1.220*
	(0.696)	(0.730)	(1.044)	(0.735)	(0.787)	(0.638)	(0.686)	(0.672)
Scope restrictions	–	−0.225	–	–	–	–	–	–
		(0.153)						
Government-ownership	–	–	−0.043***	–	–	–	–	–
			(0.015)					
Cap. req. stringency	–	–	–	−0.149*	–	–	–	–
				(0.081)				
Supervisory independence	–	–	–	–	−0.186	–	–	–
					(0.218)			

Deposit insurance	–	–	–	–	–	−0.438 (0.447)	–	–
Private monitoring	–	–	–	–	–	–	0.274 (0.205)	–
Credit information	–	–	–	–	–	–	–	−0.130 (0.126)
Constant	13.785*** (2.685)	13.357*** (2.971)	17.426*** (4.388)	12.341*** (4.128)	13.844*** (2.771)	10.841*** (3.534)	8.839** (4.050)	11.496*** (2.610)
Observations	129	119	69	119	129	119	119	117
F-test (second-stage)	6.926	5.521	6.895	3.516	5.686	3.675	3.489	5.350
...p-value	0.000	0.000	0.000	0.003	0.000	0.002	0.003	0.000
Hansen J-test for overidentification	0.287	2.377	3.290	2.647	0.536	0.730	0.352	2.011
...p-value	0.866	0.305	0.193	0.266	0.765	0.694	0.839	0.366
Cragg-Donald test for weak id.(> 9.08)	11.07	9.827	15.01	8.701	11.97	9.172	11.76	15.28

Notes: ***, **, * represent statistical significance at 1%, 5%, and 10% levels (p-values), respectively.

Among the regulatory factors, government ownership has a weak but consistent impact, reducing growth in all three tables. More specifically, countries in which the state-owned banks are predominant grow less quickly. These findings are by and large supported in the literature. Barth et al. (1999) find evidence that government ownership of banks is associated with a low level of financial development, as measured by the available of credit to private enterprises. La Porta et al. (2002) find that government ownership of banks is associated with lower subsequent financial development and growth in per capita income. Beck et al. (2004) use firm-level data to show that public bank ownership tends to exacerbate market power of the incumbents and thus constrains credit to private enterprises.[14]

Other regulatory factors have a less consistent impact. The strongest impact is with private monitoring, which is positively associated with capital income growth when private credit is considered but not in other cases. Scope restrictions tend to have a negative impact on growth when bank efficiency is considered but not when the two financial development factors are considered. Lastly, capital requirement stringency has a weak negative impact when the presence of stock market turnover is considered as an endogenous variable.

These findings imply that the government's role most likely serves as a proxy for other activities that are detrimental to growth – possibly unrelated to the financial markets. In turn, the impact of private monitoring, scope restrictions and capital requirements are mostly indirect, operating through the financial development variables, since their independent effects become insignificant when some of the financial development factors are controlled for.

6.4   Conclusions

According to our specifications, financial regulations have a relatively limited direct impact on growth. Among the seven regulatory areas considered throughout the paper, only government ownership – a proxy for entry obstacles and market conditions – appears to have a consistent and significant negative impact on growth. Moreover, there is limited evidence that financial development leads to economic development. Although efficiency and stock market turnover appear to increase income per capita growth, private credit appears to have little (and possibly negative) impact.

These results show that regulatory factors operate mostly through the financial variables. Based on the results reviewed in this chapter, the regulatory factors considered in the paper have at best an indirect impact on growth, working their way through financial development. Moreover, lack of corruption has a clear impact on growth, which underlines its importance as a precondition for growth.

Several technical shortcomings have to be noted at this stage. First, due to the small sample size considered in the study, panel estimations were not feasible. Second, the similarities between the countries considered might have generated sampling biases, which imply that the results have to be interpreted with care and should be adequately re-assessed before applying to other regions. Third, the similarities between countries also make the task of finding strong indicators more difficult as the cross-country variation is relatively limited. This is indeed one of the main causes for the apparent weaknesses of the instruments for the share of private credit in GDP. Lastly, the regulatory variables are assumed to remain fixed over long periods; although this assumption is unlikely to lead to substantial biases, it creates another source of homogeneity.

7
Conclusions

This book sheds light on the evolving monetary policy and central bank practices and the changing regulatory environment in the South and East Mediterranean countries. Over the past two decades, central banks in the SEMCs have engaged in price stability objectives and financial sector reforms, with varying degrees of depth, engagement and success. Many countries have achieved more success as compared to the others (for example Morocco and Turkey), maintaining price stability, eliminating interest rate subsidies and controls, reinforcing the responsibilities and roles of the supervisor, improving the risk-management practices in line with the state-of-the-art, successfully implementing a deposit insurance scheme, and introducing a credit information system that may well serve as a best-practice for other developing financial systems.

The other SEMCs have been less successful in controlling interest rates as an operational objective and implementing key financial reforms. Such poor performance resulted in relatively poor asset qualities, as evidenced by high rates of non-performing loans (NPLs). The policies put in place to respond to low asset quality have either led to limited improvement, a decline of credit availability or both. The privatisation efforts have been only partly successful and at times have not led to any change in the market conditions and financial development. In Algeria, the publicly-owned banks continue to dominate the banking sector, accounting for over 90 per cent of total assets. In Egypt, although privatisation efforts have been partly successful, public loans and debt represent a substantial proportion of the portfolios of banks, which hampers financial development and growth opportunities. In Tunisia, a majority of the top three banks remain owned by the state.

As for the financial reforms in the SEMCs, despite some improvements, key weaknesses remain in deposit insurance, entry obstacles and the strength of legal rights. Moreover, some disparities have also become more apparent, especially in the potential for political interference and private monitoring.

Turning to the cost efficiency analysis, results indicate an overall improvement in efficiency levels for the EU-MED and SEMCs in the later stages of the analysis, from 2005 onwards (with the exception of Egypt). For the SEMCs, this improvement is particularly remarkable for Moroccan and Algerian banks, but for different reasons. The overall mean efficiency in the region is improving, once more driven by improvements in the best practice. EU-MED banks, in particular the Spanish banks, dominate the region, with average efficiency scores of 80.4 per cent against the region's average of 63.5 per cent. Spanish banks also exhibit the highest meta-technology ratios and the ratios increase overtime. This indicates that Spanish banks consistently improved their performance, and their banking technology became best practice. Nonetheless, during this period of analysis, the average meta-technology ratio has been increasing, which indicates an ability of banks in all countries to appropriate the best available technology. These results are supported by the estimation of β-convergence. The β coefficient is always negative and statistically significant, thus indicating that convergence in efficiency scores has occurred across countries in the MED-11 area. Furthermore, results for the σ-convergence suggest an increase in the speed of convergence as the σ coefficient is always negative and statistically significant. This indicates that, although the technological gap is still wide, the gap is narrowing at a faster speed.

When examining the impact of a stable monetary policy and sound regulatory and supervisory practices on cost efficiency of banks, the results clearly show that low inflation and a sound regulatory structure are forceful contributors to an efficient system. The case of Morocco is revealing in this respect. In particular, deposit insurance schemes, adequate disclosure requirements and credit information availability seem to improve the efficiencies of banks. A broader definition of the banking market by imposing fewer scope restrictions and removing entry obstacles also improves efficiency, albeit less significantly than the previous factors. The rapid deployment of private credit bureaus, possibly modelled after the regional best-practice as evidenced by Morocco's brand new system, is also important in enhancing efficiency.

Lastly, the pro-growth impact of regulatory adequacy appears to operate mainly though its impact on financial development. Persistent government ownership in banking is detrimental to growth, even outside the scope of financial development and other finance-related variables. Moreover, more restrictive disclosure and capital requirements as well as less limited scope restrictions have pro-growth impacts by enhancing financial development.

It is important to note that the regulatory practices and adequacy factors should not be treated in a vacuum. Institutional quality, measured in the study by a variety of political and governance-related factors, is a substantially important factor in all of the regressions. The control of corruption and the presence of democratic institutions are also important factors, which need to be considered alongside the regulatory conditions.

To sum up, the book highlights some of the key shortcomings of the banking regulations of the SEMCs. It appears that some of the newer standards, such as the Basel II capital requirements, have been conceived with developed nations in mind and may not be appropriate, due to a variety of deficiencies in information-sharing and institutional and disclosure mechanisms. A key aim of the upcoming reforms should be to look for ways to reduce the role of government in the banking sector while ensuring that the regulatory framework and the relevant institutional development adequately respond to the market imperfections.

Notes

Introduction

1. The European Mediterranean countries considered in the study are Cyprus, Spain, Greece, Italy, Malta and Portugal (referred to as 'EU-MED').

1 Monetary Policy and Central Banking Independence

This chapter and its annexes are authored by Sami Mouley and revised by Rym Ayadi. Other original contributions were published under Mouley, S. (2012).

1. In 2008 Jordan ended subsidies on petrol and gas products. This led to a sharp rise in the prices of these products in the local market and contributed to the rise in inflation.
2. According to Article 4 of the law on the Central Bank of Jordan, the central bank of this country, founded in 1950, is tasked with maintaining monetary stability, ensuring convertibility of the Jordanian dinar and helping to promote sustained economic growth.
3. This is due first to several obvious obstacles, in particular the practice of managed prices and the absence of economic and institutional independence of the CBT, and second, the necessary migration at first to a system of fully flexible exchange rate regime, which is not technically possible at present.
4. Nevertheless, the multipliers of the monetary base (and of the adjusted monetary base) for the M3 aggregate were, especially in recent years, higher than the projected multipliers, without correcting the accumulated differences on a monthly basis. Therefore the divergence between the monthly target for the monetary base, which is estimated from the target for M3 monthly growth, and monetary policy interventions are not eliminated between one month and the next, from whence derive the increasing cumulative differences between M3 and its intermediate target.
5. As for example open-market transactions, repurchase options repo, allowances uptakes, credit standing facilities or deposit standing facilities.
6. But also of some of its internal components including national savings, the external debt, the balance of payments outcome as well as the parameters for public finances; all provided by specialised agencies (namely ITCEQ, on the basis of its computable general equilibrium model used for compiling macroeconomic forecasts).

7. The target may be revised regularly according to occasional intra-annual updates on the development plan.

8. In particular, econometric studies on this question show that income and interest elasticities, which are estimated on the basis of this money demand function, although positive, reveal the relative weakness of the second parameter compared to the first due to the continuing incapacity of monetary policy to use interest rates as an operational objective.

9. Intermediate target used by CBT since 1989.

10. Regarding projected multipliers, see Chailloux, A., Durré, A. and Laurens, B. J. (2009).

11. At the M3 level, the average deviation in the period 2004–10, for example, was 1301 MDT, which also coincides with the global surplus liquidity in the banking system.

12. Cf. Chailloux. A, Durré, A and B.J. Laurens (op.cit).

13. Since the mid-1990s, Tunisia has been suffering from a "structural investment gap" (or a structural deficit of savings in relation to investment).

14. The CBT's circular N°86–42 of 1 December 1986 first introduced partial liberalisation of debtors' interest rates in a margin of 3 per cent around the money market rate, with the exception of those applicable to loans for priority activities. On the other hand, the credit interest rates, with the exception of those linked to returns on small savings (deposits in special savings accounts) and to sight deposits does not exceed 2 per cent.

15. The inflation rate stabilised in double digits. It also reached unusual peaks, sometimes exceeding 100 per cent (as was the case in 1994 at 104.3 per cent).

16. The flexibility of salaries and prices in the long-term means that output and employment converge towards their potential levels or their natural rates. The inflation is then explained by the Non-Accelerating Inflation Rate of Unemployment (NAIRU).

17. For a survey on the literature of this issue, see Grauwe (de), P. and Polan, M. (2005).

18. The formalisation method then consists of passing from a dynamic monetary model with a structural base to a reduced form one of the type $\pi_t = \alpha + \beta.\pi_{t-1} + \gamma.x_t + \mu_t$, where π_i (i = t, t–1) refers to current or past inflation, xt refers to a vector of empirical determinants of inflation and μ_t is a random variable or white noise.

19. For a summary see Chagny and Döpke (2001).

20. In this context, for example, the concepts of potential output and output gaps are assimilated as those of trends and residual components of a historical series.

21. The only drawback to this linear filter method is that it supposes that trends and cycles are determinist or are based on the hypothesis of independence between cyclical and trending components. On the other hand, the Beveridge and Nelson decomposition is based on purely stochastic definitions of trend and cycle, while Harvey's method (1985) allows determinist and stochastic elements to be combined both for trends and cycles.

22. See Guay and St-Amant (1997), Chagny, Lemoine and Pelgrin (2003), Chagny and Lemoine (2004), Ladiray, Mazzi and Sartori (2003) for a comparative analysis of these linear methods and Pedersen (2004) for an analysis of the non-linear filter methods.

23. As proposed by Laxton and Tetlow (1992), by incorporating additional constraints such as those resulting from the Phillips curve, from NAIRU and so on.

24. It is also useful to study the construction of an early composite indicator.

25. Another important component of domestic demand is price inflation for foodstuffs, in a free or managed (subvention) system.

26. In all studies on this issue, the pressures linked to domestic demand are formalised by the output gap constructed by the deviation between real GDP and its potential value or trend calculated using the HP filter of Hodrick–Prescott.

27. These data are available only on an annual and quarterly basis (since 2000). In particular the use of monthly values for the output gap calculated from filtered trends of industrial production index (as a proxy for monthly GDP) does not allow satisfactory econometric estimations to be established (cf. Infra).

28. To this is added, of course, price inflation for foodstuffs as a determinant of inflation in Tunisia, and incidentally visible from the comparison between inflation (headline inflation) and underlying inflation (core inflation) cf. Supra.

29. A specific methodology was used to calculate the TCEN on a monthly basis. For details, see Mouley, S. (2007).

30. We have used the international Brent oil price in dollars. The volatility of imported energy prices (Brent oil price) can in fact be used as a valid proxy for imported inflation.

31. Previous studies have already demonstrated that these are the obvious causes of inflation in Tunisia (see, in particular, IMF in 2008).

32. This is a suitable approximation of the cyclical position of the economy due to the absence of data on a monthly or quarterly basis for productivity.

33. Globally, the same results for estimates are obtained when the IPI is used to establish a monthly frequency from the quarterly GDP according to the Chow and Lin method (1971).

34. The output gap, calculated from the gaps between the industrial production index on a monthly basis compared with its potential value (confirming the argument of Stock and Watson, 1999), can also provide a determinant for the behaviour of aggregate demand where data are available only on an annual basis but which, however, are nevertheless fundamental to detect inflationary movements due to the rise in demand. However, the consideration of the output gap on a monthly basis did not provide appropriate statistical adequation in the models used.

35. The IPC is an index of Laspeyres (base 100:2000) calculated from a basket containing 952 products divided into six groups (food, housing,

clothing, health, transport, services and others) and 43 subgroups of products. The weightings are linked to the last survey on budget and household consumption.

36. See Favero (2001) on the utility of VAR models in literature.

37. The restrictions on the estimated coefficients deducted from a cointegration relationship permit construction of a structural model based on the estimation of a VECM shape with error correction. The imposition of long-term restrictions deducted from a cointegration relationship improves the quality of VAR estimates appreciably. We can convert the model to VAR-S by using a Cholesky decomposition applied to the residual vector $Y_t = \sum_{i=1}^{\alpha} C_t . e_{t-1}$. This decomposition ensures orthogonality of the individual shocks or that the $V(e_t)$ variance-covariance matrix is diagonal. In fact, this avoids the bias linked to the arbitrary selection of the order of introduction of endogenous variables into the VAR model.

38. Akaike's AIC criterion increases when passing from VAR(1) to VAR(2), which considerably reduces the number of statistically significant parameters. The number of degrees of freedom does not allow going beyond VAR(1). To evaluate the strength of the model, we modified the order of introduction of endogenous variables in the VAR model. The results obtained did not change significantly.

39. Cf. Chailloux, A., Durré, A. and Laurens, B. J. (2009), Kandil, M. (2006), Mishkin (1995), Égert and MacDonald (2006) for a survey on the transmission channels of monetary policy applied to economies in transition and Montiel (1990) for developing countries.

40. Impacts of volatility of exchange rate on prices (pass-through).

41. In what follows, this will be the nominal effective exchange rate because of the specificities of the exchange arrangements and restrictions in Tunisia (basket of currencies with managed floating) and daily interventions managed by the CBT, although specialised literature generally uses the real effective exchange rate.

42. Or regarding investment decisions (q of Tobin).

43. This effect returns to the approach of portfolio selection from Tobin. J.

44. The repercussions of this transmission channel cannot be established without data on the volume of collateral required by banks in Tunisia. According to inquiries made on the competitiveness of Tunisian companies (essentially SMEs), it seems that the main obstacle to private investment in Tunisia mainly consists of constraints posed by the volume of collateral required by banks for loans (cf. World Bank, Financing of SMEs in Tunisia, strategic study, Ministry of Industry, Energy and SMEs, Tunis, December 2009).

45. In particular, in an analysis of the transmission mechanisms of monetary policy, the use of VAR level models is justified due to the fact that transmission mechanisms of monetary policy are by essence short-term phenomena.

46. See the following impulse response functions instead of variance's decompositions.
47. This fundamental result illustrates the difficulty of using the interest rate as an operational objective, a primordial prerequisite to the migration towards a strategy of direct inflation targeting.
48. Considering the weak capacity for using the interest rate as an operational objective, the current framework of monetary policy, based on broad monetary aggregates targeting and supported by an active exchange rate policy, can effectively be used to control inflation, including imported inflation.
49. The contractionary effect of exchange rate depreciation is explained in theory by the hysteresis effect (cf. Edwards, S. 1997).
50. Base 100:2000.
51. In this case CPI: Log (IPC), ER: Log (TCEN), TB: 3 months treasury bonds rate and GDP: Log (PIB).
52. According to Akaike's AIC criteria.
53. In the following this also refers to impulse functions and not variance decomposition.
54. For a survey on this issue, see Olsen, K., Qvigstad, J. F. and Røisland, O. (2002).
55. The original rule of Taylor, applied to the USA for period 1987–92, attributes arbitrary coefficients $\alpha = 1.5$ and $\beta = 0.5$ although the inflation target is fixed at 2 per cent.
56. Or 'accelerationist Phillips curve'.
57. Unemployment gap rule.
58. The augmented McCallum rule, with inflation predicted according to Phillips' curve (or sacrifice ratio), doesn't provide good statistical estimation for the case of Tunisia due to the fact that monthly output gap that is deduced from industrial production index used as a proxy of monthly GDP is not significant and explains only a small part of inflation variability. Phillips' curve cannot therefore be used to generate reliable forecasts for inflation.
59. Technical details can be found in Annex 1.
60. Cf. Mouley, S. (2007, 2011).
61. On this question, see Loisel, O. (2006).
62. Hence, the Bank of Canada, for example, attributes a weighting of 1 to the interest rate and a weighting of 1/3 to the exchange rate. These weightings take into account the relative incidence of variations in short-term interest and exchange rates on production. The ICM is obtained by adding the variation shown by the 90 days commercial paper rate (PC90) since January 1987 (8.67) and the third of the variation (in log) defined as a percentage (×100), recorded for the exchange rate of the Canadian dollar in relation to the currencies of its main commercial partners (TCEN, 1992 = 100), also since 1987 (91.33): ICM = (PC90 – 8.67) + (100/3) × (log (TCEN) – Log (91.33)).
63. See Annex 2.

64. For more details, see Mouley, S. (2009).
65. The Bank of Canada has a standard of variations from 1 to 3 per cent for a time horizon of 18 months; the Bank of England had a standard from 1 to 4 per cent with the low range as the objective (that is 1 to 2 per cent) from October 1992 to the spring of 1997, then of 2.5 per cent or less since then, and the Reserve Bank of New Zealand had a standard from 0 to 2 per cent until November 1996 and 0 to 3 per cent since with a horizon of one year.
66. It took two years for another FED governor, Greenspan A., to convince private agents (financial markets, economic operators and so on) to believe in his indefectible commitment to fight inflation, based on monitoring its activities ("Learning process" or "Fed-watching").
67. But this idea is not new; it was first formulated in the studies of Blinder, A. (1982), Pindyck, R. (1976) and Kydland, A. (1976), which appear to be precursors.
68. The same methodology was developed in Tunisia by Laurens, B. J., Chailloux, A., Simard, D. and Durré, A. (2007), Renforcement du cadre stratégique et opérationnel de la politique monétaire, IMF – MCM Department, Doc. Usage officiel.
69. Blanchard et al. (2010).
70. Political stability is another way of solving the problem of credibility of monetary authority, in particular in a situation of information asymmetry. In an analysis of electoral policy which is a matter of "public choice" (Tullock, 1978), credibility positively depends on the length of decision makers' mandates.
71. Cf. Bade and Parkin: "Central bank laws and monetary policy"– Manuscript ; Department of Economics, University of Western Ontario (1980), quoted in Cukierman (1995). See also Parkin (1986), Leone (1991) and Castello-Blanco and Swinburne (1991).
72. In the approach of Alesina and Summers, it even seems that a higher degree of autonomy can restrict growth.
73. Cf. Annex 3.
74. Cf. Annex 4.
75. Cf. Annex 5.
76. Roll, E. (1993).

2   Overview of the National Banking Systems and Reforms

Chapter co-authored by Rym Ayadi, Emrah Arbak and Willem Pieter De Groen. Original contribution was published in Ayadi et al. (2011, 2013a).

1. See Levine (1997, 2004) and Demirgüç-Kunt and Levine (2008) for a review of the literature on financial development and growth.
2. Although alternative theories exist, financial development is often thought to improve income equality by enabling a more just capital

accumulation or skills development (Banerjee and Newman, 1993; Galor and Zeira, 1993). See Liang (2006) for empirical support and a recent review of the relevant literature.

3. Algeria's banking sector was partly liberalised in 1990 with the entry into force of the Monetary and Credit Law (Law No. 90–10), which abolished the interest rate controls. Other parts of the economy were also liberalised over the late 1980s and early 1990s.

4. The annual change in CPI grew from approximately 10 per cent in 1989 to over 30 per cent in 1992, only to stabilise at around 2 to 4 per cent in the late 1990s.

5. The financial reform index is a normalised measure built by aggregating the extent of reforms in seven policy areas, comprising (i) credit controls and ceilings, (ii) interest rate controls, (iii) entry barriers, (iv) privatisation, (v) capital markets, (vi) banking regulation and (vii) international capital restrictions. For more details on the construction of the sub-indexes, see Abiad et al. (2008), Appendix I, pp. 14–19.

6. The banking regulatory index, which is from Abiad et al. (2008), is constructed by aggregating indicators on whether (i) the country has adopted Basel I standards, (ii) the regulatory authority is independent, (iii) on- and off-site examinations are effective and (iv) the regulations and supervision cover all banks without exception.

7. The Law and Order index, provided by PRS Group, measures the strength and impartiality of the legal system as well as the popular observance of the law. For example, a country suffers a low rating if the law is routinely ignored without effective sanctions.

8. The most notable private banks include Calyon-Algeria (France), Société Générale (France), BNP Paribas El Djazair (France), Natixis (France), Gulf Bank Algeria (Kuwait), Arab Banking Corporation (Bahrain), Citibank (US), HSBC (UK), Al Baraka Bank (Bahrain) and Fransabank El Djazair (Lebanon).

9. Other elements of Ordinance No. 09–01, Art. 58 that relate to the FDI inflows include (i) a requirement to obtain approval from the National Investment Development Agency (ANDI) for all new investments; and (ii) the rights granted to the state and public enterprises to have a "pre-emptive purchase right for all sales by or to foreign investors" (see IMF, 2010a).

10. According to *Euromoney* magazine's recent bi-annual survey, Algeria ranked in 101st place worldwide among 185 countries in September 2010, the lowest among the four Southern Mediterranean countries.

11. Order No. 03–10 for Money and Credit.

12. The 2009 Action Plan is available in French at http://www.premier-ministre.gov.dz/images/stories/dossier/Plan_action_2009_fr.pdf.

13. The 2011–13 EU-Algeria NIP is available at http://ec.europa.eu/world/enp/pdf/country/2011_enpi_nip_algeria_en.pdf.

14. Since 2004, the Egyptian Treasury bills have often had yields exceeding 9 per cent, significantly above the overnight and short-term (3-month)

deposit rates, which remain around 6 to 7 per cent. These conditions allow the Egyptian banks to earn handsome amounts by simply collecting deposits and investing them in public debt.

15. As translated from Article 9 of Law no. 76–03 on the status of Bank Al-Maghrib.

16. The fiscal conditions have deteriorated in 2008–10 due to a jump in subsidies and lower tax revenues. These conditions are not expected to threaten the long-term conditions (IMF, 2010c).

17. There are several outward capital controls in place in Morocco; inward controls have been lifted in recent years. For currency transactions, exporters can deposit up to 50 per cent of foreign exchange receipts in the foreign exchange accounts. For capital inflows, commercial banks may only borrow abroad to finance foreign trade or investment transactions or for covering currency risks for customers. Also, outward direct investments of resident firms and citizens are subject to approval.

18. It is not entirely clear to what extent Morocco's credit guarantee scheme serves smaller firms. According to 2009 figures, the average value of guarantees currently stand at $155,000, or 60 times per capita income, which are much larger than regional and global averages (Saadani et al., 2010).

19. Currently, microcredit institutions are not allowed to take retail deposits.

20. Partly owing to their rapid expansion and diminishing asset quality in recent years, the Moroccan microcredit institutions have been hit hard by the 2007–9 financial crisis, facing unprecedented levels of non-performing and problem loans. In consequence, the sector has shrunk by 6 per cent in 2008 and is likely to face consolidation in the upcoming years (MIX, 2009).

21. In the IMF's (2008) assessment, the country's regulatory structure was compliant or largely compliant with 21 of the 25 BCP principles.

22. The tier 1 requirements have been defined by Regulation No. 24/G/2006 on the prudential capital requirements for credit institutions on individual and consolidated bases. Upon receiving interest from several banks on the use of internal model-based approach to risk, BAM has started work on preparing the guiding principles with a preliminary implementation date of 2011–12.

23. The coverage was raised from 50,000 DH by the 2006 banking law.

24. Regulations 27/G/2007 and 28/G/2007 of BAM. For more information on the fundamental aspects of the private credit bureaus in Morocco, see the document entitled "Enjeux et Modes Opératoires de la Délégation de la Centrale des Risques de Bank Al-Magrhip", 26 November 2007 (available at http://www.bkam.ma/wps/wcm/resources/file/eb455a459c84942/Dpliant%20Dlgation%20de%20la%20gestion%20du%20Service%20Central%20des%20Risques.pdf).

25. As noted in Madeddu (2010, pp. 22–23), this innovative "delegated model" implemented by BAM is attractive as it (i) prevents market segmentation

through the formation of credit bureaus that have data from only some creditors ("vertical informational silos"); (ii) can facilitate entry by other private information providers; (iii) prevents lenders' reluctance to share data directly with the private bureaus and (iv) supplements the central bank's supervisory role by creditor information.

26. The market capitalisation and turnover of the Tunis Stock Exchange remains at 15 per cent and 4 per cent, according to the 2009 year-end figures.

27. Other credit institutions, including development banks and microfinance institutions, are not included in the figures and constitute a negligible proportion of the financial system.

28. Law no. 58–90 of 1958 on the creation and organisation of the BCT was amended in 2006 (Law No. 2006–26) and in 2007 (Law No. 2007–69). The law on credit institutions (Law no. 2001–65) was amended in 2006 (Law No. 2006–19).

29. Regulation No. 91–24 of 1991 on prudential regulations concerning banks was revised in 2001 by Regulation 2001–4.

30. BCT's supervisory powers are defined by Law No. 2001–65 and its amendment Law No. 2006–19.

31. Detailed information requirements for large exposures were set by Regulation No. 2001–12.

32. CAMEL-type regulatory tools combine ratios on Capital adequacy, Asset quality, Management, Earnings, and Liquidity to develop a composite rating score that is used to assess the soundness of financial institutions.

33. According to the Tunisian authorities, an Early Warning System that permits the BCT to rapidly intervene in banks in difficulty is being created.

3 Convergence of Banking Sectors Regulations

Chapter co-authored by Rym Ayadi, Emrah Arbak and Willem Pieter De Groen. Original paper was published under Ayadi et al. (2013b).

1. For the discussion of the results and other aspects of the data, see Barth et al. (2006, 2008, 2012).

2. The number of countries responding to the survey varied over time. The original survey of Barth et al. (2001) had 117 country respondents, including a wide diversity of developed, developing and underdeveloped countries. The later revisions achieved greater participation, with 152 in 2003, 142 in 2007 and 125 countries participating in 2011.

3. The Banking Activity Restrictiveness Index is constructed by summing up the scores for the World Bank Guide (WBG) questions 4.1–4.3, as detailed in Appendix 2 of Barth et al. (2006).

4. In 2012, Commissioner Michel Barnier nominated a group of experts chaired by Erkki Liikanen to examine the need for reforms in the

structure of the EU's banking sector. In the final report published in October 2012, the experts advised the European Commission among other things to curb investment banking activities.

5. Denials of domestic banks are not considered here as they are more likely to arise from prudential concerns, including funding deficiencies or other financial problems, which are commonplace for home-grown banks in countries with less developed financial systems that have limited access to external capital.

6. Aside from their potentially negative impact on entry, state-owned banks may fulfil an important developmental role in under-developed regions. Recent evidence shows that in the Middle East and North Africa (MENA) region, public banks compensate for the low private bank involvement in the small- and medium-sized enterprise (SME) sector, engaging in more risky loan issuance, although they seem to have less than sufficient capacity to manage such risks (Rocha et al., 2010). See also Andrianova et al. (2010) for recent evidence that government ownership of banks is associated with higher long-run growth rates in developing countries.

7. The entry in the banking requirements index is constructed by summing up the scores for the WBG questions 1.8.1–1.8.8, as detailed in Appendix 2 of Barth et al. (2006).

8. The share of foreign denials are addressed by WBG question 1.10, as detailed in Appendix 1 and 2 of Barth et al. (2006).

9. The share of government-controlled banks is addressed by WBG question 3.8.1, as detailed in Appendix 1 of Barth et al. (2006).

10. The stringency of the capital requirements index is addressed by WBG questions 3.1.1, 3.2, 3.3, 3.9.1, 3.9.2, 3.9.3, and 1.5–1.7. The calculation of the index is detailed in Appendix 2 of Barth et al. (2006), pp. 337–8. One question (WBG 3.7) on the fraction of revaluation gains allowed as part of capital has been omitted from the calculation of the index because the responses were not available for most of the countries in our sample.

11. These results are largely in line with the key regulatory shortcomings identified for the region in Tahari et al. (2007), using compliance of European countries with Basel Core Principles (BCPs) on prudential regulations and requirements (BCPs 6 to 15) as a benchmark.

12. The official supervisory power index is addressed by WBG questions 5.5–5.7, 6.1, 10.4, 11.2, 11.3.1–11.3.3, 11.6, 11.7, and 11.9.1–11.9.3. The calculation of the index is detailed in Appendix 2 of Barth et al. (2006), pp. 339–42.

13. In these cases, the aggregate score is augmented by only half points; for more details, see the calculation of the index in Appendix 2 of Barth et al. (2006), pp. 339–42.

14. The independence from political interference index is addressed by WBG questions 12.2, 12.10, and 12.2.2. The calculation of the index is slightly different from the specification in Appendix 2 of Barth et al. (2006), pp. 349–50, in that to score a point in question 12.2, the supervisory bodies should be accountable to no one other than a legislative body, such as the parliament or congress.

15. In the case of Morocco, the governor of the Bank Al-Maghrib serves at the discretion of the king.
16. See Kane (2000) and Demirgüç-Kunt et al. (2005) for a review of the potential effects and key design features of the deposit insurance schemes.
17. Empirical evidence shows that the coverage limits and co-insurance practices serve to reduce the likelihood of bank failure substantially (Demirgüç-Kunt and Detragiache, 2002).
18. See Directive 2009/14/EC, which amended the Deposit Guarantee Directive 94/19/EC. The minimum amount of €100,000 has been in force since 31 December 2010.
19. In Egypt, although the legal framework allows for the establishment of an autonomous deposit insurance fund, no scheme has been set up yet.
20. The calculation of the deposit insurance scheme index follows the format detailed in Barth et al. (2006, p. 354), except that a score of zero is assigned to countries with no explicit insurance scheme. Three separate sources were used for the information on the deposit insurance scheme. First, the BRSS provided the basic information and evaluation for 2003 and 2007. Whenever the BRSS gave conflicting or incomplete results, the information contained in Demirgüç-Kunt et al. (2005), the European Commission's (2010) assessment of EU deposit guarantee schemes, and the legal documents from the websites of Bank Al-Maghrib and Banque d'Algérie were used.
21. Gropp and Vesala (2004) shows that credible implicit guarantees operating through the expectation of public intervention at times of distress can aggravate the moral hazard problem when compared with explicit deposit guarantee schemes. As the authors note, the key issue is whether the institutional and fiscal conditions would make the inherent guarantees credible. It is assumed here that the three countries with no explicit systems, namely Egypt, Israel and Tunisia, have ample fiscal resources and the necessary institutional framework that could make such guarantees credible.
22. Under Law no. 90–10 of 1990 regarding money and credit, the Algerian treasury was a contributor to the deposit guarantee fund (Art. 170). More recently, the government's funding role has been replaced with full funding by banks under the amending Law no. 03–11 of 2003 regarding money and credit (Art. 118).
23. This was amply demonstrated during the fall of Northern Rock in 2007, when the UK Treasury extended the existing guarantees on bank deposits – with a maximum payout of £31,700 at the time – to cover all deposits.
24. The private monitoring index is addressed by WBG questions 5.1, 5.3, 10.7.1–2, 10.1, 10.1.1, 10.3, 10.6, 3.5–6, 10.4.1, 10.5, and 11.1.1. The calculation of the index is slightly different from the specification in Appendix 2 of Barth et al. (2006, pp. 350–52), excluding a question on the presence of an explicit deposit insurance, which is already covered in another index.
25. The observation for Morocco is from the 2007 survey, since the Moroccan authorities did not report the equivalent number in the most recent survey.

26. These results may also arise from a small or highly concentrated banking sector. In such a case, only a handful of top banks will dominate the banking sector while the other (smaller) banks will be subject to less investor scrutiny.

27. First started in 2003, the World Bank's Doing Business surveys cover over 180 countries, providing a snapshot of regulatory and legal conditions and their effects on businesses, especially on SMEs. Each year, the surveys are sent out to a large number of local experts specialising in different fields, including lawyers, consultants, officials and other professionals who are in close contact with the legal and regulatory structures of the covered countries (the results of the surveys are available at http://www.doingbusiness.org/).

28. See the World Bank's Doing Business website for more details on the methodology (http://www.doingbusiness.org/methodology/getting-credit).

29. Rocha et al. (2010) note the essential role that public banks fulfil in the region by providing financing to the SMEs. The authors note that private banks are unable to fill this gap, largely owing to the generally weak quality of the financial infrastructure, including the availability and reliability of information on potential borrowers.

30. Morocco may serve as an interesting example, by effectively combining the data collection roles and capacities of the Bank Al-Maghrib, which operates the public registry, with the newly established private credit bureau, Experian-Morocco. For a comparative analysis of the Moroccan and Egyptian credit information systems, see Madeddu (2010, pp. 21–3).

4   Analysis of Banking Efficiency and Convergence

This Chapter chapter is authored by Barbara Casu. Original work published under Ayadi et al. (2011).

1. See Baele et al. (2004) for a review of different measures of financial market integration.

2. Similar specifications have been estimated, among others, by Fung (2006), Parikh and Shibata (2004), Weill (2009) and Casu and Girardone (2010).

3. Overheads comprise Personnel Expenses, Other Administrative Expenses and Other Non-Interest Costs.

5   Impact of Monetary policy and Bank Regulations on Efficiency

This chapter is co-authored by Rym Ayadi and Emrah Arbak. Original work was published under Ayadi et al. (2011).

1. The literature has obtained mixed results on the impact of bank size or scale on efficiency, although most studies have found that large banks

are either more efficient than or equally efficient to smaller banks. See DeYoung (1998) for a general discussion. For results that are applicable to the Middle East and the North Africa (MENA) region, see Olson and Zoubi (2010), who provide evidence for scale economies.

2. Using data on 25 emerging countries, Brown and Dinc (2005) find that bank failures are significantly less likely to occur prior to an election, pointing to a concern for loss of votes and increased attention paid to stability. Indeed, among the failures observed in the sampled countries in the authors' dataset, only 10 per cent have taken place within a year before the election. The study also raises another interesting point on crisis management: banks that are taken over by the government almost never fail, reflecting the underlying guarantees.

3. For more details on the scope restrictions index, see Chapter 3.

4. Although public banks may have a development role (Gerschenkron, 1962; Stiglitz, 1994; Hakenes and Schnabel, 2006) and may even be more stable than their commercial peers (Garcia-Marco and Robles-Fernandez, 2008; Ayadi et al., 2009), there is a general agreement that is backed by substantial evidence that undue public interference leads to an inefficient allocation of credit and risk-taking (Sapienza, 2004; Dinc, 2005; Khwaja and Mian, 2005; Cole, 2009).

5. For more details on the capital requirement stringency index, see Chapter 3.

6. For more details on the supervisory independence index, see section Chapter 3.

7. For more details on the private monitoring index, see Chapter 3.

8. The idea is at the core of the third pillar of the Basel II framework. Basel Committee on Banking Supervision's (1999) consultative paper on capital adequacy asserts that "[m]arket discipline imposes strong incentives on banks to conduct their business in a safe, sound and efficient manner" (BCBS, 2001, p. 1).

9. For more details on the strength of credit information index, see Chapter 3.

10. The Basel Committee on Bank Supervision comprises representatives from bank supervisory agencies from advanced countries, including Australia, Belgium, Canada, France, Germany, Italy, Japan, Luxembourg, the Netherlands, Spain, Sweden, Switzerland, the United Kingdom and the United States, as well as developing countries, including Argentina, Brazil, China, Hong Kong SAR, India, Indonesia, Korea, Mexico, Russia, Saudi Arabia, Singapore, South Africa and Turkey.

11. For a thorough review of these methodologies, see World Bank (2005).

12. The publication of the FSAP results, including the detailed Reports on the Observance of Standards and Codes (ROSCs), is voluntary. Although most developed countries have agreed to publish the detailed assessments and ROSCs, among the SEMC countries in our sample, a detailed account of compliance with BCPs is only available for Tunisia. Moreover, Egypt has agreed only to publish a summary of the FSAP 2008 report.

For these reasons, the compilation of the BCP compliance scores was not possible for our sample.

13. The covered years are approximate as the responses have been collected over several years in each one of the countries.

14. An alternative explanation is that the management of larger banks are more interested in 'building empires'. For a study documenting how such incentives may give rise to lower bank efficiency, see Hughes et al. (2003).

6 Impact of Bank Regulations on Growth

This chapter is co-authored by Rym Ayadi, Emrah Arbak and Sami Ben Naceur. Original work was published under Ayadi et al. (2011).

1. See Barth et al. (2006, pp. 21–46, 178–280) for more details on the public- and private-interest views to financial regulations.

2. For a more complete survey of the so-called "finance-growth" literature, see Levine (1997, 2004) and Demirgüç-Kunt and Levine (2008).

3. Examining a number of national surveys, Fadil (2000) finds that a general lack of access to credit markets is one of the principal constraints faced by SMEs to grow in line with their cash-flow in the MENA region.

4. For a review of criticism of studies linking finance development to growth, see Wachtel (2001, 2003) and references therein. See also Arestis and Demetriades (1997) for reasons on why cross-country empirical studies may suffer from serious methodological problems.

5. The only MED-11 country included in the sample of Demetriades and Hussein (1996) is Turkey.

6. The idea that unaccounted for factors and relationships between non-structural variables may introduce biases in the empirical assessment of policy impacts goes back to Lucas (1976).

7. See Chapter 4 for a more detailed treatment of the literature.

8. Although greater concentration in the banking sector may reduce the overall availability of credit, Cetorelli and Gambera (2001) find that it may enhance funding for firms that specialise in research and development, are highly dependent on external finance and develop long-lasting relationships with their creditors. These issues are less likely to be applicable in the Middle East and North African perspective since reliance on external financing is relatively low.

9. Using 2000–2006 figures, Turk-Ariss (2009) finds that market conditions in Algeria, Morocco and Tunisia can best be categorised as a monopoly. The banks in other MENA countries included in the study (Egyptian banks were not covered in the sample) operate under monopolistic competition.

10. These results are by and large confirmed in our sample. The three countries with elements of common British law (Cyprus, Israel and Malta)

score very high on creditors' rights and the certified audit requirement for banks.

11. For our purposes, the Cragg-Donald threshold of 9.08 (with three instruments and a single endogenous variable) corresponds to a maximum bias of 10 per cent at the 5 per cent significance level. For more information, see Stock and Yogo (2001, Table 1).

12. For more details on entry obstacles, see Chapter 3.2.2. The pairwise correlation coefficients between the market share of state-owned banks on the one hand and the licensing requirement and foreign denial scores on the other are 0.270 and 0.435, respectively.

13. Several studies linking the impact of financial development to growth have used black market premia to account for corruption-related factors (Beck et al., 2000; Beck and Levine, 2004; Ben Naceur and Ghazouani, 2007).

14. Part of the literature argues that excessive government ownership can be harmful because politicians use government-owned banks to further their own political goals (Shleifer and Vishny, 1994; La Porta et al., 2002). Dinc (2005) provides support to this 'political view' that public bank policies are often politically-oriented in finding that public banks increase their lending in election years. Caprio and Peria (2000) show that state ownership of banking is associated with a greater likelihood of crises. The latter finding should also be considered in light of evidence that public banks in developing countries are often more stable than their privately-owned counterparts (Ayadi et al., 2009).

Annex

1. The Autoregressive Integrated Moving Average (ARIMA) models are generalizations of autoregressive models AR(p). For useful details, see Hamilton (1994).

2. These conclusions confirm previous results established by Senhadji, Saadi Sedik and Kpodar, IMF (2007).

3. See below.

4. Here, $k>0$ means that the employment notional objective is higher than the natural rate normalised to zero.

References

Abiad, A., T. Tressel and E. Detragiache (2008), *A New Database of Financial Reforms*, IMF Working Paper No. 08/266, International Monetary Fund, Washington, D.C.

Abrams, R., R. Froyen and R. Waud (1980), Monetary policy reaction functions, consistent expectations and burn Era, *Journal of Money, Credit and Banking*, Vol. 12 (pp 30–42), February.

Adams, C. and D. Gros (1986), The Consequences of Real Exchange Rate Rules for Inflation: Some Illustration Examples, IMF Staff papers, Vol. 33 (pp 439–76), September.

Aglietta, M. (1992), L'indépendance des banques centrales: Leçons pour la banque centrale européenne, *Revue d'économie financière*, Vol. 22, No. 3 (pp 37–56).

Aglietta, M. (1993), Crises et cycles financiers. Une approche comparative, *Revue d'économie financière*, Vol. 26, automne (pp 5–50).

Agénor, P.R. (1994), Credibility and exchange rate management in developing countries, *Journal of development economics*, Vol. 45 (pp 1–15), August.

Agénor, P.R., J. Bhandari and R. Flood (1992), Speculative Attacks and Models of Balance of Payments Crises, IMF Staff Papers, Vol. 39, No. 2, June.

Agénor, P.R. and M.P. Taylor (1992), Testing for Credibility Effects, IMF Staff Papers, Vol. 39, No. 3 (pp 545–71).

Agliata, M. (1992), L'indépendance des Banques centrales. Leçons pour la Banque Centrale Européenne, *Revue d'Economie Financière*, No. 22 (pp 37–56), Autumn.

Al Nowaihi, A. and P. Levine (1996), Independent but accountable: Walsh contracts and the credibility Problem, CEPR discussion paper, No. 1387, April.

Alba, P., L. Hernandez and D. Klingebiel (1999), Financial Liberalisation and the Capital Account: Thailand 1988–1997, World Bank, Policy Research Working Paper Series, No. 2188.

Alesina, A. (1988), Macroeconomics and Politics, *NBER Macroeconomics Annual*, edited by Stanley Fischer, Cambridge, Mass., MIT Press, pp. 17–52.

Alesina, A. (1989), Politics and business cycles in industrial democracies, Economic Policy – A European Forum No. 8 (pp 57–98), April.

Alesina, A. and R. Gatti (1995), How independent should the Central Bank be? *American Economic Review*, Vol. 85, No. 2 (pp 196–200), May.

Alesina, A. and V. Grilli (1991), The European Central Bank: reshaping monetary politics in Europe, CEPR discussion papers N563, July (also appeared in *Establishing a Central Bank: Issues in Europe and Lessons from The United States*, Canzoneri, M., V. Grilli, and P. Masson (eds) (pp 49–77), Cambridge University Press).

Alesina, A. and V. Grilli (1992), The European Central Bank: reshaping monetary politics in Europe. *Establishing a Central Bank: Issues in Europe and Lessons from the US*, p. 49.

Alesina, A. and L. Summers (1993), Central Bank independence and Macroeconomic performance: some comparative evidence, *Journal of Money, Credit and Banking*, Vol. 25, No. 2 (pp 151–62).

Alesina, A. and G. Tabellini (1988a), Credibility and politics, *European Economic Review*, Vol. 32.

Alesina, A. and G. Tabellini (1988b), Rules and discretion with non-coordinated monetary and fiscal policies, *Economic Inquiry*, Vol. 33.

Alesina, A. and G. Tabellini (1990), A positive theory of Fiscal deficit and government Debt, *Review of Economic Studies*, Vol. 57 (pp 403–14), July.

Al-Mashat, R. (2007), Exchange Rate Pass-Through in Egypt, Central Bank of Egypt, mimeo.

Alper, E.C. and Z. Onis (2003), The Turkish Banking System, Financial Crises and the IMF in the Age of Capital Account Liberalisation: A Political Economy Perspective, Paper presented at the Fourth Mediterranean Social and Political Research Meeting, Florence-Montecatini Terme, 19–23 March.

Andersen, T.M (1986), Rules versus discretion in monetary policy: the case of asymmetric information, *Journal of Economic Dynamics and Control*, Vol. 10 (pp 169–74).

Andersen, T.M. (1989), Credibility of policy announcements: the output and inflation costs of disinflationary policies, *European Economic review*, Vol. 33, No. 1 (pp 13–30).

Andersen, T.M. and O. Risager (1991), The role of credibility for the effects of a change in the exchange-rate policy, *Oxford Economic Papers* Vol. 41 (pp 85–98), January.

Andrianova, S., P. Demetriades and A.K. Shortland (2010), Government Ownership of Banks, Institutions and Economic Growth, *Discussion Papers in Economics*, No. 11/01, Department of Economics, University of Leicester.

Arellano, M. and O. Bover (1995), Another look at the instrumental variables estimation of error components models, *Journal of Econometrics*, Vol. 68.

Arestis, P. and P.O. Demetriades (1997), Financial development and economic growth: assessing the evidence, *Economic Journal*, Vol. 107, No. 442.

Arnone, M., J.B. Laurens and J.F. Segalotto (2006), Measures of Central Bank Autonomy: Empirical Evidence for OECD, Developing and Emerging Market Economies, IMF Working Paper No. 06–228, October.

Artus, P. (1987), Fixation de l'objectif monétaire et réputation de la Banque Centrale, *Revue Economique*; Vol. 38, No 4 (pp 807–35), July.

Artus, P. (1995), Pourquoi le gradualisme des politiques monétaires, Cahiers économiques et monétaires No. 44, Banque de France.

Artus, P. (1996), La spéculation, *Revue économique*, Vol. 47, No. 3, May.

Artus, P. (2009), Quelques lecons de la crise pour les politiques monétaires, Recherche Economique, Natixis, Flash Economie No. 379, August.

Aubin, C. (1994), Union monétaire et hétérogénéité des préférences inflationnistes, GRIEF- cahier de recherches de l'université de Poitiers.

Aubin, C. (1995), Indépendance de la Banque Centrale: l'argument du conservatisme reconsidéré, *Revue d'Economie Politique*, Vol. 105, No. 3.

Auernheimer, L. (1974), The honest government's guide to the revenue from the creation of money. *Journal of political economy*, Vol. 82 (pp 598–606).

Auernheimer, L. (1987), On the outcome of inconsistent programs under exchange rate and monetary rules, *Journal of Monetary Economics*, Vol. 19 (pp 279–305).

Aumann, R.J. (1976), Agreeing to disagree, *Annals of Statistics*, Vol. 4.

Ayadi, R., Schmidt, R., Carbo-Valverde, S., Arbak, E., & Rodríguez-Fernández, F. (2009), *Investigating Diversity in the Banking Sector in Europe: The Performance and Role of Savings Banks,* CEPS Paperback, CEPS.

Ayadi, R., E. Arbak, S. Ben Naceur and B. Casu (2011), *Convergence of Bank Regulation on International Norms in the Southern Mediterranean: Impact on Performance and Growth*, Centre for European Policy Studies (CEPS), Brussels.

Ayadi, R., E. Arbak, S. Ben Naceur, W.P. De Groen (2013a), Determinants of financial development across the Mediterranean, MEDPRO Technical Report, N° 29, Mediterranean Prospects (MEDPRO).

Ayadi, R., E. Arbak, W.P. De Groen (2013b), Convergence and Integration of Banking Sector Regulations in the Euro-Mediterranean area: Trends and Challenges, MEDPRO Technical Report, No. 34, Mediterranean Prospects (MEDPRO).

Backus, D. and J. Driffill (1985b), Inflation and Reputation, *American Economic Review*, Vol. 75, No. 3 (pp 530–38), June.

Bade, R. and M. Parkin (1980, 1985), Central Bank Laws and Monetary Policy, Manuscript, Department of Economics, University of Western Ontario. Cited in Cukierman, A. (1995).

Baele, L.M., A. Ferrando, P. Hordahl, E. Krylova and C. Monnet (2004), Measuring financial integration in the euro area, ECB Occasional Paper No. 14, European Central Bank, Frankfurt.

Bahmani-Oskooee, M. and I. Domac (2003), On the link between dollarisation and inflation: evidence from Turkey, *Comparative Economic Studies*, Vol. 45, No. 3 (pp 306–328).

Bailey, M. (1956), The welfare cost of inflationary finance, *Journal of political Economy*, Vol. 64 (pp 93–110).

Balino, T.J. and C. Cottarelli (1994), Frameworks for Monetary Stability: Policy Issues and Country Experiences, IMF, Washington D.C.

Ball, L. (1990), Credible Disinflations with Staggered Price Setting, NBER Working Paper No. 3555, December.

Ball, L. (1999), Policy rules for open economies, in J.B. Taylor (ed.), *Monetary Policy Rules*, Chicago, Chicago University Press.

Banerjee, A.V. and A.F. Newman (1993), Occupational choice and the process of development, *Journal of Political Economy*, Vol. 101, No. 2.

Banker, R.D. and R. Natarajan (2008), Evaluating contextual variables affecting productivity using data envelopment analysis, *Operations Research*, Vol. 56, No. 1.

Banker, R.D., A. Charnes and W.W. Cooper (1984), Some models for the estimating technical and scale inefficiency in data envelopment analysis, *Management Science*, Vol. 30.

Banque Centrale de Tunisia (2011a), Réglementation bancaire.

Banque Centrale de Tunisia (2011b), Réglementation des changes.

Bårdsen, G., E. Jansen and R. Nymoen (1999), Econometric Inflation Targeting, Norges Bank Working Paper, No 99–05.

Barro, R.J. and Sala-i-Martin, X. (1991), Convergence across states and regions, Brooking Papers on Economic Activity, Vol. 1, No. 4 (pp 107–182).

Barro, R.J. and Sala-i-Martin, X. (1992), Convergence, Journal of Political Economy, Vol. 100, No. 2 (pp 223–51).

Barro, R.J. and Sala-i-Martin, X. (1995), Economic Growth, New York, McGraw-Hill.

Barro, R. (1976), Rational expectations and the role of monetary policy, *Journal of Monetary Economics*, Vol. 2, No. 1 (pp 1–32).

Barro, R. (1979), On the determination of the public debt, *Journal of Political Economy*, Vol. 87 (pp 940–71).

Barro, R. (1983), Inflationary finance under discretion and rules, *The Canadian Journal of Economics*, Vol. XVI, No. 1 (pp 1–17), February.

Barro, R. (1986a), Recent developments in the theory of rules vs discretion, *Economic Journal – Supplement*, Vol. 96 (pp 23–37).

Barro, R. (1986b), Reputation in a model of monetary policy with incomplete information, *Journal of Monetary Economics*, Vol. 17 (pp 3–20).

Barro, R.J. (1991), Economic growth in a cross section of countries, *Quarterly Journal of Economics*, Vol. 106, No. 2.

Barro, R.J. and D. Gordon (1983a), A positive theory of monetary policy in a natural rate model, *Journal of Political Economy*, Vol. 91 , No. 4 (pp 589–610).

Barro, R.J. and D. Gordon (1983b), Rules, discretion and reputation in a model of monetary policy, *Journal of Monetary Economics*, Vol. 12 (pp 101–21).

Barro, R.J. and X.X. Sala-i-Martin (1991), Convergence across states and regions, Brookings Papers on Economic Activity, No. 1, Brookings Institution, Washington, D.C.

Barro, R.J. and X.X. Sala-i-Martin (1992), Convergence, *Journal of Political Economy*, Vol. 100.

Barro, R.J. and X.X. Sala-i-Martin (1995), *Economic growth*, New York, McGraw Hill.

Barth, J.R., G. Caprio Jr. and R. Levine (1999), Banking Systems around the Globe: Do Regulation and Ownership Affect Performance and Stability?, Policy Research Working Paper No. 2325, World Bank, Washington, D.C.

Barth, J.R., G. Caprio Jr. and R. Levine (2001), The Regulation and Supervision of Banks Around the World: A New Database, Policy Research Working Paper No. 2588, World Bank, Washington, D.C.

Barth, J.R., G. Caprio Jr. and R. Levine (2004), Bank regulation and supervision: What works best?, *Journal of Financial Intermediation*, Vol. 13, No. 2.

Barth, J.R., G. Caprio Jr. and R. Levine (2006), *Rethinking Bank Supervision and Regulation: Till Angels Govern*, Cambridge, Cambridge University Press.

Barth, J.R., G. Caprio Jr. and R. Levine (2008), Bank regulations are changing: but for better or worse? Policy Research Working Paper No. 4646, World Bank, Washington, D.C.

Barth, J.R., G. Caprio Jr. and R. Levine (2012), *The Evolution and Impact of Bank Regulations*, Policy Research Working Paper No. 6288, World Bank, Washington, D.C.

Batini, N., R. Harrison and S. Millard (2001), Monetary Policy Rules for an Open Economy, Bank of England Working Paper, no 91.

Battese, G.E. and T.J. Coelli (1995), A model for technical inefficiency effects in a stochastic frontier production function for panel data, *Empirical Economics*, Vol. 20.

Battese, G.E., D.S. Prasada Rao and C.J. O'Donnell (2004), A meta-frontier production function for estimation of technical efficiencies and technology gaps for firms operating under different technologies, *Journal of Productivity Analysis*, Vol. 21, No. 1.

Baxter, M. and R.G. King (1995), Measuring Business-Cycles: Approximate Band-Pass Filters for Economic Time Series, Working Paper No. 5022, National Bureau of Economic Research.

Baxter, M. and R.G. King (1999), Measuring business cycles: approximate band-pass filters for economic time series, *The Review of Economics and Statistics*, Vol. 81 (pp 575–93).

BCBS (Basel Committee on Banking Supervision) (2001), Working Paper on Pillar 3 – Market Discipline, Bank for International Settlements (BIS), Geneva, September.

Beck, T. and A. Demirgüç-Kunt (2009), Financial Institutions and Markets Across Countries and over Time: Data and Analysis, Policy Research Working Paper No. 4943, World Bank, Washington, D.C.

Beck, T., A. Demirgüç-Kunt and V. Maksimovic (2004), Bank competition and access to finance: international evidence, *Journal of Money, Credit, and Banking*, Vol. 36, No. 3.

Beck, T. and R. Levine (2004), Stock markets, banks, and growth: panel evidence, *Journal of Banking and Finance*, Vol. 28, No. 3.

Beck, T., R. Levine and N. Loayza (2000), Finance and the sources of growth, *Journal of Financial Economics*, Vol. 58, Nos. 1–2.

BEI-FEMIP (2010), Crise et voies de sortie de crise dans les pays méditerranéens

Ben Naceur, S. and S. Ghazouani (2007), Stock markets, banks, and economic growth: empirical evidence from the MENA region, *Research in International Business and Finance*, Vol. 21, No. 2.

Ben Naceur, S., H. Ben-Khedhiri and B. Casu (2011), What Drives the Performance of Selected MENA Banks? A META-frontier Analysis, IMF Working Paper No. 11 WP/11/34, International Monetary Fund, Washington, D.C.

Berger, A.N. (2007), International comparisons of banking efficiency, *Financial Markets, Institutions and Instruments*, Vol. 16, No. 3.

Berger, A.N., R. DeYoung, H. Genay and G.H. Udell (2000), Globalization of financial institutions: evidence from cross-border banking performance, Brookings-Wharton Papers on Financial Services.

Berger, A.N. and T.H. Hannan (1998), The efficiency cost of market power in the banking industry: a test of the 'Quiet Life' and related hypotheses, *Review of Economics and Statistics*, Vol. 80, No. 3.

Berger, A.N. and D.D. Humphrey (1997), Efficiency of financial institutions: international survey and directions for future research, *European Journal of Operational Research*, Vol. 98.

Berger, A.N. and L.J. Mester (2003), Explaining the dramatic changes in performance of US banks: technological change, deregulation, and dynamic changes in competition, *Journal of Financial Intermediation*, Vol. 12, No. 1.

Berkmen, P. and N. Gueorguiev (2004), Macroeconomic Implications of the Transition to Inflation Targeting and Capital Account Liberalisation in Romania, IMF Working Paper, No.04/232, December.

Bernanke, B. (1987), *Readings and Cases in Macro-economics*, Mc-Graw Hill Book Company.

Bernanke, B. and A.B. Abel (2001), *Macroeconomics*, Addison Wesley Longman Inc.

Bernanke, B. and M. Gertler (2001), Should central bank respond to movements in asset prices? *American Economic Review*, Papers and Proceedings Vol. 91, No. 2 (pp 253–57).

Bernanke, B.S. and I. Mihov (1995), Measuring monetary policy, *Quarterly Journal of Economics*, 3 August.

Bernanke, B. and F. Mishkin (1992), Central Bank Behavior and Strategy of Monetary Policy: Observations from Six Industrialized Countries, NBER Working Papers Series No. 4082, May.

Berndt, M. and D. Ottolenghi (2009), Vulnerability of the Mediterranean region to the Financial Crisis, Banque Européenne d'Investissement.

Beveridge, S. and C.R. Nelson (1981), A new approach to decomposition of economic time series into permanent and transitory components with particular attention to measurement of the business cycle, *Journal of Monetary Economics*, Vol. 7 (pp 151–74).

Bhattacharya, S. and A.V. Thakor (1993), Contemporary banking theory, *Journal of Financial Intermediation*, Vol. 3, No. 1.

Bikker, J.A. (2004), *Competition and Efficiency in a Unified European Banking Market*, Cheltenham, UK, Edward Elgar.

Blackburn, K. and M. Christensen (1989), Monetary policy and policy credibility: theories and evidence, *Journal of Economic Literature*, Vol. XXVII (pp 1–45), March.

Blanchard, O. (2009), The Crisis: Basic Mechanisms and Appropriate Policies, IMF Working paper No. 09–80, April.

Blanchard, O. (1984), The Lucas critique and the Volcker deflation, *American Economic Review, Papers and Proceedings*, Vol. 74 (pp 211–15).

Blanchard, O., G. Dell'Ariccia, Paolo Mauro (2010), Rethinking Macroeconomic Policy, IMF Staff Position Note, February 12.

Blinder, A. (1982), Issues in the Coordination of Monetary and Fiscal Policy, NBER Working Paper No. 982.

Blundell, R. and S.R. Bond (1998), Initial conditions and moment restrictions in dynamic panel data models, *Journal of Econometrics*, Vol. 87.

Bollerslev, T., R.Y. Chou and K.F. Kroner (1992), Arch modeling and empirical evidence, *Journal of Econometrics*, Vol. 52 (pp 5–59).

Bordes, C. and M.O. Strauss-Kahn (1987), Dix ans de politique d'objectifs en France ou le targeting, à la française. SUERF Papers on Monetary Policy and Financial Systems, No. 4, Tilburg.

Bordo, M.D. (2007), The Crisis of 2007: The Same Old Story, Only the Players Have Changed, Federal Reserve Bank of Chicago and International Monetary Fund Conference 'Globalization and Systemic Risk', Chicago, Illinois, 28 September, 2007

Bordo, M.D. and A. Redish (1990), Credible commitment and exchange rate stability: Canada's interwar experience, *Canadian Journal of Economics*, Vol. 23 (pp 357–80), May.

Bos, J.W.B., F. Heid, M. Koetter, J.W. Kolari and C.J.M. Kool (2005), Inefficient or just different? effects of heterogeneity on bank efficiency scores, Discussion Papers Series 2, *Banking and Finance Studies*, Vol. 15, Deutsche Bank, Research Center.

Bos, J.W.B. and C.J.M. Kool (2006), Bank efficiency: the role of bank strategy and Local Market Conditions, *Journal of Banking and Finance*, Vol. 30, No. 7.

Bos, J.W.B. and H. Schmiedel (2007), Is there a single frontier in a single European banking market*Journal of Banking and Finance*, Vol. 31.

Boyd, J.H., C. Chang and B.D. Smith (1998), Moral Hazard under commercial and universal banking, *Journal of Money, Credit, and Banking*, Vol. 30, No. 3.

Brainard, W. (1967), Uncertainty and the effectiveness of policy, *American Economic Review; Papers and Proceedings*, LVII, N2 (pp 411–25).

Brown, C.O. and I.S. Dinc (2005), The politics of bank failures: evidence from emerging markets, *Quarterly Journal of Economics*, Vol. 120, No. 4.

Brown, M., T. Jappelli and M. Pagano (2009), Information sharing and credit: firm-level evidence from transition countries, *Journal of Financial Intermediation*, Vol. 18, No. 2.

Bry, G. and C.H. Boschan (1971), Cyclical Analysis of Economic Time Series: Selected Procedures and Computer Programs, NBER Technical Working Paper No. 20.

Bullard, J. and K. Mitra (2002), Learning about monetary policy rules, *Journal of Monetary Economics*, Vol. 49, No. 6 (pp 1105–29), September.

Canzoneri. M, V. Grilli. and P. Masson (1992), Establishing a Central Bank: issues in Europe and lessons from the United States, Cambridge University Press.

Caprio, G. and P. Honohan (2004), Can the Unsophisticated Market Provide Discipline? Policy Research Working Paper No. 3364, World Bank, Washington, D.C.

Caprio, G. and M.S.M. Peria (2000), Avoiding Disaster: Policies to Reduce the Risk of Banking Crises, ECES Working Paper No. 47, Egyptian Center for Economic Studies (ECES), Cairo.

Carare, A. and R. Tchaidze (2005), The Use and Abuse of Taylor Rules: How Precisely Can We Estimate Them? IMF Working Paper, WP/05/148

Cargill, T. and M. Hutchison (1990), Monetary Policy and Political Economy: The Federal Reserve and the Bank of Japan, In Thomas Mayer, ed., *The Political Economy of American Monetary Policy*, New York, Cambridge University Press.

Cartapanis, A. and M. Bassoni (1995), Autonomie des Banques Centrales et Performances macroéconomiques: Un réexamen, Working paper No. 1994–8, CEFI-Avril 1994. (also appeared in *Revue Economique*, Vol. 46, No. 2, March).

Castello-Branco, M. and M. Swinburne (1991), Central Bank independence and Central Bank functions, in Downes, P. and R. Vaez-Zadeh (eds) *The Evolving Role of Central Banks*, Washington, D.C., IMF (pp 414–44).

Castello-Branco, M. and M. Swinburne (1992), L'indépendance des Banques Centrales peut-elle faciliter la Maîtrise de l'inflation? Problèmes théoriques et pratiques, Finances et développement, FMI, Vol.29, No. 1, March.

Casu, B. and A. Ferrari (2013), The dynamics of bank efficiency in the European Union and the Southern Mediterranean: Is there convergence? MEDPRO Technical Report No. 33, Centre for European Policy Studies (CEPS), Brussels.

Casu, B. and C. Girardone (2010), Integration and efficiency convergence in EU banking markets, *OMEGA, The International Journal of Management Science*, Vol. 38, No. 5.

Cetorelli, N. and M. Gambera (2001), Banking market structure, financial dependence and growth: international evidence from industry data, *Journal of Finance*, Vol. 56, No. 2.

Cetorelli, N. and P.E. Strahan (2006), Finance as a Barrier to entry: bank competition and industry structure in local U.S. markets, *Journal of Finance*, Vol. 61, No. 1.

Chaffai, M.E., M. Dietsch and A. Lozano-Vivas (2001), Technological and environmental differences in the European banking industries, *Journal of Financial Services Research*, Vol. 19.

Chagny, O. and J. Döpke (2001), Measures of the Output Gap in the Euro-Zone: An Empirical Assessment of Selected Methods, Kiel Working Paper, 1053, Kiel Institute of World Economics.

Chagny, O. and M. Lemoine (2004), The Impact of the Macroeconomic Hypothesis on the Estimation of the Output Gap Using a Multivariate Hodrick-Prescott Filter: The Case of the Euro Area, Monographs of Official Statistics, Papers and Proceedings of the Third Colloquium on Modern Tools for Business Cycle Analysis, G.L. Mazzi and G. Savio (Eds).

Chagny, O., M. Lemoine and F. Pelgrin (2003), An Assessment of Multivariate Output Gap Estimates in the Euro Area, Working Papers and Studies, Eurostat, Luxembourg.

Chailloux. A., A. Durré and B.J. Laurens (2009), Requirements for Using Interest Rates As an Operating Target for Monetary Policy: The Case of Tunisia, IMF Working Paper No. 09/149, July.

Charnes, A., W.W. Cooper and E. Rhodes (1978), Measuring efficiency of decision making units, *European Journal of Operational Research*,Vol. 2.

Chiang, A.C. (1984), Fundamental methods of mathematical economics, 3éd, Mc-Graw Hill.

Chow, G.C. and Lin, A.L. (1971), Best linear unbiased interpolation, distribution, and extrapolation of time series by related series. *The Review of Economics and Statistics,* Vol. 53, No. 4 (pp 372–75).

Cho, I. and D. Kreps (1987), Signalling games and stable equilibria, *Quarterly Journal of Economics* C II, No. 2 (pp 179–221).

Christensen. M. (1990), Policy credibility and the Lucas critique – some new tests, in Artus. P,Y. Barroux, and G. Mckenzie (eds) *Monetary and Financial Models*, Dordrecht; Boston, Kluwer Academic publishers.

Christiano, L. and M. Eichenbaum (1992), Liquidity effects and the monetary transmission mechanism, *American Economic Review*, Vol. 82 (pp 346–53).

Christiano, L., M. Eichenbaum and C. Evans (2005), Nominal rigidities and the dynamic effects of a shock to monetary policy, *Journal of Political Economy*. Vol. 113 (pp 1–45), February.

Christiano, L. and T.J. Fitzgerald (2003), The band pass filter, *International Economic Review*, Vol. 44 (pp 435–65).

Christiansen, A.B. and J.F. Qvigstad (1997), Choosing a monetary policy target, Scandinavian University Press.

Čihák, M. and A.F. Tieman (2008), Quality of Financial Sector Regulation and Supervision Around the World, IMF Working Paper No. 08/190, International Monetary Fund, Washington, D.C.

Claessens, S., A. Demirgüç-Kunt and H. Huizinga (2001), How does foreign entry affect domestic banking markets? *Journal of Banking and Finance*, Vol. 25, No. 5.

Claessens, S. and L. Laeven (2004), What drives bank competition? some international evidence, *Journal of Money, Credit, and Banking*, Vol. 36, No. 3.

Clarida, R., J. Gali and M. Gertler (1998), Monetary policy rules in practice: some international evidence, *European Economic Review*, Vol. 42 (pp 1033–67).

Clarida, R. and M. Gertler (1997), How the Bundesbank conducts monetary policy, in Romer C. and D. Romer (eds) *Reducing Inflation*, University of Chicago Press.

Cole, S. (2009), Fixing market failures or fixing elections? agricultural credit in India, *American Economic Journal: Applied Economics*, Vol. 1, No. 1.

Cooper, R.N. (1985), Economic interdependence and coordination of economic policies, in R.W. Jones and P.B. Kennen (eds) *Handbook of International Economics, Vol. II*, (Chapter 23), Elsevier science publishers.

Cottarelli, C. and C. Giannini (1995), Credibility without rules – Monetary frameworks in the post Bretton Woods Era, XI world congress of the International Economic Association; Tunis (18–22 December), Tunisia.

Creane, S., R. Goyal, A.M. Mobarak and R. Sab (2004), *Financial Sector Development in the Middle East and North Africa*, IMF Working Paper No. WP/04/201, International Monetary Fund, Washington, D.C.

Cukierman, A. (1986), Central bank behavior and credibility: some recent theoretical developments, Quarterly review, Federal reserve bank of st. Louis, Vol. 68, No. 3 (pp 5–16) May.

Cukierman, A. (1992), Central bank strategy, credibility and independence: theory and evidence, The MIT Press, Cambridge, MA.

Cukierman, A. (1994), Central bank independence and monetary control, *Economic Journal*, Vol. 104, (pp 1437–48), November.

Cukierman, A. (1995), The Economics of Central Banking, XIth world congress of the International Economic Association (IEA), 18–22 December 1995, Tunis, Tunisia.

Cukierman, A. (2008), Central bank independence and monetary policy-making institutions – Past, present and future, *European Journal of Political Economy*, Vol 24, No. 4 (pp 722–36).

Cukierman, A., P. Kalaitzidakis, L.H. Summers and S.B. Webb (1993), Central bank independence, growth, investment and real rates, *Carnegie-Rochester Conference Series on public Policy*, Vol. 39 (pp 95–145), Autumn.

Cukierman, A. and N. Liviatan (1991), Optimal accommodation by strong policymakers under incomplete information, *Journal of Monetary Economics*, Vol. 27 (pp 99–127).

Cukierman, A. and A.H. Meltzer (1986a), A theory of ambiguity, credibility, and inflation under discretion and asymmetric information, *Econometrica*, Vol. 54, No. 5 (pp 1099–128), September.

Cukierman, A. and A. Meltzer (1986b), A positive theory of discretionary policy, the cost of a democratic government, and the benefits of a constitution, *Economic Inquiry*, Vol. 24 (pp 367–88), July.

Cukierman, A. and S.B. Webb (1995), Political influence on the Central Bank: international evidence, *The World Bank Economic Review*, 9, No 3 (pp 397–423), September.

Cukierman, A., S.B. Webb and B. Neyapti (1992), Measuring the independence of central banks and its effects on policy outcomes, *World Bank Economic Review*, Vol. 6, No. 3, September.

Cukierman, A., S. Edwards and G. Tabellini (1992), Seignorage and political instability, *American Economic Review*, Vol. 82 (pp 537–55).

Currie, D.A., P. Levine. and J. Pearlman (1995), Can delegation be counter-productive ?: The choice of conservative bankers in open economies, CEPR discussion paper, N 1148.

Currie, D.A., P. Levine. and J. Pearlman (1996), The choice of conservative bankers in open economies: monetary regime options for Europe, *Economic Journal*, Vol. 106, No. 435 (pp 345–58).

Daniel, J.-M., A. Gubian, and H. Harasty (1993), Finances publiques en Europe: un blocage généralisé? *Revue de l'OFCE*, Vol 46, No. 1 (pp 175–209).

Das, U.S., P. Iossifov, R. Podpiera and D. Rozhkov (2005), *Quality of Financial Policies and Financial System Stress*, IMF Working Paper No. 05/173, International Monetary Fund, Washington, D.C.

Debelle, G. (1996), Central Bank Independence: A Free Lunch, IMF Working paper No. 96/1, January.

Debelle, G. and S. Fischer (1994), How independent should a Central Bank be? in J.C. Fuhrer (ed.) *Goals, Guidelines and Constraints Facing Monetary Policymakers*, Federal Reserve Bank of Boston.

Debonneuil, M., M. Feroldi and Sterdyniak (1984), Interdépendance et autonomi: variation sur un thème de Mundell, Document de travail INSEE.

Deidda, L. and B. Fattouh (2002), Non-linearity between finance and growth, *Economics Letters*, Vol. 74, No. 3.

Demetriades, P.O. and K.A. Hussein (1996), Does financial development cause economic growth? Time-series evidence from 16 countries, *Journal of Development Economics*, Vol. 51, No. 2.

Demirgüç-Kunt, A. and E. Detragiache (2002), Does deposit insurance increase banking system stability? an empirical investigation, *Journal of Monetary Economics*, Vol. 49, No. 7.

Demirgüç-Kunt, A. and E. Detragiache (2010), Basel Core Principles and Bank Risk: Does Compliance Matter? IMF Working Paper No. 10/81, International Monetary Fund, Washington, D.C.

Demirgüç-Kunt, A. and E.J. Kane (2002), Deposit insurance around the globe: where does it work? *Journal of Economic Perspectives*, Vol. 16, No. 2, Spring.

Demirgüç-Kunt, A., B. Karacaovalı and L.A. Laeven (2005), *Deposit Insurance around the World Dataset*, Policy Research Working Paper No. 3628, World Bank, Washington, D.C.

Demirgüç-Kunt, A., L. Laeven and R. Levine (2004), Regulations, market structure, institutions, and the cost of financial intermediation, *Journal of Money, Credit, and Banking*, Vol. 36, No. 3.

Demirgüç-Kunt, A. and R. Levine (2008), Finance, Financial Sector Policies, and Long-Run Growth, Policy Research Working Paper No. 4469, World Bank, Washington, D.C.

Demopoulos, G.D., G.M. Katsimbris and S.M. Miller (1987), Monetary policy and central – bank financing of government budget deficit, *European Economic Review*, Vol. 31 (pp 1023–50).

Desormeaux, J., K. Fernandez and P. Garcia (2008), Financial implications of capital outflows in Chile: 1998–2008, *Economic Policy Paper*, Central Bank of Chile, No. 23, March.

DeYoung, R. (1998), Management quality and X-inefficiency in national banks, *Journal of Financial Services Research*, Vol. 13, No. 1.

Diamond, D.W. and P.H. Dybvig (1983), Bank runs, deposit insurance, and liquidity, *Journal of Political Economy*, Vol. 91, No. 3.

Dietsch, M. and A. Lozano-Vivas (2000), How the environment determines banking efficiency: a comparison between French and Spanish industries, *Journal of Banking and Finance*, Vol. 24, No. 6.

Dinc, I.S. (2005), Politicians and banks: political influences on government-owned banks in emerging markets, *Journal of Financial Economics*, Vol. 77, No. 2.

Djankov, S., C. McLiesh and A. Shleifer (2007), Private credit in 129 countries, *Journal of Financial Economics*, Vol. 84, No. 2.

Dornbusch, R., and S. Fischer (1993), Moderate Inflation, *World Bank Economic Review*, Vol. 7 (pp 1–44).

Downes. P. and R. Vaez-Zadeh, (eds) (1991), *The Evolving Role of Central Banks*, IMF, Washington, DC.

Driscoll, M. (1992), The transmission mechanisms and effects of monetary policy in Europe, Cahiers Economiques et Monétaires, Banque de France No. 40 (pp 115–43).

Durand, J. (1988), Stratégies et crédibilité des autorités monétaires, Cahiers Economiques et Monétaires de la Banque de France, No. 32 (pp 127–46).

Edison, I. Hali, M.W. Klein, L.A. Ricci and T. Sløk (2004), Capital Account Liberalisation and Economic Performance: Survey and Synthesis. IMF Staff Papers, *International Monetary Fund*, Vol. 51, No. 2 (pp 220–56).

Edwards, S. (1997), Exchange rate issues in developing and transitional economies, *Journal of African Economies*, Vol.6, No. 3 (pp 37–73).

Edwards, S. and J.D. Ostry (1990), Anticipated protectionist policies, real exchange rates and the current account, *Journal of International Money and Finance*, Vol. 9 (pp 206–19).

Edwards, S. and M. Savastano (2000), Exchange rates in emerging economies: what do we know? what do we need to know? in Krueger, A. (ed.) *Economic Policy Reform: The Second Stage*, Chicago, University of Chicago, Press.

Egebo. T and A. S. Englander (1992), Engagements institutionnels et crédibilité de la politique économique: Etude critique et analyse économetrique du mécanisme de change du SME, Revue économique de l'OCDE, N 18, printemps 1992.

Égert, B. and R. Macdonald (2006), Monetary Transmission Mechanism in Transition Economies: Surveying the Surveyable, CESifo Working Paper 1739, Munich: CESifo.

Eichengreen, B. (1986), Book review: rational expectations and inflation, *Journal of Economic Literature*, Vol. 24 (pp 1812–15).

Eichengreen, B. (1999), *Toward a New International Financial Architecture: A Practical Post-Asian Agenda*, Washington, Institute for International Economics.

Eichengreen, B. and C. Artanda (2000), *Banking Crises in Emerging Markets: Presumptions and Evidence*, Institute of Business and Economic Research, Center for International and development Economics Research, University of California.

Eichengreen, B. and D. Leblang (2002), Capital Account Liberalisation and Growth: Was Mr. Mahathir Right? Working Paper No. 9427, National Bureau of Economic Research, December.

Eijffinger, S.C.W. and P.M. Geraats (2006), How transparent are central banks, *European Journal of Political Economy*, Vol. 22, No. 1 (pp 1–21), March.

Emerging Markets Group (2006), Strengthening Egypt's Credit Reporting System – Phase 2: Final Report, report prepared by Emerging Markets Group, Ltd., prime contractor for the FIRST Initiative, under Contract #49 C343, November.

Epstein, G.A. and J.B. Schor (1986), The Political Economy of Central Banking, Harvard Institute for Economic Research, Discussion Paper #1281, November 1986.

European Commission (2010), Impact Assessment Accompanying Document to the Proposal on Deposit Guarantee Schemes, Commission Staff Working Document, SEC(2010) 834/2, Brussels.

Fadil, M.A. (2000), *A Survey of the Basic Features and Problems of the Informal Small and Micro-Enterprises in the Arab Region*, FEMISE Research Programme.

Fanizza, D., N. Laframboise, E. Martin, R. Sab and I. Karpowicz (2002), Tunisia's Experience with Real Exchange Rate Targeting and the Transition to a Flexible Exchange Rate Regime, IMF Working Paper No. 02–190, November.

Faugere, J.P. (1991), Les règles monétaires génératrices de crédibilité. Eléments de critique des thèses des nouveaux classiques, *Revue Française d'économie*, Vol. 6, No. 4 (pp 227–80).

Favero, C. (2001), *Applied Macroeconometrics*, Oxford University Press

Fazio, A. (1991), Role and Independence of Central Banks, in Downes, P. and R. Vaez- Zadeh (eds)., *The Evolving Role of Central Banks*, Washington, D.C., IMF.

Femise (2004a), Exchange rates, trade and FDI flows, Femise Research Program No. FEM 21–13, Neaime et alii.

Femise (2004b), FDI inflows to the MENA region, Femise Research Program No. FEM 21–15

Femise (2008–2010), Rapports sur le partenariat euro-méditerrannén.

Fischer, S. (1987), The Israeli stabilization program, 1985–86, *American Economic Review*, Vol. 77, No. 2 (pp 275–78).

Fisher, R. (1995), Central Bank independence, *American Economic Review*, Vol. 85, No. 2 (pp 201–6).

Flood, R., and P.M. Garber (1983), A model of stochastic process switching, Econometrica, Vol. 51 (pp 537–51).

Forbes, K.J. (2007), One Cost of the Chilean Capital Controls: Increased Financial Constraints for Smalles Traded Firms, NBER Working Paper Series, No. 9777.

Freedman, C., M. Kumhof, D. Laxton and J. Lee (2009), The Case for Global Fiscal Stimulus, IMF Staff Position Note, No. SPN/09/03, March

References 247

Freedman, C. and I. Ötker-Robe (2009), Country Experiences with the Introduction and Implementation of Inflation Targeting, IMF Working Paper, No. 09/161, July.

Fries, S. and A. Taci (2005), Cost efficiency of banks in transition: evidence from 289 banks in 15 post-communist countries, *Journal of Banking and Finance*, Special Issue, Vol. 29, No. 1.

Fung, M.K. (2006), Scale economies, X-efficiency, and convergence of productivity among bank holding companies, *Journal of Banking and Finance*, Vol. 30.

Funke, N. (1993), Timing and sequencing of reforms: competing views and role of credibility, *KYKLOS*, Vol. 46.

Galor, O. and J. Zeira (1993), Income distribution and macroeconomics, *Review of Economic Studies*, Vol. 60, No. 1.

Garcia, R. and H. Schaller (1995), Are the effects of monetary policy asymmetric? Université de Montréal, document de travail No. 0595.

Garcia-Marco, T. and M.D. Robles-Fernandez (2008), Risk-taking behaviour and ownership in the banking industry: the Spanish evidence, *Journal of Economics and Business*, Vol. 60, No. 4.

Genberg, H. and A. Swoboda (2005), Does What Countries Say Matter? IMF Staff Papers 52 (Special Issue) (pp 129–41).

Gerlach, S. and G. Schnabel (1999), The Taylor Rule and Interest Rates in the EMU Area: A Note, Bank for International Settlements, Working Paper No. 73.

Gerschenkron, A. (1962), *Economic Backwardness in Historical Perspective*, Cambridge, MA: Harvard University Press.

Giannini, C. (1992), *Topics in Structural VAR Econometrics*, Springer-Verlag.

Giavazzi, F. and A. Giovannini (1986), Monetary Policy Interactions under Managed Exchange Rates, CEPR Discussion Paper Series No. 123, August.

Giavazzi, F. and A. Giovannini (1987), Models of the EMS: is Europe a greater Deutschmark area? in Bryant, R.C. and R. Portes (eds) *Global Macroeconomics – Policy Conflict and Cooperation*, CEPR. Mc Millan press, London.

Giavazzi, F. and A. Giovannini (1988), Modèles du SME: l'Europe n'est-elle qu'une zone-Deutschmark, Revue Economique, Vol. 39, No. 3 (pp 641–66), May.

Giavazzi, F., S. Micossi and M. Miller (Dir. Pub) (1988), *The European Monetary System*, Cambridge University Press.

Giavazzi, F. and M. Pagano (1988), The advantage of tying one's hands: EMS discipline and Central Bank credibility, *European Economic Review*, Vol. 32, No. 5 (pp 1055–1082), June.

Goodhart, C. (1988), *The Evolution of Central Banks*, Cambridge, Mass., MIT Press.

Goodhart, C. (1992), The draft statute of the European central banks: a commentary, *Cahiers économiques et monétaires, Banque de France*, Vol. 40, (pp 335–48).

Goodhart, C. (1993), La politique monétaire dans les années 90. Objectifs et moyens d'action, Cahiers économiques et monétaires, *Banque de France*, Vol. 41 (pp 5–20).

Goddard, J.A., P. Molyneux and J.O.S. Wilson (2001), *European Banking: Efficiency, Technology and Growth*, London, John Wiley and Sons.

Goddard, J.A., P. Molyneux, J.O.S. Wilson and M. Tavakoli (2007), European banking: an overview, *Journal of Banking and Finance*, Vol. 31.

Goodhart, C. (1992), La politique monétaire dans les années 1990: objectifs et moyens d'action, Cahiers économiques et monétaires, No. 41 (pp 5–20), Banque de France.

Goodhart, C. (1994), The draft statute of the European system of central Banks: a commentary, cahiers economiques et monétaires No. 40, Banque de France.

Grauwe, P. de and M. Polan (2005), Is inflation always and everywhere a monetary phenomenon? *Scandinavian Journal of Economics*, Vol. 107, No. 2 (pp 239–59).

Griffith-Jones, S. and J.A. Ocampo (2009), The Financial Crisis and its Impact on Developing Countries, United Nations Development Programme, Discussion, Paper PG/2009/001, January.

Grigorian, D.A. and V. Manole (2006), Determinants of commercial bank performance in transition: an application of data envelopment analysis, *Comparative Economic Studies*, Vol. 48.

Grilli, V., D. Masciandaro and G. Tabellini (1991), Political and monetary institutions and public finance policies in the industrial countries, *Economic Policy*, Vol. 13 (pp 341–92), October.

Gropp, R. and J. Vesala (2004), Deposit insurance, moral hazard and market monitoring, *Review of Finance*, Vol. 8, No. 4.

Guay, A. and P. St-Amant (1997), Do the Hodrick-Prescott and Baxter-King Filters Provide a Good Approximation of the Business Cycles?, Université du Quebec a Montreal, Working Paper 53.

Hakenes, H. and I. Schnabel (2006), The Threat of Capital Drain: A Rationale for Public Banks? Working Paper No. 11, Max Planck Institute for Research on Collective.

Hamilton, J. D., and Susmel, R. (1994), Autoregressive conditional heteroskedasticity and changes in regime, *Journal of Econometrics*, Vol. 64, No. 1 (pp 307–33).

Hansen, L.P. (1982), Large sample properties of generalized method of moments estimators, *Econometrica*, Vol. 50, No. 4.

Harvey, A.C. (1985), Trends and cycles in macroeconomic time series, *Journal of Business and Economic Statistics*, 3, 216001E227.

Harvey, A.C. (1989), *Forecasting. Structural Time Series Models and the Kalman Filter*, Cambridge University Press, Cambridge.

Harvey, C., G. Bekaert and Ch. Lundblad (2006), Growth volatility and financial liberalisation. *Journal of International Money and Finance*, Vol. 25 (pp 370–403).

Haselmann, R., K. Pistor and V. Vig (2010), How law affects lending, *Review of Financial Studies*, Vol. 23, No. 2.

Hauner, D. (2008), Credit to government and banking sector performance, *Journal of Banking and Finance*, Vol. 32, No. 8.

Hauner, D. (2009), Public debt and financial development, *Journal of Development Economics*, Vol. 88, No. 1.

Hicks, J.R. (1935), Annual survey of economic theory: the theory of monopoly, *Econometrica*, Vol. 3, No. 1.

Hodrick, R.J. and E.C. Prescott (1997), Postwar U.S. business cycles: an empirical investigation, *Journal of Money, Credit and Banking*, Vol. 29 (pp 1–16).

Hughes, J.P., W.L. Lang, L.J. Mester, C. Moon and M.S. Pagano (2003), Do bankers sacrifice value to build empires? managerial incentives, industry consolidation, and financial performance, *Journal of Banking and Finance*, Vol. 27, No. 3.

Hughes, J.P. and L.J. Mester (2010), Efficiency in banking: theory, practise and evidence, in A. Berger, P. Molyneux and J.O.S. Wilson (eds), *The Oxford Handbook of Banking*, Oxford, Oxford University Press.

Huybens, E. and B.D. Smith (1999), Inflation, financial markets and long-run real activity, *Journal of Monetary Economics*, Vol. 43, No. 2.

Icard, A. (1992), Les effets de la politique monétaire dans un environnement financier en mutation, *Cahiers économiques et monétaires, Banque de France*, Vol. 40 (pp 27–43).

IMF (2002), Tunisia: Financial System Stability Assessment, including Reports on the Observance of Standards and Codes on the following topics: Monetary and Financial Policy Transparency, and Insurance Regulation, IMF Staff Country Reports, No. 02/119, International Monetary Fund, Washington, D.C.

IMF (2007a), Tunisia – Renforcement du cadre stratégique et opérationnel de la politique monétaire, Laurens B J, Chailloux A, Simard D et A Durré, May.

IMF (2007b), Global Financial Stability Report, Chapter 2. Washington, International Monetary Fund.

IMF (2007c), Tunisia: Financial Sector Assessment Program Update – Detailed Assessment of Compliance of the Basel Core Principles for Effective Banking Supervision, IMF Staff Country Reports, No. 07/98, International Monetary Fund, Washington, D.C.

IMF (2008), Morocco: Financial System Stability Assessment – Update, IMF Staff Country Reports, No. 08/333, International Monetary Fund, Washington, D.C.

IMF (2009a), Tunisia: 2009 Article IV Consultation – Staff Report, IMF Country Reports, No. 09/329, International Monetary Fund, Washington, D.C.

IMF (2009b), *Requirements for Using Interest Rates as an Operating Target for Monetary Policy: The Case of Tunisia*, Chailloux. A, Durré, A and B. J. Laurens (eds), IMF WP/09/149, July.

IMF (2010a), Algeria: 2009 Article IV Consultation – Staff Report; and Public Information Notice, IMF Country Report, No. 10/57, International Monetary Fund, Washington, D.C.

IMF (2010b), Arab Republic of Egypt: 2010 Article IV Consultation – Staff Report Public Information Notice on the Executive Board Discussion; and Statement by the Executive Director for the Arab Republic of Egypt, IMF Country Report, No. 10/94, International Monetary Fund, Washington, D.C.

IMF (2010c), Morocco: 2009 Article IV Consultation – Staff Report; Public Information Notice on the Executive Board Discussion; and Statement by the Executive Director for Morocco, IMF Country Report, No. 10/58, International Monetary Fund, Washington, D.C.

IMF (2010d), Tunisia: 2010 Article IV Consultation – Staff Report; Public Information Notice on the Executive Board Discussion; and Statement by the Executive Director for Tunisia, IMF Country Report, No. 10/282, International Monetary Fund, Washington, D.C., September.

IMF (2010e), The Role of Indicators in Guiding the Exit from Monetary and Financial Crisis Intervention Measures, MCM department, January.

Isik, I. and M.K. Hassan (2003), Financial deregulation and total factor productivity change: an empirical study of Turkish commercial banks, *Journal of Banking and Finance*, Vol. 27.

Jaillet, P. (1998), "Stratégies de politique monétaire. Quelques enseignements du passé récent et pistes pour l'avenir". *Revue économique*, pp. 629–41.

Jappelli, T. and M. Pagano (2002), Information sharing, lending and defaults: cross-country evidence, *Journal of Banking and Finance*, Vol. 26, No. 10.

Johansen, S. (1988), Statistical analysis of cointegration vectors, *Journal of Economic Dynamics and Control*, Vol. 12 (pp 231–54).

Johansen, S. (1991), Estimation and hypothesis testing of cointegration vector autoregressive models , *Econometrica*, Vol. 59 (pp 1551–80).

Johansen, S. and K. Juselius (1990), Maximum likelihood estimation and inference on cointegration with applications to the demand for money, *Oxford bulletin of economics and statistics*, Vol. 52.

Judd, J.P., G.D. Rudebusch (1998), Taylors rule and the fed: 1970–1997, *Federal Reserve Bank of San Francisco economic review*, No 3

Kahn, G.A. (1988), Nominal GDP: An Anchor for Monetary Policy, *Economic Review*, Federal Reserve Bank of Kansas City (pp 18–35).

Kandil, M. (2006), *On the Transmission Mechanism of Policy Shocks in Developing countries*, Mimeo, Economic Research Forum, Egypt.

Kane, E. (2000), Designing Financial Safety Nets to Fit Country Circumstances, Policy Research Working Paper No. 2453, World Bank, Washington, D.C.

Kasman, A. and C. Yildirim (2006), Cost and profit efficiencies in transition banking: the case of new EU members, *Applied Economics*, Vol. 38, No. 9.

Kaufmann, D., A. Kraay and M. Mastruzzi (2009), Governance Matters VIII: Governance Indicators for 1996–2008, World Bank Policy Research, World Bank, Washington, D.C.

Khwaja, A.I. and A. Mian (2005), Do lenders favor politically connected firms? rent provision in an emerging financial market, *Quarterly Journal of Economics*, Vol. 120, No. 4.

King, R.G. and R. Levine (1993), Finance and growth: Schumpeter might be right, *Quarterly Journal of Economics*, Vol. 108, No. 3.

Klein, M.W. (2005), Capital Account Liberalisation, Institutional Quality and Economic Growth: Theory and Evidence, NBER Working Paper, No. 11112.

Klein, M.W. and G.P. Olivei, (2008), Capital account liberalisation, financial depth, and economic growth, *Journal of International Money & Finance*, Vol. 27, No. 6 (pp 861–75).

Kozicki, S. (1999), How useful are Taylor rules for monetary policy?, *Economic Review*, Second Quarter, Federal Reserve Bank of Kansas City.

Kydland, F.E. (1976), "Decentralized stabilization policies: optimization and the assignment problem", *Annals of Economic and Social Measurement*, Vol. 5 (pp 249–61).

Kydland, F. and E.C. Prescott (1977), Rules rather than discretion. *The Inconsistency of Optimal Plans Journal of Political Economy*, Vol. 85–1977 (pp 473–91).

Kydland, F. and E.C. Prescott (1982), Time to build and aggregate fluctuations, *Econometrica*, Vol. 50, No. 6 (pp 1345–70), November.

La Porta, R., F. Lopez-de-Silane, A. Shleifer and R.W. Vishny (1997), Legal determinants of external finance, *Journal of Finance*, Vol. 52, No. 3.

La Porta, R., F. Lopez-de-Silanes and A. Shleifer (1998), Law and finance, *Journal of Political Economy*, Vol. 106, No. 6.

La Porta, R., F. Lopez-de-Silanes and A. Shleifer (2002), Government ownership of banks, *Journal of Finance*, Vol. 57, No. 1 (pp 265–301).

Ladiray, D., G.L. Mazzi and F. Sartori (2003), Statistical Methods for Potential Output Estimation and Cycle Extraction, Working Papers and Studies, Eurostat, Luxembourg.

Laeven, L. and R. Levine (2008), Bank Governance, Regulation, and Risk Taking, NBER Working Paper No. 14113, National Bureau of Economic Research, Cambridge, MA.

Laurens, B. and A. Sarr (2003), Tunisia – Strengthening the Monetary Framework and Instruments SM/03/246, Annex, July.

Laurens, B.J., A. Chailloux, D. Simard and A. Durré (2007), Renforcement du cadre stratégique et opérationnel de la politique monétaire, IMF, May

Lavigne, A. and P. Villieu (1996), La politique monétaire: nouveaux enjeux; nouveaux débats, *Revue d'économie politique*, Vol. 106, No. 4, July-August.

Laxton, D. and R. Tandlow (1992), A Simple Multivariate Filter for the Measurement of Potential Output, Technical Report, 59, Bank of Canada.

Leitemo, K. and I. Lønning (2001), Simple monetary policymaking without the output gap, Manuscript, Norges Bank.

Leone, A. (1991), Effective and implications of limits on Central bank credit to the Government. In Patrick Downes and Reza Vaez-Zadeh, eds., *The Evolving Role of Central Banks*, Washington D.C., IMF.

Levine, R. (1997), Financial development and economic growth: views and agenda, *Journal of Economic Literature*, Vol. 35, No. 2.

Levine, R. (1998), The legal environment, banks, and long-run economic growth, *Journal of Money, Credit, and Banking*, Vol. 30, No. 3.

Levine, R. (2004), Finance and Growth: Theory and Evidence, NBER Working Paper No. 10766, National Bureau of Economic Research, Cambridge, MA.

Liang, Z. (2006), Financial development and income distribution: a system GMM panel analysis with application to Urban China, *Journal of Economic Development*, Vol. 31, No. 2.

Liikanen, E. (2012), High-level Expert Group on reforming the structure of the EU banking sector – Final Report, European Commission, Brussels.

Lohmann, S. (1992), Optimal commitment in monetary policy: credibility versus flexibility, *American Economic Review*, Vol. 82 (pp 273–86).

Loisel, O. (2006), L'élaboration de la politique monétaire dans la zone euro et aux Etats-Unis, Bulletin de la Banque de France, No. 156, December.

Lucas, R.E. (1972a), Econometric testing of the naturel rate hypothesis, in *The Econometric of Price Determination* O. Eckstein (ed.), Board of Governors of the Federal Reserve System, Washington D.C, (pp 50–59).

Lucas, R.E. (1972b), Expectations and the neutrality of money, *Journal of Economic Theory*, 4, No. 2 (pp 103–24), April.

Lucas, R.E. (1973), Some International evidence on output-inflation trade offs, *American Economic Review*, Vol. LXIII, No. 3 (pp 326–34), June.

Lucas, R.E., Jr. (1976), Econometric policy evaluation: a critique, *Carnegie-Rochester Conference Series on Public Policy*, Vol. 1.

Lucas, R.E. (1981), Econometric policy evaluation: a critique, in *Studies in Business Cycle Theory*, MIT Press; Cambridge Massachusetts.

Madeddu, O. (2010), The Status of Information Sharing and Credit Reporting Infrastructure, MENA Financial Sector Flagship Report, Improving Access to Finance while Maintaining Stability in the Middle East and North Africa, World Bank, Washington, D.C.

Mankiw, N.G. (ed.) (1994), *Monetary Policy*, Chicago, University of Chicago Press for NBER.

Masciandaro, D. (1995), Modelling a Central Bank: Benevolent Policy Maker, Conservative Player, Monetary Agent, XI World Congress of the International Economic Association. Tunis (18–22 December).

Maudos, J. and J.F. de Guevara (2007), The cost of market power in banking: social welfare loss vs. cost inefficiency, *Journal of Banking and Finance*, Vol. 31, No. 7.

Mauro, P. (1995), Corruption and growth, *Quarterly Journal of Economics*, Vol. 110, No. 3.

Mc. Callum, B.T. (1984), Credibility and Monetary Policy, N.B.E.R. Working paper No. 1490, November.

Mc. Callum, B.T. (1987), The case for rules in the conduct of monetary policy: a concrete example, *Economic Review*, Federal Reserve Bank of Richmond, (pp 10–18), September–October.

Mc. Callum, B.T. (1988), Robustness properties of a rule for monetary policy, *Carnégie-Rochester Conference Series on Public Policy*, Vol. 29 (pp 173–203).

Mc. Callum, B.T. (1993), Discretion versus policy rules in practice: two critical points – a comment, *Rochester Conference Series on Public Policy*, Vol. 39.

Mc. Callum, B.T. (1995a), Rules for monetary policy, NBER Reporter, spring.

Mc. Callum, B.T. (1995b), Two fallacies concerning Central bank independence, *American Economic Review*, Papers and Proceedings, Vol. 85, No. 2 (pp 207–21) May.

Mc. Callum, B.T. (1998), Issues in the design of monetary policy rules, in J. Taylor and M. Woodford (eds) *Handbook of Macroeconomics*, North Holland.

Merton, R.C. (1977), An analytic derivation of the cost of deposit insurance and loan guarantees: an application of modern option pricing theory, *Journal of Banking & Finance*, Vol. 1, No. 1.

Miao, Y. (2009), In Search of Successful Inflation Targeting: Evidence from an Inflation Targeting Index, IMF Working Paper, No. 09/148, July.

Mishkin, F.S. (1982), Does anticipated monetary policy matter? an econometric investigation, *Journal of Political Economy*, Vol. 90, No. 1 (pp 22–51).

Mishkin, F.S (1995), Symposium on the monetary transmission mechanism *Journal of Economic Perspectives*, Vol. 9, No. 4 (pp 3–10).

Mishkin, F.S (1995), On the transmission mechanism of policy shocks in developing countries, *Oxford Development Studies*, Vol. 34 No. 2 (pp 117–149).

Mishkin, F.S. (2008), Globalization, Macroeconomic Performance, and Monetary Policy, NBER Working Paper, No. 13948.

Mishkin, F.S. and Schmidt-Hebbel, K. (2001), One Decade of Inflation Targeting in The World: What do We Know and What do We Need to Know? NBER Working Paper 8397, Cambridge, National Bureau of Economic Research.

MIX (2009), Arab Microfinance Analysis and Benchmarking Report, report from Microfinance Information Exchange (MIX), Sanabel and the Consultative Group to Assist the Poor (CGAP).

Montiel, Peter J. (1990), The Transmission Mechanism for Monetary Policy in Developing Countries. *IMF Working Paper*, pp. 1–30.

Mouley, S. (2012), The Role of Monetary Policies and Macroeconomic Convergence in the Development of Financial Systems in South Mediterranean Countries, MEDPRO Technical Report, No. 12, Mediterranean Prospects (MEDPRO).

Mouley, S. (2011), Economie du central banking: théorie et application, (éds) Imprimerie Officielle de la République Tunisienne, July

Mouley, S. (2009), Finance internationale et politiques macroéconomiques, (eds) Imprimerie Officielle de la République Tunisienne, Tunis.

Mouley, S. and H. Fehri (2009), Théorie de la politique monétaire (éds). Imprimerie Officielle de la République Tunisienne, Tunis

Mouley, S. (2007), Inflation targeting and exchange rate policy in Tunisia: pre-requisites and economic prospects, Research Papers, Central Bank of Tunisia, Issue 1, March.

Mukherjee, K., S.C. Ray and S.M. Miller (2001), Productivity growth in large us commercial banks: the initial post-deregulation experience, *Journal of Banking and Finance*, Vol. 25.

Murinde, V., J. Agung and A.W. Mullineux (2004), Patterns of corporate financing and financial system convergence in Europe, *Review of International Economics*, Vol. 12.

Neaime, S. (2000), *The Macroeconomics of Exchange Rate Policies, Tariff Protection and the Current Account: A Dynamic Framework*, APF Press, Toronto, Canada.

Neaime, S., (2008), Monetary Policy Transmission and Targeting Mechanisms in the MENA Region, ERF Working Paper No. 395, April.

ODonnel, C.J., D.S. Prasada Rao and G.E. Battese (2008), Meta-frontier Frameworks for the study of firm level efficiencies and technology ratios, *Empirical Economics*, Vol. 34.

Obstfeld, M., J. Shambaugh and Taylor, A. (2004), The Trilemma in History: Tradeoffs among Exchange Rates, Monetary Policies, and Capital Mobility, NBER Working Paper no. 10396.

Olsen, K., J.F. Qvigstad and O. Røisland (2002), Monetary policy in real time: the role of simple rules, Autumn Economist's Meeting, BIS, October.

Olson, D. and T.A. Zoubi (2010), Efficiency and Bank Profitability in MENA Countries, School of Business and Management, American University of Sharjah, Sharjah, United Arab Emirates.

Orphanides, A. (1998), Monetary Policy Evaluation with Noisy Information, Finance and Economics Discussion Series, no 1998–50, Board of Governors of the Federal Reserve System.

Orphanides, A. (1999), The quest for prosperity without inflation. Paper presented at the workshop on Inflation targeting and exchange rate fluctuations at Sveriges Riksbank, Stockholm.

Orphanides, A., R.D. Porter, D. Reifschneider, R. Tandlow and F. Finan (2000), Errors in the measurement of the output gap and the design of monetary policy, *Journal of Economics and Business*, Vol. 52 (pp 117–41).

Orphanides, A. and J.C. Williams (2002), Robust monetary policy rules: the case of unknown natural rates of interest and unemployment. Paper presented at the ECB workshop on monetary policy in Frankfurt, March.

Oulidi, N., & Allain, L. (2009), Credit Market in Morocco: A Disequilibrium Approach, *IMF Working Papers*, pp 1–18.

Pagano, M. and T. Jappelli (1993), Information sharing in credit markets, *Journal of Finance*, Vol. 48, No. 5.

Pandit, J.P. (1992), Contenu et critères de l'indépendance des Banques Centrales, *Revue d'Economie Financière*, No. 22.

Panzar, J.C. and J.N. Rosse (1987), Testing for 'Monopoly' equilibrium, *Journal of Industrial Economics*, Vol. 35, No. 4.

Parikh, A. and M. Shibata (2004), Does trade liberalisation accelerate convergence in per capita incomes in developing countries? *Journal of Asian Economics*, Vol. 15.

Parkin, M. (1986), Domestic Monetary Institutions and Deficits, in J.M. Buchanan, C.K. Rowley and R.D. Tollison, eds., *Deficits*. New York, Brasil Blackwell.

Pasiouras, F. (2008), International evidence on the impact of regulations and supervision on banks technical efficiency: an application of two-stage data envelopment analysis, *Review of Quantitative Finance and Accounting*, Vol. 30, No. 2.

Pasiouras, F., S. Tanna and C. Zopounidis (2009), The impact of banking regulations on banks cost and profit efficiency: cross-country evidence, *International Review of Financial Analysis*, Vol. 18, No. 5.

Patat, J.P. (1992), Quelques remarques sur la question de l'indépendance de la Banque Centrale, *Revue d'Economie Financière*, No. 22, Autumn.

Patat, J.P. and J. Bozzi (1993), Les politiques monétaires au cours du cycle économique, *Revue d' Economie Financière*, No. 26 (pp 51–64).

Pedersen, T.M. (2001), The Hodrick–Prescott filter, the Slutzky effect, and the distortionary effect of filters. *Journal of Economic Dynamics and Control*, Vol. 25, No. 8 (pp 1081–1101).

Pindyck R. (1976), The cost of conflicting objectives in policy formulation, *Annals of Economic and Social Measurement*, Vol. 5, No. 2 (pp. 239–248).

Plihon, D. (1992), La Banque Centrale et les mutations de l'économie monétaire et bancaire – Synthèse des travaux, Cahiers économiques et monétaires, No. 40 (pp 335–48), Banque de France.

Podpiera, R. (2006), Does Compliance with Basel Core Principles Bring Any Measurable Benefits? IMF Staff Papers, Vol. 53, No. 2, International Monetary Fund, Washington, D.C.

Pollard, P.S. (1993), Central bank independence and economic performance. *The Federal Reserve Bank of Saint-Louis Review*, Vol. 75, No. 4 (pp 21–36), July–August.

Quah, D. (1996), Twin peaks: growth and convergence in models of distribution dynamics, *Economic Journal*, Vol. 106.

Qvigstad, J.F. (2001), Monetary Policy in Real Time, Norges Bank Working Paper, No. 01-01.

Rioja, F. and N. Valev (2004), Does one size fit all?: a reexamination of the finance and growth relationship, *Journal of Development Economics*, Vol. 74, No. 2.

Rocha, R., S. Farazi, R. Khouri and D. Pearce (2010), The Status of Bank Lending to SMEs in the Middle and North Africa Region: The Results of a Joint Survey of the Union of Arab Banks and the World Bank, World Bank, Washington, D.C.

Rocha, R., S. Farazi, R. Khouri and D. Pearce (2010a), The Status of Bank Lending to Small and Medium Enterprises, MENA Financial Sector Flagship Report, Improving Access to Finance while Maintaining Stability in the Middle East and North Africa, World Bank, Washington, D.C.

Rodrik, D. (1989), Promises: credible policy reform via signalling, *Economic Journal (99)*, No. 397 (pp 756–72).

Rogoff, K. (1985), The optimal degree of commitment to an intermediate monetary target, *Quarterly Journal of Economics*, Vol. 100, No. 4 (pp 1169–90).

Rogoff, Nowaihi and Levine (1996), "Independent but accountable: Walsh contracts and the credibility Problem," CEPR Discussion Papers No 1387.

Roll, E. (Report) (1993), A report of an independent panel chaired by Roll –Independent and Accountable: A New Mandate for the Bank of England-, CEPR, London.

Romer, C. and D.H. Romer (1989), Does monetary policy matter? a new test in the spirit of Friedman and Schwartz, in Blanchard, O.J. and S. Fisher (eds) *NBER Macroeconomics Annual 1989* (pp 121–70), Cambridge, Mass, MIT press.

Rose-Ackerman, S. (1975), The economics of corruption, *Journal of Public Economics*, Vol. 4, No. 2.

Saadani, Y., Z. Arvai and R. Rocha (2010), A Review of Credit Guarantee Schemes, MENA Financial Sector Flagship Report, Improving Access to Finance while Maintaining Stability in the Middle East and North Africa, World Bank, Washington, D.C.

Samy Ben Naceur, Hichem Ben-Khedhiri, and Barbara Casu (2009), What Drives The Efficiency Of Selected Mena Banks? A Meta-Frontier Analysis, Working Papers 499, Economic Research Forum, revised Aug 2009.

Sapienza, P. (2004), The effects of government ownership on bank lending, *Journal of Financial Economics*, Vol. 72, No. 2.

Sargent, T. J., and Wallace, N. (1981), Some unpleasant Monetarist arithmetic, *Federal Reserve Bank of Minneapolis Quarterly Review*, Vol. 5, No. 3, Fall (pp 1–17).

Sargent, T.J., and N. Wallace (1981), Some unpleasant Monetarist arithmetic, *Federal Reserve Bank of Minneapolis Quarterly Review*, Vol. 5, No. 3, Fall (pp 1–17).

Schmidt-Hebbel, K. and M. Tapia (2002), Monetary Policy Implementation and Results in Twenty Inflation-targeting Countries, Central Bank of Chile Working Paper No. 166 (Santiago).

Schumpeter, J.A. (1934), *The Theory of Economic Development*, Cambridge, MA: Harvard University Press.

Sealey, C. and J.T. Lindley (1977), Inputs, outputs and a theory of production and cost at depositary financial institutions, *Journal of Finance*, Vol. 32.

Senhadji, A., T. Saadi Sedik and K. Kpodar (2007), Prévisions de l'inflation et transmission des variations du taux de change aux prix à la consommation, Tunisia: Questions générales, Rapport du FMI No. 07/319.

Shleifer, A. and R.W. Vishny (1993), Corruption, *Quarterly Journal of Economics*, Vol. 108, No. 3.

Shleifer, A. and R.W. Vishny (1994), Politicians and firms, *Quarterly Journal of Economics*, Vol. 109, No. 4.

Silver, M. (2006), Core Inflation: Measurement and Statistical Issues in Choosing Among Alternative Measures, International Monetary Fund (IMF), Working Paper WP/06/97, Washington, D.C., IMF.

Stiglitz, J.E. (1994), The role of the state in financial markets, in *Proceedings of the World Bank Annual Conference on Development Economics*, World Bank, Washington, D.C.

Stock, J.H. and M. Yogo (2001), *Testing for Weak Instruments in Linear IV Regression*, unpublished manuscript, Harvard University.

Stock, J.H. and M.W. Watson, (1988), Variable trends and economic fluctuations, *Journal of Economic Perspectives* (pp 147–74), Summer.

Stock, J.H. and M.W. Watson, (1989), New Indexes of Coincident and Leading Economic Indicators, NBER Macroeconomic Annual Report (pp 351–94), Cambridge, Massachusetts, National Bureau of Economic Research.

Stock, J.H. and M.W. Watson, (1998), Business Cycle Fluctuations in U.S. Macroeconomic Time Series, NBER Working Paper No. 6528.

Stock, J.H. and M.W. Watson, (1999), Forecasting inflation, *Journal of Monetary Economics*, Vol. 44 (pp 293–335).

Stock, J.H. and M.W. Watson, (2003), Forecasting output and inflation: the role of asset prices, *Journal of Economic Literature*, Vol. XLI (pp 788–829).

Sundararajan, V., D. Marston and R. Basu (2001), Financial System Standards and Financial Stability – The Case of Basel Core Principles, IMF Working Paper No. 01/62, International Monetary Fund, Washington, D.C.

Tabellini, G. (1987), Secrecy of monetary policy and the variability of interest rates, *Journal of Money, Credit and Banking*, Vol. 19, No. 4 (pp 425–35), November.

Tahari, A., P. Brenner, E.D. Vrijer, M. Moretti, A. Senhadji, G. Sensenbrenner and J. Solé (2007), Financial Sector Reforms and Prospects for Financial Integration in Maghreb Countries, IMF Working Paper No. 07/125, International Monetary Fund, Washington, D.C.

Tavéra, C., I. Cadorand and N. Payelle (1998), La convergence des asymétries dans les effets réels des impulsions monétaires, ouvrage coordonné par C. Tavéra La convergence des économies européennes, *Economica* (pp 121–37).

Taylor, J. and M. Woodford (eds) (1998), *Handbook of Macroeconomics*, North Holland.

Taylor, J.B. (1993), Discretion versus policy rules in practice, *Carnegie-Rochester Conference Series on Public Policy*, Vol. 39 (pp 195–214).

Taylor, J.B. (ed.) (1999), *Monetary Policy Rules*, Chicago, University of Chicago Press.

Tortosa-Ausina, E. (2002), Exploring efficiency differences over time in the Spanish banking industry, *European Journal of Operational Research*, Vol. 139, No. 3.

Tullock, Gordon (1978), Achieving deregulation: a public choice perspective. *Regulation*, Vol. 2 (p 50).

Turk-Ariss, R. (2009), Competitive behavior in Middle East and North Africa banking systems, *Quarterly Review of Economics and Finance*, Vol. 49, No. 2.

Vander Vennet, R. (2002), Cost and profit efficiency of financial conglomerates and Universal banks in Europe, *Journal of Money, Credit, and Banking*, Vol. 34, No. 1.

Vickers, J. (1986), Signalling in a model of monetary policy with incomplete information, *Oxford Economic Papers*, Vol. 38 (pp 443–55).

Villa, P. (1995), Policy Mix et indépendance des Banques Centrales, *Economie Internationale*, Vol. 61 (pp 71–97).

Vives, X. (1990), Trade association disclosure rules, incentives to share information, and welfare, *RAND Journal of Economics*, Vol. 21, No. 3, Autumn.

Wachtel, P. (2001), Growth and finance: what do we know and how do we know it? *International Finance*, Vol. 4, No. 3, Winter.

Wachtel, P. (2003), How much do we really know about growth and finance?, *Federal Reserve Bank of Atlanta Economic Review*, 1st Quarter, Vol. 88, No. 1.

Waller, C.J. (1992), A bargaining model of partisan appointments to the central bank, *Journal of Monetary Economics*, Vol. 29, No. 3 (pp 411–428).

Walsh, C. (1993), Central bank strategies, credibility and independence: a review essay, *Journal of Monetary Economics*, Vol. 32, No. 2 (pp 287–302).

Walsh, C. (1995), Optimal contracts for independent Central bankers, *American Economic Review*, Vol. 85, No. 1 (pp 150–167), March.

Weber, A. (1991), Reputation and Credibility in the European Monetary System, *Economic Policy: A European Forum*, No. 6 (pp 57–102), April.

Weill, L. (2009), Convergence in banking efficiency across European countries, *Journal of International Financial Markets, Institutions & Money*, Vol. 5.

Woodford, M. (1994), Nonstandard indicators for monetary policy: can their usefulness be judged from forecasting regressions?, in N G Mankiw (ed.) *Monetary Policy*, Chicago, University of Chicago Press for NBER.

World Bank (2004), Algeria: Financial Sector Assessment Staff Report, Financial Sector Assessment Program (FSAP), Washington, D.C.

World Bank (2005), Financial Sector Assessment: A Handbook, jointly published by the World Bank and the International Monetary Fund, Washington, D.C.

World Bank (2008), Egypt: Financial Sector Assessment, Washington, D.C.

World Bank (2009), Program Document for a proposed integration and competitiveness development policy loan – DPL, Report No. 47556-TN, February.

World Bank (2010a), Cadre de Partenariat Stratégique pour la République Tunisienne, Rapport No. 50223 – TUN, Washington, January.

World Bank (2010b), République de Tunisie – Revue des politiques de développement, Promouvoir l'innovation pour accélérer la croissance de la productivité, Report No. 50487-TN, February.

Yashiv, E. (1994), Money demand in a high inflation economy: the case of Israel, *Review of Economics and Statistics*, Vol. 76, No. 1 (pp 186–191).

Zhao, T., B. Casu and A. Ferrari (2010), The impact of regulatory reforms on cost structure, ownership and competition in Indian banking, *Journal of Banking and Finance*, Vol. 34.

Windmeijer, F. (2005), A finite sample correction for the variance of linear efficient two-step GMM estimators, *Journal of Econometrics*, Vol. 126, No. 1 (pp 25–51).

Annex 1: The Autoregressive Moving Average Model (ARMA)

The *Autoregressive Moving Average* (ARMA) process $(p,q)^1$ is a generalisation of autoregressive models (AR) of the order (p), AR(p), and of the moving average (MA) of the order (q), MA(q):

$AR(1): x_t = \theta \cdot x_{t-1} + \xi_t$
$MA(1): x_t = \theta \cdot \xi_{t-1} + \xi_t$
$AR(p): x_t = \theta_1 \cdot x_{t-1} + \theta_2 \cdot x_{t-2} + \ldots\ldots\ldots + \theta_p \cdot x_{t-p} + \xi_t$
$MA(q): x_t = \theta_1 \cdot \xi_{t-1} + \theta_2 \cdot \xi_{t-2} + \ldots\ldots\ldots + \theta_q \cdot \xi_{t-q} + \xi_t$

The ARMA model (p,q) is expressed as follows:

$$ARMA(p,q): x_t = \theta_1 \cdot x_{t-1} + \theta_2 \cdot x_{t-2} + \ldots\ldots + \theta_p \cdot x_{t-p}$$
$$+ \theta_1 \cdot \xi_{t-1} + \theta_2 \cdot \xi_{t-2} + \ldots\ldots + \theta_q \cdot \xi_{t-q} + \xi_t, \quad \xi_t \to N(0, \sigma_\xi^2)$$

or

$$x_t = \sum_{i=1}^{p} \theta_i \cdot x_{t-1} + \sum_{i=1}^{q} \theta_q \cdot \xi_{t-q} + \xi_t .$$

The ARMA processes can be represented using a delay operator which delays the data of one time unit:

$Lx_t = x_{t-1},$
$L^2 x_t = LLx_t = Lx_{t-1} = x_{t-2},$

or, when generalising

$$L^j x_t = x_{t-j},$$
$$L^{-j} x_t = x_{t+j}.$$

It is also possible to keep polynomials from the delay operator. This gives us:

$$a(L)x_t = (a_0 \cdot L^0 + a_1 \cdot L^1 + a_2 \cdot L^2 + \ldots\ldots + a_p \cdot L^p).x_t$$
$$= a_0 \cdot x_t + a_1 \cdot x_{t-1} + a_2 \cdot x_{t-2} + \ldots\ldots + a_p \cdot x_{t-p}.$$

By using this notation, the ARMA model can now be expressed as follows:

$$AR(1) : (1 - \theta \cdot L) \cdot x_t = j_t,$$
$$MA(1) : x_t = (1 + \theta \cdot L) \cdot j_t,$$
$$AR(p) : (1 - \theta_1 \cdot L^1 - \theta_2 \cdot L^2 - \ldots\ldots - \theta_p \cdot L^p) \cdot x_t = \xi_t,$$
$$MA(q) : x_t = (1 + \theta_1 \cdot L^1 + \theta_2 \cdot L^2 + \ldots\ldots + \theta_p \cdot L^p) \cdot \xi_t,$$
$$ARMA(p,q) : (1 - \theta_1 \cdot L^1 - \theta_2 \cdot L^2 - \ldots\ldots - \theta_p \cdot L^p) \cdot x_t$$
$$= (1 + \theta_1 \cdot L^1 + \theta_2 \cdot L^2 + \ldots\ldots + \theta_p \cdot L^p) \cdot \xi_t.$$

ARMA models may also be used for projecting inflation simply by using mathematical expectation. By way of illustration and within a simple process AR(1), the projection of a variable x, let $\hat{x}_t$ operate as follows:

$$x_t = \theta \cdot x_{t-1} + \xi_t \text{ where } \xi_t \to N\left(0, \sigma_\xi^2\right),$$

$$\hat{x}_{t+1} = E\left[x_{t+1} | x_t\right] = \theta \cdot x_t,$$
$$\hat{x}_{t+2} = E\left[x_{t+2} | x_t\right] = \theta \cdot E\left[x_{t+1} | x_t\right] = \theta^2 \cdot x_t,$$
$$\hat{x}_{t+k} = \theta^k \cdot x_t.$$

ARMA processes may be considered as a means of making series stationary, bypassing the autocorrelation problem of residues. Here, in addition to the Durbin and Watson test, we favour the following iterative approach.

* Study of model specification by tests of simple autocorrelations (ACF) and partial autocorrelations (PACF). A good specification means zero autocorrelations (p-value = 0).
* Study of the so-called 'coat-rack' statistics according to its two variants (test of Box–Pierce and test of Ljung–Box). The (ACF) test of white noise should not reveal non-zero autocorrelations.
* Selection of orders of delays of processes (AR) and (MA), either in view of the autocorrelograms of processes used for estimation (method of Box–Jenkins), or from the minimisation of information criteria SC of Schwartz or AIC of Akaike, or finally from the minimisation of the criterion of Hanan-Quinn, where the statistics are expressed by the following formula:

$$HQ(p,q) = T.\log(\sigma_t^2) + (p+q).\log\left[\frac{\log(T)}{T}\right].$$

The identification approach deduced from an investigation of all possible combinations of AR and MA from delay orders sufficiently high in autoregressive terms (p) and moving averages (q), (p = 0, ...,5 and q = 1,.....,5), demonstrated that the best dynamics specification for inflation in Tunisia is an ARMA process (2,2). Besides inflation delays and residues the model includes advanced indicators as explanatory variables (in first difference) relative to the channels of bank credit and interest rate, while formalising the impact of exogenous factors by fluctuations in the international price of imported energy. The ARMA specification for inflation in Tunisia (log of IPC) shows good statistical appropriateness. The variation predicted by LIPC (in first difference, DLIPC) allows for signposting of inflexion points, which strengthens the validity of forecasts on retrospective series[2]. Moreover, the root-mean-square error (RMSE) on a projected horizon of 12 months for global inflation is low, as is the predicted variation of DLIPC.

Annex 2: Construction of the Capital Account Liberalisation Indicator

We adopted the approach of Klein and Olivei (2008) which is based on information included in the *Codes of liberalisation of capital movements from the OECD* to construct a synthetic index of capital account liberalisation in Tunisia following changes in exchange regulation of the Central Bank of Tunisia (CBT).

We only took into consideration the categories of international transactions where restrictions were relaxed. As a consequence, we used information on the degree of restrictions applied to eleven types of transaction, namely: foreign investment in Tunisia, current transactions relating to return on capital, other current transactions, operations in the money market in foreign currency, import and export of means of payment, Tunisian investment abroad or in non-resident companies settled in Tunisia, foreign lending, exchange market in cash and futures, non-resident accounts, execution of payments with foreigners and residents' accounts.

For each of these categories, we calculated a specific index designated I_{it}, belonging to the interval [0,1], which takes into account all liberalisation measures relating to it. The indicator of global liberalisation, designated I_t, which also belongs to the interval [0,1], is calculated as the arithmetic average of eleven specific indices. It should be emphasised that a unit value of this index does not mean a total capital account liberalisation. This index only traces the progressive evolution over time of the liberalisation process for capital accounts. In particular, it does not allow any international comparison of the degree of liberalisation. Formally, if n_i is the total number of liberalisation measures specific to category i over the whole period and n_{is} is the number of these measures decided on date s, this gives:

$$I_{it} = \frac{1}{n_i}\sum_{s=1}^{t} n_{is} \quad t = 1, 2, ..., T.$$

The global index for the whole economy is given by:

$$I_t = \frac{1}{n} \sum_{i=1}^{n} I_{it} \quad t = 1, 2, ..., T.$$

Annex 3: Flexibility – Cons – Credibility: Solution via a Contract with a Punitive Dismissal Threat

Walsh (1995) considers that the economy consists of two sectors: the first one establishes the level of nominal wages before the observation of supply shocks, and the second after their transmission. The hypothesis of the asymmetry of information then becomes partial if we assume that the second sector consists of a proportion *(1–s)* of the public who has access to the same information as the governor about the nature of the shocks (only the interpretation of the signal differs). The government has the following quadratic loss function:

$$S = \frac{1}{2}\left(y - y^c - k\right)^2 + \frac{1}{2} \cdot \beta \cdot \pi^2 \tag{1}$$

where
y^c = equilibrium production;
k = the gap between notional production objective and equilibrium production;
y = the current production;
π = the current inflation.

In every sector i (i = 1, 2), the level of production (y_i) is defined by a Cobb-Douglas function (Y) with the form:

$$y_i = Y + \alpha \cdot n_i + e \tag{2}$$

where
e = the supply shock;
n_i = the work demand of sector (i).

Furthermore,

$$y_i = f(y^c, (\pi - \pi^e))$$
$$= y^c + \left(\frac{\alpha}{1-\alpha}\right) \cdot (\pi - \pi^e) + \left[\frac{1+\alpha(1-s)}{(1-\alpha)}\right] \cdot e \tag{3}$$

where

$\pi - \pi^e$ = unexpected inflation;

$1 - S$ = the proportion in the second sector of agents informed about the supply shocks (agents of the first sector are therefore not informed); π^e = the weighted average of expected inflation rate by each sector, so that $\pi^e = s\pi_1^e + (1-s)\pi_2^e$.

The error of control of the monetary instrument by the central bank (or velocity shock) is given by:

$$\pi = m + v \tag{4}$$

where
v = the error of control or velocity shock;
m = the monetary instrument.

The authorities only observe the evolution of an monetary aggregate (M) in volume, but cannot directly observe the instrument used (m):

$$M = m + \omega \tag{5}$$

where

ω = white noise $\left(\omega \to N\left(0, \sigma_\omega^2\right)\right)$.

We also consider that the measure of inflation is unpredictable due to a measurement bias (b) and a measurement error (ξ). Therefore, the observed inflation (π^m) is equal to:

$$\pi^m = \pi + b + \xi \tag{6}$$

For all these types of imperfections, wages contracts cannot therefore be established on only disinflationary performance. The optimum policy from the perspective of the authorities is then deduced from the minimisation of its loss function:

$$Min\ E(S)\ \ S/C\ \ \pi^a = m + v = 0 \tag{7}$$

where π^a = zero average inflation.

The optimum solution consists in respecting a zero inflation rule, while stabilising the economy in case of supply or velocity shocks:

$$m^c\left(e, v^f\right) = -\delta^c \cdot e - v^f \tag{8}$$

where v^f = the forecast of velocity shock (v) by the central bank.

Annex 3

In the case of a supply shock, $(1-s)$ employees in the second sector rationally anticipate the stabilisation strategy of the central bank, while employees in the first sector will be "surprised" by an inflation which is automatically generated by a monetary easing policy in periods of weak economic performance (supply shock). The intertemporal inconsistency of this optimal policy of stabilisation is corrected by a credibilisation in terms of a contract including a punitive threat of dismissal if an inflation threshold is exceeded. The incentive ensues from the utility for the governor of the central bank for his appointment to be renewed for a new mandate; he will then try to maximise the following utility function:

$$W = Z - E(S) + \rho \cdot r \cdot U_0 \tag{9}$$

where
Z = utility of the "agent" (Governor) to be renewed;
S = function of loss of "main" operator (Authorities);
r = probability of renewal;
ρ = discount rate;
U_0 = utility hoping to be renewed at (t+1).

The threshold of inflation or threshold of performance fixed by the 'main' operator, π^* (e), is a function of the supply shock (e). In other words, the authorities authorise the central bank to implement a policy of monetary easing to react to the supply shock by creating inflation lower than π^* (e), without making the objective of disinflation totally redundant. This partial and sustainable reaction is favoured by the threat of dismissal. The central banker is then encouraged to adapt his behaviour to a partisan politico-economic cycle, his objective being renewal with a probability equal to:

$$
\begin{aligned}
r &= prob(\pi^m \leq \pi^*(e, v^f)) \\
&= prob(m + v + b + \xi \leq \pi^*(e, v^f)) \\
&= F(\pi^* - m - v^f - b)
\end{aligned}
\tag{10}
$$

where F = the function of distribution of variable $(v - v^f + \xi)$.

The central banker then maximises (W) to determine the optimum value of the monetary instrument (m^{rd}) so that $m^{rd} = m^c$, where (r) means renewal.

Annex 4: Optimal Contract with Linear Reward on Inflation

Applied to relations between government and central bankers, this literature tries to formalise in "main operator–agent" models an optimal incentive contract in which the moral hazard of the central bank agent ensues from the asymmetric information which he has, with a signal of an unexpected productivity shock[3]. By returning to the formalisation of ROGOFF, Walsh (1995) develops a simple "main operator – agent" model where the "main operator" aggregates the behaviour of the public which is reduced to that of the government, and the "agent" aggregates the behaviour of the central bank which is reduced to its governor. He supposes that the "agent" receives a budget (t) and minimises a loss function equal to:

$$L^b = L - t$$

$$\Rightarrow L^b = \left\{1/2\,(\pi_t)^2 + 1/2 \cdot b \cdot (y_t - k)^2 - t\right\}. \tag{1}$$

The "main operator" tries to determine the optimum incentive plan or optimum budgetary reward (t^*) by encouraging the "agent" to implement a credible policy knowing that he has private information about the shock (ξ) hitting the economy. Expectations are created before the shock is observed, while the "agent" chooses his instrument (setting the inflation rate) after observing a signal (θ) of a random shock:

$$\xi = \theta + \phi \tag{2}$$

where ϕ = term of error $(E_\theta(\phi) = 0; \sigma_\phi^2 = V(\phi))$,

$E_\theta\,(\xi) = 0$ (expectation of shock conditional to its signal – ξ).

Under these conditions, the contract depends only on variables which are observable by the 'main operator' and the 'agent', that is, ξ, y and π. But as π is the only independent variable, the budget then depends, without loss of generality, on the implemented inflation rate $t(\pi)$.

The central bank agent minimises the conditional expectation with the signal θ, that is E_θ, of anticipated loss L^b:

$$\underset{\pi^b}{MIN}\, E_\theta(L^b) = MIN\, E_\theta\left\{1/2(\pi_t)^2 + 1/2 \cdot b \cdot (y_t - k)^2 - t(\pi)\right\}. \tag{3}$$

Considering inflation expectations as given, the first order condition is expressed as:

$$\pi + b \cdot (\pi - \pi^e + \xi - k) - E_\theta \cdot \left(\frac{\delta t}{\delta \pi}\right) = 0$$

$$\Rightarrow \pi + b \cdot \left[\pi - \pi^e + \theta + E_\theta(\phi) - k\right] - E_\theta\left[\frac{\delta t}{\delta \pi}\right] = 0$$

$$\Rightarrow \pi + b \cdot \left[\pi - \pi^e + \theta - k\right] - E_\theta\left[\frac{\delta t}{\delta \pi}\right] = 0$$

By applying the operator of rational conditional expectations to the information state in $(t-1)$, E_{t-1}, that is by endogenising inflation expectations, we permute the first order condition which becomes:

$$\pi + b\left[\pi - E_{t-1}(\pi) + \theta - k\right] - E_\theta\left[\frac{\delta t}{\delta \pi}\right] = 0$$

$$\Rightarrow (1 + b) \cdot \pi = b \cdot E_{t-1}\left(\frac{\delta t}{\delta \pi}\right) - b \cdot \theta + b \cdot k + E_\theta\left(\frac{\delta t}{\delta \pi}\right)$$

$$\Rightarrow \pi^b = \left(\frac{b}{1+b}\right) \cdot k - \left(\frac{b}{1+b}\right) \cdot \theta + \left(\frac{b}{1+b}\right) E_{t-1}\left(\frac{\delta t}{\delta \pi}\right) + \left(\frac{1}{1+b}\right) E_\theta\left(\frac{\delta t}{\delta \pi}\right)$$

$$\Rightarrow \pi^b = \left(\frac{b}{1+b}\right) \cdot k - \left(\frac{b}{1+b}\right) \cdot \theta + E_\theta\left(\frac{\delta t}{\delta \pi}\right) + \left(\frac{b}{1+b}\right) \cdot \left[E_{t-1}\left(\frac{\delta t}{\delta \pi}\right) - E_\theta\left(\frac{\delta t}{\delta \pi}\right)\right]$$

For a contract to be optimum the following must apply:

$$\pi^b = \pi^t$$

$$\Rightarrow \pi^b = -\left(\frac{b}{1+b}\right) \cdot \xi = -\left(\frac{b}{1+b}\right) \cdot \theta \tag{4}$$

(because ϕ is white noise, $E_\theta(\phi) = 0$)

$$\Rightarrow \left(\frac{b}{1+b}\right)k + E_\theta\left(\frac{\delta t}{\delta \pi}\right) + \left(\frac{b}{1+b}\right)\cdot\left[E_{t-1}\left(\frac{\delta t}{\delta \pi}\right) - E_\theta\left(\frac{\delta t}{\delta \pi}\right)\right] = 0$$

$$\Rightarrow b\cdot k + (1+b)\cdot E_\theta\left(\frac{\delta t}{\delta \pi}\right) + b\cdot\left[E_{t-1}\left(\frac{\delta t}{\delta \pi}\right) - E_\theta\left(\frac{\delta t}{\delta \pi}\right)\right] = 0$$

$$\Rightarrow -b\cdot k = (1+b)E_\theta\left(\frac{\delta t}{\delta \pi}\right) + b\left[E_{t-1}\left(\frac{\delta t}{\delta \pi}\right) - E_\theta\left(\frac{\delta t}{\delta \pi}\right)\right] = 0$$

An optimum contract $t(\pi^b) = t(\pi^r)$ which introduces a linear reward (or a sanction) on the inflation rate, and verifies this optimum condition, is expressed as:

$$t(\pi) = t_0 - b\cdot k\cdot\pi \qquad (5)$$

$$\Rightarrow \left(\frac{\delta t}{\delta \pi}\right) = -b\cdot k$$

and

$$E_{t-1}\left(\frac{\delta t}{\delta \pi}\right) = E_\theta\left(\frac{\delta t}{\delta \pi}\right) = -b\cdot k$$

In other words, the optimum contract consists in increasing the marginal cost of inflation in the loss function of a number amount proportional to the inflation bias of the discretionary strategy.

The incentive plan with a reward is due to the fact that the "main operator" ignores the "type" (or preferences) of the "agent" who possesses private information or an information advantage on the exogenous variables (or shocks) of supply. The incentive contract reveals the real "type" of central banker by relaxing this situation of "adverse selection" lined to the asymmetry of information. Any temptation to deceive would increase the marginal cost of inflation, in other words it would reduce the transfer of income.

Annex 5: Credibility versus Flexibility

The argument is formalised in a static model with stochastic supply shocks with symmetrical information (absence of retention), in which the economy is formalised by Lucas's supply function:

$$y_t = (\pi_t - \pi_t^e) + \xi_t \tag{1}$$

where
y_t = level of production (given as a gap with regard to a natural level of anticipated output normalised to zero);
π_t = current inflation rate;
π_t^e = expected inflation rate;
ξ_t = 'white noise' or random shock ($E(\xi) = 0; V(\xi_t) = \sigma_j^2$)).

The public rationally forms its expectations (or salary contracts) before the shock ξ and the choice of π_t as an instrument of monetary policy are observed:

$$\pi_t^e = E_{t-1}\left(\pi_t / \Omega_{t-1}\right)$$

The government (or public authorities) minimises an objective function of quadratic loss (L) representing social wealth, which is a function of marginal inflation cost and marginal earnings in terms of employment of surprise-inflation, measured by the gap between the level of unemployment (y_t) and its notional objective[4] (k):

$$L = \left\{ \frac{1}{2} \cdot (\pi_t)^2 + \frac{1}{2} \cdot b \cdot (y_t - k)^2 \right\} \tag{2}$$

where b = relative weighting attributed to stabilisation of economic activity with regard to disinflation.

When the government does not commit credibly to a rule of monetary policy or choice of inflation rate, its discretionary strategy is determined by the minimisation of the loss function (L) by considering inflationary expectations as data:

$$\underset{\pi_t}{\text{MIN}} \ \ L = \left\{ 1/2\,(\pi_t)^2 + 1/2 \cdot b(y_t - k)^2 \right\}$$

$$= \left\{ 1/2\,(\pi_t)^2 + 1/2 \cdot b(\pi_t - \pi_t^e + \xi_t - k)^2 \right\},$$

which leads to the following first order solution:

$$\frac{\delta L}{\delta \pi_t} = 0 \Rightarrow (1+b)\cdot \pi_t - b\pi_t^e + b\cdot\xi_t - b\cdot k = 0$$

By taking the rational anticipation of this relation, we obtain the following discretionary inflation rate:

$$\pi_t^d = -\left(\frac{b}{1+b}\right)\cdot\xi_t + b\cdot k \tag{3}$$

$$\Rightarrow \pi_t^{e,d} = E(\pi_t^d) = b\cdot k \tag{4}$$

$$\Rightarrow y_t^d = -\left(\frac{b}{1+b}\right)\cdot\xi_t + \xi_t = \left(\frac{1}{1+b}\right)\xi_t \tag{5}$$

Therefore, the discretionary optimum monetary policy is incoherent over time since it leads to an inflationary bias ($b\,k$) and a stabilisation term [$(b/1 + b)\cdot\xi_t$]. When the government commits to a rule of deflation, it 'internalises' the impact of this choice on expectation. The loss function is then minimised under constraint, not only of the state of the economy, but also of the rationality of expectations:

$$\underset{\pi_t}{\text{MIN}} \ \ L = \left\{ 1/2\cdot(\pi_t)^2 + 1/2\cdot b\cdot(\pi_t - \pi_t^e + \xi_t - k)^2 \right\},$$

$$\text{S/C } \pi_t^e = E_{t-1}\left(\pi_t/\Omega_{t-1}\right)$$

This provides the following first order condition:

$$\frac{\delta L}{\delta \pi_t} = 0 \Rightarrow \pi_t + b(y_t - k) - b\cdot E_{t-1}(y_t - k) = 0.$$

By taking the rational expectation for this relation, we get the optimum rule of the inflation rate:

$$\pi_t^r = -\left(\frac{b}{1+b}\right)\cdot\xi_t \tag{6}$$

$$\Rightarrow \pi_t^{e,r} = E(\pi_t^r) = 0 \tag{7}$$

$$\Rightarrow y_t^r = -\left(\frac{b}{1+b}\right)\cdot\xi_t + \xi_t = \left(\frac{1}{1+b}\right)\cdot\xi_t \tag{8}$$

Finally, we note that:

$$y_t^r = y_t^d = y_t = \left(\frac{1}{1+b}\right)\xi_t$$

$$\Rightarrow E(y_t^r) = E(y_t^d) = E(y_t) = 0$$

et $V(y_t^r) = V(y_t^d) = \sigma_{y_t^r}^2 = \sigma_{y_t^d}^2 = V(y_t) = \sigma_y^2$

$$\Rightarrow V(y_t) = E\left[y_t - E(y_t)\right]^2 = E(y_t^2) - \left[E(y_t)\right]^2 = E(y_t^2)$$

$$\Rightarrow V(y_t) = E\left[\frac{1}{(1+b)^2}\xi_t^2\right] = \frac{1}{(1+b)^2}\cdot E(\xi_t^2) = \frac{1}{(1+b)^2}\cdot\sigma_\xi^2$$

Likewise, similar reasoning for the inflation rate leads to:
$\pi_t^d = \pi_t^r + b\cdot k$ (bk being the inflation bias).

$$\Rightarrow E(\pi_t^d) = E(\pi_t^r) + b\cdot k = bk,$$

because $E(\pi_t^r) = 0$, and

$$V(\pi_t^r) = E\left[\left(\frac{-b}{1+b}\right)^2\cdot\xi_t^2\right] = \left(\frac{b}{1+b}\right)^2\cdot\sigma_\xi^2$$

$$= E(\pi_t^{d2}) - (b\cdot k)^2$$

$$= E\left[\pi_t^{r2} + 2\cdot\pi_t^r\cdot b\cdot k + (bk)^2\right] - (bk)^2$$

$$= E(\pi_t^{r2}) = V(\pi_t^r) = \left(\frac{b}{1+b}\right)^2\cdot\sigma_\xi^2.$$

The disinflation strategy is thus analysed through the following system:

$$E(y^r) = E(y^d) = 0 , \tag{9}$$

$$V(y^r) = V(y^d) = \frac{1}{(1+b)^2} \sigma_j^2 , \tag{10}$$

$$E(\pi^r) = 0 , \tag{11}$$

$$V(\pi^r) = V(\pi^d) = \frac{b^2}{(1+b)^2} \cdot \sigma_\xi^2 , \tag{12}$$

$$E(\pi^d) = b \cdot k . \tag{13}$$

The optimal rule for the inflation rate reduces output variance $(V(y^r) < V(\pi^r))$, eliminates inflation bias $(E(\pi^r) = 0)$ but leads to a stationary average output identical to the discretionary strategy $(E(y^r) = E(y^d) = 0)$. A discretionary monetary policy reduces output variance $(V(y^d) < V(\pi^d))$ but led to a positive average inflation $(E(\pi^d) = b \cdot k))$ with no increase in average output. The inflation bias in this flexibility strategy is higher when the weighting (b) applied to the stabilisation of activity is strong. The government can thus ensure required flexibility when stabilising supply shocks if it resigns itself to throttling inflation.

Only a conservative central banker can arbitrate in an optimal manner between flexibility and credibility of disinflation. To that end, the government has to look for a central banker to whom it delegates implementation of monetary policy, and who has the constant conservatism as defined by Rogoff (1985) under the two following conditions: i) he must have the same function objective ($\hat{L}$) as that of the government (L); but ii) a lower and non-zero relative aversion to unemployment ($\hat{b} < b$).

The independent central bank is thus defined by the selection of the optimum *ex ante* coefficient ($\hat{b}$), considering that the appointed banker will nevertheless apply discretionary solutions (π^d, $\pi^{e,d}$, y^d), based on minimisation by the government of expectation of the following social loss:

$$\hat{L} = \underset{b}{MIN}\ E\left\{\frac{1}{2}(\pi^d)^2 + \frac{1}{2}\cdot b\cdot(y^d - k)^2\right\} = \underset{b}{MIN}\ E(L)$$

$$\Rightarrow \hat{L} = \underset{b}{MIN}\ E\left\{\frac{1}{2}\left[\hat{b}\cdot k - \left(\frac{\hat{b}}{1+\hat{b}}\right)\xi_t\right]^2 + \frac{1}{2}b\cdot\left[\left(\frac{1}{1+\hat{b}}\right)\cdot\xi - k\right]^2\right\}. \tag{14}$$

The choice of the level of conservatism of the central bank is given by the first order solution as follows:

$$2\cdot\hat{b}\cdot(1+\hat{b})^4 - 2\hat{b}\cdot(1+\hat{b})^3\cdot(\sigma_\xi^2)^{-1}\cdot k^2 = b$$

$$\Rightarrow 0 < \hat{b} < b. \tag{15}$$

Demonstration:

From the following general rule of variance for all variables (X):

$$V(X) = E[X - E(X)]^2 = E(X^2) - [E(X)]^2$$

$$\Rightarrow E(X^2) = V(X) - [E(X)]^2$$

we obtain

$$\hat{L} = E\left\{1/2\left[\hat{b}\cdot k - \left(\frac{\hat{b}}{1+\hat{b}}\right)\cdot\xi_t\right]^2 + 1/2.b\left[\left(\frac{1}{1+\hat{b}}\right).\xi - k\right]^2\right\}$$

$$\Rightarrow \hat{L} = E\left\{1/2\cdot C^2 + 1/2\cdot b\cdot D^2\right\}$$

where $C = \hat{b}\cdot k - \left(\dfrac{\hat{b}}{1+\hat{b}}\right)\cdot\zeta_t,\ D = \left(\dfrac{1}{1+\hat{b}}\right)\cdot\zeta_t - k,$

$$\Rightarrow \hat{L} = 1/2\cdot E(C^2) + 1/2\cdot b\cdot E(D^2)$$

$$= 1/2\left\{V(C) + E[(C)]^2 + 1/2\cdot b\left\{V(D) + E[(D)]^2\right.$$

$$= 1/2\left\{\left[(\hat{b}\cdot k)^2 - \frac{\hat{b}^2}{(1+\hat{b})^2}\cdot\sigma_\xi^2\right] + (\hat{b}k)^2\right\} + 1/2\cdot b\left\{\left[\frac{1}{(1+\hat{b})^2}\sigma_\xi^2 - k^2\right] + k^2\right\}$$

$$= \frac{1}{2}\left\{2(\hat{b}\cdot k)^2 - \frac{\hat{b}^2}{(1+\hat{b})^2}\cdot\sigma_\xi^2\right\} + \frac{1}{2}\cdot b\left\{\frac{1}{(1+\hat{b})^2}\sigma_\xi^2\right\}.$$

The first order condition then gives us:

$$\frac{\delta\hat{L}}{\delta\hat{b}} = 0 \Rightarrow 2\cdot\hat{b}\cdot k^2 - \sigma_\xi^2\left[(2\hat{b})\cdot(1+\hat{b})^2 - (2\hat{b}^2)(1+\hat{b})\right] + \frac{b}{2}\cdot\sigma_\xi^2\cdot\left[\frac{2(1+\hat{b})}{(1+\hat{b})^4}\right] = 0$$

$$\Rightarrow 2\hat{b}\cdot k^2 - \sigma_\xi^2\left[2\hat{b}(1+\hat{b})\right] + b\cdot\sigma_\xi^2\cdot\frac{1}{(1+\hat{b})^3} = 0$$

$$\Rightarrow b\cdot\sigma_\xi^2\cdot\frac{1}{(1+b)^3} = -2\hat{b}\cdot k^2 + 2\hat{b}(1+\hat{b})\cdot\sigma_\xi^2$$

$$\Rightarrow b = 2\hat{b}\cdot(1+\hat{b})^4 - 2\hat{b}(1+\hat{b})^3\cdot(\sigma_\xi^2)^{-1}\cdot k^2.$$

Yet this condition of choice leads to indecision over the optimum degree of conservatism. Nothing is said on the initial argument of this formalisation which aims to know if the appointment of a more conservative central banker than the median preferences of society would allow stabilisation of productivity shocks. The model of Rogoff (1985) ultimately only demonstrates the comments already given relating to credibility of monetary policy being able to reduce inflationary bias $(\hat{b}\cdot k < b\cdot k)$. Flexibility is not ensured since this strategy only increases output variability because:

$$\hat{\pi}_t = \frac{-\hat{b}}{1+\hat{b}}\cdot\xi_t + \hat{b}\cdot k < \pi_t^d \tag{16}$$

$$\hat{\pi}_t^e = \hat{b}\cdot k < \pi_t^{e,d} = b\cdot k. \tag{17}$$

But

$$\hat{y}_t = \left(\frac{1}{1+\hat{b}}\right)\cdot\xi_t > y_t^d = \left(\frac{1}{1+b}\right)\cdot\xi_t \tag{18}$$

$$V(\hat{y}_t) = \frac{1}{(1+\hat{b})^2}\cdot\sigma_\xi^2 > V(y_t^d) = \frac{1}{(1+b)^2}\cdot\sigma_\xi^2. \tag{19}$$

Index

Lightning Source UK Ltd.
Milton Keynes UK
UKHW022229080620
364668UK00010B/874